Jean QUELLIEN

THE AMERICANS IN NORMANDY

OREP
EDITIONS

CONTENTS

Aboard an LCA, these rangers are preparing to board the troop transport vessel that will take them to Normandy.

INTRODUCTION

On the 6th of June 1944, the Americans landed on the Normandy beaches, launching what General Eisenhower was later to refer to as the «Crusade in Europe», aimed at liberating enslaved populations from the Nazi oppression. Today, the event is so deep-rooted in our memories that the fact that boys from Texas, Maryland, Virginia or New York found themselves on the shores of *Utah Beach* and *Omaha Beach* appears almost «obvious», as if it had been their long-awaited destiny. However, in contrast with their British and Canadian colleagues, this was far from the case for the American troops.

In September 1939, the United States was, as yet, very much detached from events in Europe. Public opinion showed little concern for the war and the idea of participating had occurred to but a tiny minority of the population. In the spring of 1940, President Roosevelt was impervious to pleas for help sent by France, which was on the verge of defeat. Even if he had been in favour of American military intervention, it was impossible for him to accept. Despite its potential power, the small American army was incapable of defying anyone, for its economy was far from having totally recovered from the Wall Street crash in October 1929. Despite the «New Deal», the country still had millions of unemployed, a problem that aroused considerably more concern in the average American than the war in Europe.

On the 7th of December, the Japanese attack on Pearl Harbor was to hasten the United States' involvement in the conflict. In just a few years, the immense war effort deployed by the world's most powerful nation was to irreversibly tip the scales in favour of the Allies. The first American soldiers arrived in Belfast as early as January 1942. By the spring of 1944, 1,700,000 were posted in the United Kingdom. Some of them spent months there before heading for Normandy to contribute to the liberation of France and Western Europe. This book offers an account of their long journey.

Considerable attention is, of course, paid to the hostilities that marked the summer of 1944, of D-Day - of the heavy losses sustained on *Omaha Beach* and among paratroopers - up to the Americans' victorious charge through France late summer, 1944, via the capture of Cherbourg - an essential strategic target - late June, and the terrible war of the hedgerows amidst the hell of the Normandy bocage, in July.

This work also covers aspects which are often left in the shadows, such as how an army operates out in the field, the vital importance of logistics, the day-to-day lives of the GIS, their relationships with the local population or the great burden of the presence of the Americans in Normandy; by late July, there were three times as many GIs in the Cotentin and Bessin as there were inhabitants! Beyond pure historical analysis, it also includes many accounts by participants and witnesses to the events, from major military chiefs to simple GIs. «There are really two wars and they haven't much to do with each other," the writer John Steinbeck was keen to stress. "There is the war of maps and logistics, of campaigns, of armies, divisions and regiments – and that is the general's war. Then there is the war of homesick, weary, funny, violent, common men who wash their socks in their helmets, complain about the food, whistle at the girls, and lug themselves through as dirty a business as the world has ever seen and do it with dignity and courage.»

THE AMERICAN WAR
MACHINE MOVES INTO ACTION

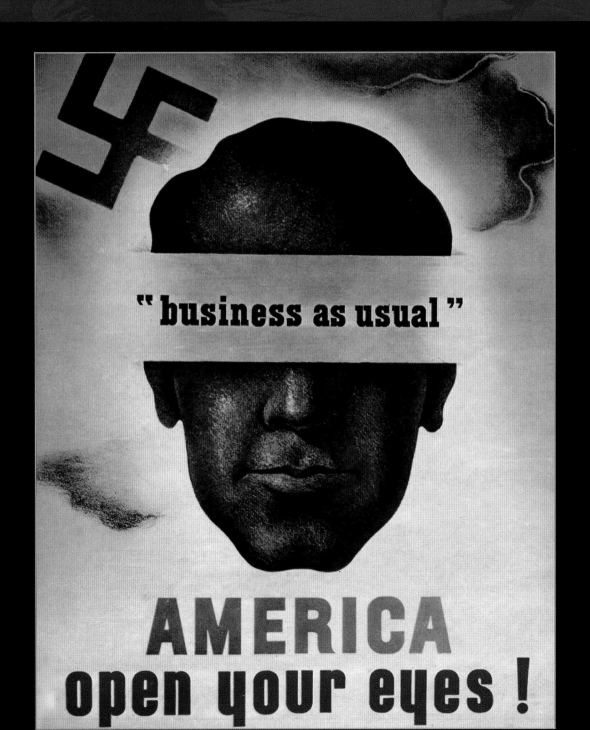

Did the United States make the right decision when it joined World War I in 1917? A question to which the Senate's Special Committee on Investigation of the Munitions Industry replied, "No" in 1934; opinion was believed to have been influenced by banking institutions and gun sellers. Was the sound of marching boots from old Europe not likely to rekindle similar erring ways? A comprehensive legislative framework was established to avoid this. The *Johnson Act* (1934) formally prohibited the granting of any further credit to nations that had, as yet, failed to reimburse the debts they had contracted twenty years previously. From 1935 to 1937, whilst Mussolini attacked Ethiopia and the Spanish Civil War was raging, the Congress voted a series of neutrality acts. An embargo was set on weapons deliveries to nations at war. For other nations, the *Cash and Carry* principle was applied to all goods purchased from the United States: pay up front and organise your own shipping.

Chicago, April 1941, America First Committee meeting in favour of the United States' strict neutrality and against any financial or military support for the United Kingdom. The aviator Charles Lindbergh is at the rostrum.

◄ Propaganda poster promoting the United States' involvement in the war.

Isolationism or interventionism?

This overcautious stance strove at all costs to protect from the danger from without. America's traditional isolationism, although temporarily thwarted under President Wilson, had never been so vigorous, whilst the entire world was advancing towards catastrophe. Yet the Americans were far from insensitive to the Japanese attack on China in 1937, to Hitler's annexation of Austria the following year or to the dismembering of Czechoslovakia; nor did they close their eyes to Jewish persecution and to the arrival of Nazi-fleeing exiles. Yet military intervention remained out of the question.

Already under severe criticism for his interior policy due to economic decline, President Roosevelt was keen to avoid seeing his exterior policy generate further hostility. Although perfectly aware of the emergent danger, his position appeared somewhat timorous and hesitant. When war broke out in Europe in September 1939, he upheld the principle of neutrality. A Gallup survey revealed that only 2.5% of the American population were in favour of their country engaging in the war

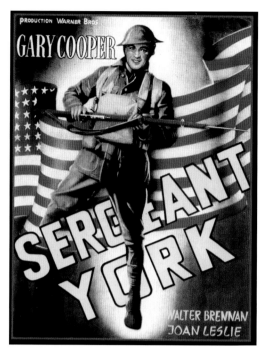

Sergeant York: an "interventionist" film.

The America First Committee highlighted the risks involved in any United States engagement in the conflict.

effort. The United States' unique gesture towards the Democracies was to lift the weapons delivery embargo in November 1939, whilst continuing to enforce the *Cash and Carry* principle.

France's collapse in June 1940 was undoubtedly to mark a capital turning point. It was an immense shock for the Americans. The army that had been considered the world's best had literally been pulverised by Hitler's hordes. The Democracies had just lost one of their strongholds. In the autumn, Britain remained isolated yet directly under threat from fierce attacks by *Luftwaffe* bombers. American opinion was deeply stirred by the moving reports - sirens and explosions booming - broadcast by the CBS offices in London. This turn for the worse in the war in Europe was to brutally arouse awareness: America's neutrality would ultimately be condemned. One form or another of military intervention appeared inevitable.

Although still strong, the nation's isolationist stance was faltering. Yet a number of uncompromising partisans remained staunchly attached. In September 1940, they joined forces in the form of the America First Committee, presided over by General Wood. In this somewhat heterogeneous conglomeration, nationalist conservatives rubbed shoulders with a few defenders of authoritarian regimes. The aviator, Charles Lindbergh, was among its most active members and was convinced that "Western Civilisation's saviour depended on Germany's strength."He invested his entire reputation, gained in 1929 during his inaugural transatlantic flight, to serve the cause of non-intervention and the United States' strict neutrality.

At the opposite extreme of public opinion, the Committee to Defend America by Aiding the Allies, founded by the journalist William Allen White, militated in favour of active support for the British. Hollywood was quick to join the bandwagon. A number of films endeavoured to influence opinion towards US intervention. Hence, in *Confessions of a Nazi Spy*, Anatole Litvak warned of the dangers of the "fifth column" in the United States. Warner studios also produced *I married a Nazi*. In *The Great Dictator*, Chaplin offered a parody of the Third Reich, bitterly satirising its glorious Fuehrer and scathingly attacking his regime's brutality and anti-Semitism. Certain critics responsive to isolationist views condemned the films as a "bellicose, Jewish and anti-American work."In 1941, the Senate established an investigation committee on "insidious propaganda aimed at influencing public opinion towards the United States' participation in the European war."Yet it did not prevent Howard Hanks from embarking on *Sergeant York*, the same year, offering a portrait of a pacifist farmer - played by Garry Cooper - metamorphosed into a World War I hero... a conspicuously timely demonstration!

France's defeat had convinced Roosevelt that he could no longer maintain his stance as a more or less engaged spectator. Almost imperceptibly, he became a key player, guided by two major concerns: to reinforce the United States' defensive potential and to offer support to the

Poster published by the Committee to Defend America by Aiding the Allies.

British, who were now alone against the Axis Powers. He nevertheless adopted a prudent, step-by-step approach, taking into account interior constraints.

The second semester of 1940 was largely occupied by preparations for the presidential elections and Roosevelt had decided to run for election for the third time. He consequently avoided taking overtly unpopular measures, to avoid jeopardising his chances of success. His interventions were purposely reassuring "I will not send your boys into any foreign wars." In November, his clear victory against the republican candidate was nevertheless to offer him free rein for an increasingly conspicuous policy in favour of both moral and material support for Great Britain.

But late 1940, Churchill appealed for help. Britain's finances were depleted. The country would shortly no longer be able to honour payment of the equipment and supplies the United States was providing. Roosevelt fully grasped the urgency and was quick to react. On the 17th of December, during a press conference, the President advocated a genuine revolution in America's trade relations with Great Britain, "What I'm trying to do is eliminate the dollar sign. Suppose my neighbor's home catches fire, and I have a length of garden hose... I don't say to him, 'Neighbor, my garden hose cost me $15. You have to pay me $15 for it'. I'll lend it to him ... and he'll give it back to me... or he'll replace it." Hence, the idea behind the *Lend Lease* law was launched. The President's proposal was approved by a large majority. Despite rearguard action by the America First Committee, the Congress agreed and the text introducing the Lend-Lease law, ingeniously baptised, "An Act to Further Promote the Defense of the United States", was promulgated on the

American rifles being delivered to the United Kingdom, under the Lend-Lease programme.

August 1941: reunited with their respective military staff aboard the *Prince of Wales* battleship, Roosevelt and Churchill drafted the bases of the Atlantic Charter.

March 1941: Comics joined the public opinion bandwagon.

11th of March 1941. Upon approval from the chambers, the President was authorised to provide weapons, ammunition and supplies to any country whose defence appeared essential to the national interest. Any question of possible reimbursement was deliberately left unanswered. Several billion dollars of credit were immediately granted to the United Kingdom. The USSR, which had been invaded by German troops in June, was also to benefit from such support as from October 1941.

Well beyond economic solidarity, the United States and the United Kingdom began to forge other, moral and ideological links. On the 9th of August 1941, the American President and the British Prime Minister met aboard a warship, off the Newfoundland coast. Their encounter was to lead to a joint policy statement in the form of the Atlantic Charter. It set down a series of general principals aimed at implementing a shared policy: the right for all populations for self-determination, the need for global cooperation to encourage economic and social advancement, the freedom of trade and of the seas, the restoration of sustainable peace thanks to the

7th December 1941: Japanese attack on Pearl Harbor. The *Tennessee* and *West Virginia* battleships ablaze.

implementation of a future general security system - all of these principles being made possible thanks to the immediate and total destruction of the Nazi tyranny. It was a fine illustration of faith in the future, whilst the vast majority of Europeans still writhed under Hitler's yoke.

During their Newfoundland encounter, Churchill also strove to engage in military negotiations. The subject of transatlantic supply convoys was broached. The severe losses sustained by the British convoys had considerably reduced the effectiveness of the American support. The United States agreed to protect transport ships as far as the coast off Iceland. Following the supposedly fortuitous attack on an American destroyer by a *U-Boot* in September 1941, Roosevelt spoke of Germany as a "venimous serpent», stating that the

time for active defence had come. The US Navy warships received orders to fire on sight whenever threatened. By November, the Congress had completed the dismantling of the neutrality acts by authorising American merchant ships to arm and to transport equipment. The United States and Germany were virtually at war without for as much declaring it.

A survey, conducted during the summer of 1941, revealed that two-thirds of American citizens were, at this stage in developments, in favour of supporting the United Kingdom, whatever the risks involved, compared to only 36% in May 1940. A share of Roosevelt's entourage urged him to take the ultimate step. Yet the President fully intended to stick to his *all aid short of war* position, failing to take any further initiative, in

8th December 1941: President Roosevelt declares war against Japan.

...we here highly resolve that these dead shall not have died in vain...

REMEMBER DEC. 7th!

keeping with his public commitments. He confided in a close friend that he would rather "be forced into the conflict"than to decide to do so of his own will. And whilst he very probably expected Germany to deliver the decisive blow... Japan entered the scene.

On the 7th of December 1941, Japanese aircraft carriers launched a brutal attack on the American base on Pearl Harbor, in Hawaii. This surprise attack - or at least surprise location - was the consequence of the increasingly tense relationship between the United States and Japan resulting from the imperialist policy adopted over several years by the latter in South-East Asia and to which Washington had retaliated via progressively severe economic retortion. On the 8th of December, upon Roosevelt's request, the Congress unanimously (with the exception of one vote) declared war against Japan. Three days later, upon Tokyo's request, Germany and Italy declared war against the United States. The conflict had become world war.

Less than a fortnight after Pearl Harbor, Roosevelt and Churchill met again in Washington (the Arcadia Conference). They decided to establish a joint military staff and to define a common war strategy. In perfect harmony, they decided to place priority on the fight against what they deemed to be their most formidable enemy, Nazi Germany (*Germany First*); which was far from an obvious choice, given the widespread condemnation against Japan. However that may be, the United States' main concern was now to put their policy into action by mobilising public opinion, by developing their weapons production and by forming an army worthy of the name.

In truth, diplomatic changes driven by Roosevelt himself since 1940 had already led to decisive decisions being made well before Pearl Harbor. Without necessarily being totally organised to face the challenge of world war, the United States was at least better prepared than it had been in 1917.

Mobilising public opinion

Pearl Harbor was to permanently eradicate the isolationist movement, provoking a genuine sacred union and stirring national fervour. Although the desire for vengeance against Japan required no further feeding, the conflict that opposed the United States with Germany and Italy was far from arousing equivalent enthusiasm. In the spring of 1942, a survey revealed that 53% of Americans had, as yet, failed to fully grasp their nation's precise aims. The Office of War Information (OWI), set up by Roosevelt at the time, was entrusted with the mission of informing them.

San Augustine (Texas): propaganda posters even made their way inside schools.

Recording of the radio series, *You can't do business with Hitler*, produced by the OWI (1942).

Children taking part in a patriotic demonstration in Southington (Connecticut).

One of its tasks consisted in inundating the country with propaganda posters. Largely distributed thanks to support from keen local volunteers, patriotic associations, boy scouts and even railway companies, these posters were to be plastered everywhere: in the street, in workshops, stores, offices, restaurants, train stations and even schools. Their aim was to convince the Americans of the necessity of the war effort in all its forms.

A series of posters was designed to highlight the threat that a Nazi attack implied for the national territory. A threat which, if truth be told, was scarcely credible given the great distance, but sufficient to increase the population's awareness of the state of war and to generate a defensive reaction. With the same objective, a curfew was initiated in certain cities such as Chicago and New York, as if they were under a genuine bombing threat. Anti-aircraft guns appeared on the roofs of certain buildings in Washington, whilst sand bags were used to protect historic monuments.

May 1942: patriotic demonstration on *Memorial Day* in a small town in north-west America.

A "*Victory Home*". The pennant with the blue star indicates that a member of the family is serving in the armed forces. In the case of a death, the star was yellow.

Other defensive measures were also deployed. The music industry also contributed to the patriotic wave with releases such as *Ballad for Americans, Bless'm all, Praise the Lord and pass the munitions…* whilst radio channels devoted a large share of their programmes to the war. Every Saturday night, virtually each and every network broadcast the series *This is War*, covering themes such as *America at War, Your Army, Mr Smith against the Axis…* Three quarters of the twenty TV series broadcast by the NBC every week were connected with the war. The OWI organised a great diversity of campaigns across the radio airwaves, ranging from planting lawns (referred to as "Victory Gardens") to the enlisting of glider pilots, via the purchase of war bonds.

Extensive use was made of the seventh art. In 1942, the filmmaker Franck Capra was entrusted by the US Army with the mission of comprising a team and of producing a series of propaganda films entitled *Why We Fight* and aimed at explaining the sense of the conflict both to new recruits and to civilians. However, rather than these documentaries, American spectators preferred

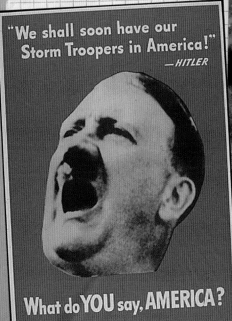

"We shall soon have our Storm Troopers in America!"
—HITLER

What do YOU say, AMERICA?

Don't Let That Shadow Touch Them
Buy WAR BONDS

IT CAN HAPPEN HERE

HE'S WATCHING YOU

WE'RE FIGHTING TO PREVENT THIS

entertaining programmes that made them laugh, cry or shudder. Hollywood consequently deployed its huge power and skill to tip the scales. Among the 1,200 films produced during the war, over 500 were on the same subject. The transition had proved to be relatively simple: the wicked gangster became a wicked Nazi, the nasty Indian became a nasty Jap, and the good guys were now the brave American or Allied soldiers.

Such mobilisation of the collective consciousness was quick to bear fruit. The call for patriotism was far from vain. In American workshops, the star spangled banner was proudly flown above machines operating at full capacity. Posters proclaiming, "*This is a Victory Home*" were affixed to house windows, bearing witness to the family's commitment to serve the nation. Alongside them, many a pennant, boasting the national colours, also indicated a son or a husband enlisted in the army.

"The Arsenal of Democracy"

America's industry found itself assigned with a gargantuan task. It was to achieve two concurrent aims: to respond to ever-increasing demands from Allied nations, without sacrificing - on the contrary - the armament of the developing US Army.

In December 1940, Roosevelt launched a new slogan that was to truly hit home: the United States was to become the "Arsenal of Democracy". The promulgation of the Lend-Lease law a few months later was to further accentuate demand from overseas. By late 1941, the President and his advisors had elaborated their famous "*Victory Program*", presented to the American people shortly after Pearl Harbor, in January 1942. "The United States' superiority in terms of weapons and ships must be overwhelming. So overwhelming that the Axis nations will lose all hope of ever challenging it." And the President then announced a long list of breathtaking figures: 60,000 planes in 1942, 125,000

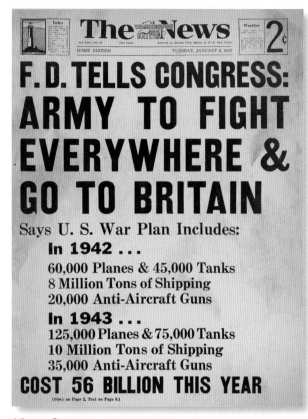

Victory Program press announcement.

in 1943. The same year, 75,000 tanks were also to be produced, along with 35,000 anti-aircraft guns. The volume of naval constructions was to be multiplied by ten in just two years.

Although by no means negligible, the results achieved in 1942 were far from the predetermined objective which had proved to be somewhat unrealistic. The move from a peaceful to a wartime economy had met with a few hurdles and hiccups. The multiplication of bureaux within the Federal administration, each with more or less well-defined responsibilities, encroaching on one another, had finally led to certain disorder. It was only in 1943, via the creation of the Office of War Production (OWP), which operated in close collaboration with major employers, that production truly and radically increased: 30,000 tanks in 1943 compared to 400 in 1940; concurrently, the production of guns increased from 1,800 to 67,000. Yet the most spectacular effort was made in the nation's aircraft production: 96,000 planes were produced in 1944 compared to 13,000 in 1940. The Americans had made the strategic choice of equipping its air force with a powerful fleet of heavy long-range bombers such as Boeing B-17 Flying Fortresses or Consolidated B-24 Liberators. Throughout the entire duration of the war, a total of 320,000 planes were delivered to the US Army, along with 88,000 tanks, 114,000 combat vehicles (half-track), 634,000 jeeps and 2,300,000 trucks of all sorts.

The powerful American military-industrial complex was now in place and it made quite an impression on outside observers, such as this Frenchman, during a trip to North-West America, "The landscape is no longer recognisable. New factories have replaced lines of trees. The planes and trucks, for which there is no more

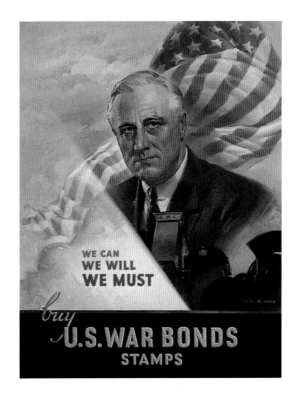

WE CAN
WE WILL
WE MUST

buy
U.S. WAR BONDS
STAMPS

B-17 bombers being assembled in Boeing's Seattle plants (in the State of Washington).

A giant *B-24* production plant in Willow Run

In the spring of 1941, in response to insistent government appeals, Henry Ford accepted to create a brand new factory, in the middle of a field in Willow Run, 30 miles to the south of Detroit, to produce *B-24 Liberator* bombers.

Built partly thanks to State funding, the plant stretched over a whole mile and, at the time, was the largest in the world. At the peak of its activity, it employed 42,000 labourers, many of whom were women and unemployed workers from southern states, essentially blacks.

Genuine cities needed to be developed to accommodate them, a highway needed to be built to ensure fast links with Detroit and a training centre with a capacity of 3,000 needed to be opened.

Ford applied to aeronautical construction the assembly techniques that had sealed his success in the automobile industry. At the height of its activity in 1944, a total of 650 planes left Willow Run's assembly lines each month, i.e. 20 to 25 every day... approximately one plane every hour!

The plant produced a total of 8,800 *B-24s*, representing around a half of the 18,000 planes of this type produced in the United States throughout the war.

space left in hangars, are lined up in the fields, wheel-to-wheel, bumper-to-bumper; creating a brown wave across the prairie. When counting up this iron harvest, when contemplating the guns that grow in the plain, a stupid, yet nagging question haunts you, 'What are they going to do with it all?' "

M3 Grant tanks being produced in Chrysler's Detroit plants (Michigan).

Victory will depend on good company relationships among all races.

Manufacturers needed to respond to massive State orders and to restructure accordingly. Chrysler gave up its car manufacture to make tanks; Ford took to mass production of planes; Chevrolet and Studebaker developed plane engines. Typewriter manufacturers were now making machine guns. Here and there, silverware was replaced by medical instruments... or bayonets, agricultural trucks by gear systems, car radiators by helmets, juke-boxes by metal lathes...

Despite the millions of men who had enlisted, the question of manpower was by no means a hurdle. Although Roosevelt's *New Deal* had generated a certain economic upturn, the 1930s depression had left many millions unemployed and immediately available on the labour market. As during World War I, the time had even come to massively call upon women and black workers, the American society's perpetually neglected citizens.

For it was one thing to mass produce weapons, but it was another to ship them overseas to feed the Allied nations and the theatres of operations in which the US Army was engaged. Hence the necessity for a merchant fleet, the *Liberty Fleet*, capable of taking on such a challenge. Such was the mission entrusted to America's shipyards. The Richmond yards (in California), run by the genius Henry Kayser, produced the famous *Liberty Ships* at an astounding rate thanks to a new assembly process consisting in putting together prefabricated parts. He also replaced welding - which demands highly qualified staff - with a much faster pneumatic rivet gun technique which required no training. From then on, the time required to complete a 10,000 tonne, 425-feet ship - excluding interior fittings - had been reduced to one month compared to the previous six months. In 1943, one team even established an all-time record of just fourteen days. A total of 2,700 *Liberty Ships* were set to sea during the war.

The Bethlehem Fairfield Shipyards in Baltimore (Maryland).

Do the job *HE* left behind

APPLY
U.S. EMPLOYMENT SERVICE

We Can

WOMEN

There's work to be done and a war to be won...
NOW!

SEE YOUR U. S. EMPLOYMENT SERVICE
WAR MANPOWER COMMISSION

U. S. ARMY
OFFICIAL POSTER

SOLDIERS *without guns*

American women during the war

In the United States, women's work was traditionally relatively poorly developed due to reluctance on two fronts: among industrial bosses, owing to their inferior physical strength; and among conservative circles who cherished traditional family values.

The war was to reverse the situation. Women massively entered the labour market. From 10 million in 1939, their numbers progressed to 20 million in 1944, i.e. 36% of the active population, including - and that's where the genuine novelty lay - a majority of married women.

Women were increasingly employed in the civil service, in the stock exchange, as bus drivers, train inspectors, policewomen... However, the most striking innovation was their spectacular integration within industrial plants, where they now represented 30% of the total workforce, occupying up to 40% of jobs in aviation factories. One could now see female crane drivers, mechanics, naval shipyard labourers... A famous poster, "Rosie the Riveter" proudly proclaimed, "We can do it.»

To satisfy industrial needs, the Office of War Information was entrusted with promoting both the aeronautical construction sector and women's work in general. The office's photographers set to producing a multitude of pictures demonstrating that women were perfectly capable of doing men's jobs, without losing their, often Hollywood-inspired, femininity.

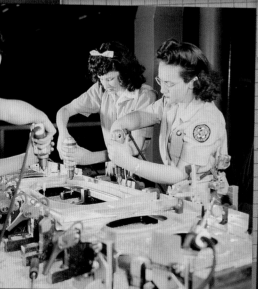

I'm Proud... my husband wants me to do my part

SEE YOUR U. S. EMPLOYMENT SERVICE
WAR MANPOWER COMMISSION

The more WOMEN at work the sooner we WIN!

WOMEN ARE NEEDED ALSO AS:

FARM WORKERS	WAITRESSES	TIMEKEEPERS	LAUNDRESSES
TYPISTS	BUS DRIVERS	ELEVATOR OPERATORS	TEACHERS
SALESPEOPLE	TAXI DRIVERS	MESSENGERS	CONDUCTORS

— and in hundreds of other war jobs!

SEE YOUR LOCAL U.S. EMPLOYMENT SERVICE

An army to build

In 1939, the United States' armed forces barely exceeded 300,000 men for a total population of some 130 million. Despite a few shortages, the US Navy nevertheless maintained a certain degree of credibility; however, the US Army, with its 165,000 infantrymen and 25,000 aviators remained the forces' poor relation. "A third-rate power,"George C. Marshall, Chief of Staff of the Army since 1939, had even dared to declare. In true Anglo-Saxon tradition, the militaristic spirit was only poorly developed in the United States, contrary to Germany or Japan. Furthermore, the country imposed no mandatory military service, simply a small professional army which, although correctly trained, was frustrated by inadequate military funding, insufficient numbers and still equipped with material dating from World War I. This Regular Army was complemented by the National Guard and the Organized Reserve.

The National Guard was raised and trained by each State; in charge of maintaining order in times of peace, it could only be mobilised in times of war. It comprised a total of 200,000 volunteers, who underwent forty-eight training periods every year. In reality, barely a few hours of exercise or firing per day, customarily followed by rowdy card games over a good few pints of beer in the company mess.

The Organized Reserve was essentially comprised of officers (115,000), some of them Great War veterans, but the majority of them younger recruits who had received military training in colleges or universities before being commissioned by the Reserve Officer Training Corps.

At the start of the war in Europe, and more particularly following France's totally unexpected collapse in June 1940, the American government multiplied its efforts to reinforce its army. Military funding was substantially

George C. Marshall (1880-1959), US Army Chief of Staff.

Recruitment poster for the regular army (1941).

increased in order to modernise the armed forces, to boost their ranks by enlisting volunteers and to intensify the production of weapons and ammunition.

In order to multiply the ranks, the National Guard was placed under federal control in the summer of 1940. Hence, the 29th Infantry Division, which was to land on *Omaha Beach* on the 6th of June 1944, was formed in February 1941 from National Guard battalions originating from Maryland and Virginia. Concurrently, reserve officers were gradually called up to reinforce supervision. Conscription (the Draft) was re-established in September, for the first time in the country's history in times of peace. The Selective Service Act provided for the registration of all men aged between 21 and 35 years. Lots were drawn and nine hundred thousand of them were incorporated for one year, a period which was extended to eighteen months in August 1941. Immediately prior to Pearl Harbor, the United States Army comprised a total of 2,500,000 men.

After America had entered the war, a new law extended the basis of military mobilisation. All men aged from 18 to 45 years were potentially eligible for enlistment for a period equivalent to the duration of the war plus a further six months. Discharge measures on the grounds of physical condition or family situation were gradually reduced. However, in order to satisfy economic needs, the entire male population was not for as much submitted to donning the military uniform. Yet voluntary enlistment continued, particularly among young men and intensely after the Japanese attack. In December 1942, all forces combined, a total of 7,000,000 were under military service, a figure that was to rise to 12,500,000 by early 1944. The US Army had become one of the world's most powerful, its figures largely measuring up to those of the Red Army. Racial segregation was still in force in the American army during World War II - only to be abolished in

Calling upon airborne troops to enlist.

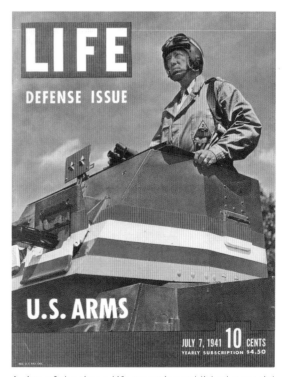

A sign of the times, Life magazine published a special issue in July 1941 focusing on the US Army and on rearmament. General Patton, Commander of the 2nd Armoured Division, appeared on the front cover.

1948 - for still commonplace in society. In 1940, Roosevelt had imposed an overall quota of 10% of black soldiers within the armed forces, i.e. in equivalent proportion to the general population. Nevertheless, despite a few accomplishments during the conflict, American blacks remained victim to racial prejudice. As such, very few of them joined combat units, due to their alleged lack of "discipline and efficiency". Essentially originating from southern States, and more than reluctant, they were only to integrate the officer corps in "dribs and drabs" What's more, blood transfusion centres used "white blood for whites" and "black blood for blacks". Since the "noble" forces, such as the Air Force and the Navy, remained extremely attached to their "*lilywhite*"tradition, the vast majority of black soldiers were posted in the Army, almost exclusively among logistic services and in separate units.

In the United States, the prospect of seeing women don a military uniform was also far from meeting with unanimous approval, still hindered by conventional

Posters encouraging nurses to enlist in the army.

General McNair (1883-1944), the "father of the US Army" talking with General Bradley (1893-1981), Commander of the Fort Benning Infantry School, during 3rd Army manoeuvres in Louisiana.

mentalities. Their proportion among recruits was consequently modest (never exceeding 2%), compared, in particular, with the United Kingdom (10%) and the USSR (12%). The Army Nurses Corps, of old origin for it dated back to the early 20th century, was relatively well-regarded. Yet the creation, during World War II, of the WAC (Women's Army Corps) within the Army and the Air Force and the WAVES (Women Accepted for Volunteer Emergency Service) within the Navy, met with increasing reservations, even if there was no question of their integration within combat units, contrary to women enlisted in the Red Army. Most often young, single or divorced, with a high level of education, these female volunteers were entrusted with a wide range of tasks among military departments: weather, mail, transmissions, transport, staff management, supplies...

From "Sammy" to GI: reorganising the armed forces

Throughout the armed forces' phenomenal growth, reorganisation and adjustments proved necessary. Following the example of the United Kingdom, and for the same strategic purposes given the conflict's international scale and the necessity to combat overseas, the Air Force and the Navy were afforded particular attention.

America's aviation, until then still incorporated within the Army, gained its independence in March 1942 with the official inauguration of the US Air Force. It was to undergo spectacular development, both in terms of the imposing equipment at its disposal and the number of its recruits: 1,800,000 men early 1944, i.e. seventy-two times more than in 1939!

The United States' military commitment on two key fronts, Europe and Asia, had rendered the creation of a "Two-Ocean Navy" absolutely necessary and had led to the US Navy's division into two distinct commands, one for the Atlantic, the other for the Pacific. In 1944, with the addition of the Coast Guards and the US Marine Corps, which had its own infantry and aviation, the Navy reunited a total of around 3 million men.

The US Army in turn reunited a powerful force of some 7,600,000 men. Yet, "victim" to competition from the nation's other two forces, the Army failed to gather the 115 divisions planned for in the Victory Plan, to finally content itself with 90 divisions.

Lieutenant General Lesley McNair, Commanding General of the Army Ground Forces, was entrusted with the huge mission of mobilising, equipping and training millions of men before sending them overseas, essentially to Europe, but also to Asia. As such, he was legitimately considered as the "father of the US Army".

The successful feats by the *Wehrmacht* in the early months of the war had inspired the military staff. Hence, the *Panzers'* victorious march through France

in June 1940 led, the very next month, to the creation of America's first two armoured divisions. Similarly, akin to the *Fallschirmjäger*, paratrooper units were progressively developed leading to the creation, in 1942, of the 82nd and the 101st Airborne that were to win fame two years later in Normandy.

Yet the US Army was far from limited to combat troops. Foreshadowing modern armies, logistic corps (engineer, transport, supply, signal, medical...) absorbed a significant share of available troops. In 1944, they represented around half of the Army Ground Forces' total numbers.

Up to early 1942, the physical appearance of American soldiers was barely distinguishable from that of their

The crew of an *M4 Sherman*, during manoeuvres at Fort Knox (Kentucky).

Up to 1941, American soldiers still looked very much like their World War I predecessors.

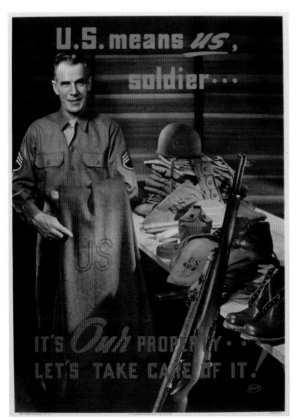

The GI's new gear.

the one that was quick to be given the nickname of "GI" after the traditional stamp on military equipment: *Government Issue.*

Re-equipped from head to toe, with a genuine "wardrobe" full of highly functional clothing, they became the best dressed soldiers in the world. In complement to the service uniform, battle dress - a khaki and beige *Field Jacket* and mustard-coloured trousers were worn both by troops and superior officers, whereas the olive green fatigue uniform was also used for combat in the summer months. The British "Brodie" helmet was replaced by the US M1 model, including a light fibre helmet covered with a heavy steel helmet. They wore laced boots with flexible rubber soles, ideal for silent manoeuvres. Their old *Springfield* rifles were replaced by automatic *Garands*, 30 calibre carbines or *Thompson* submachine guns. Their kit bag included food rations, toiletries, first-aid kit, personal belongings... and a half-tent to join up with a buddy's for camp.

After training, the American forces were now ready and equipped to be sent into combat. The US Navy served essentially in the Pacific, whilst the US Army was largely engaged in Europe. Its first objective: the United Kingdom.

forefathers, the "*Sammies*", who had fought in World War I. However, 1942 was to bring a new US soldier:

Reviewing a kit bag during 2nd Army manoeuvres in Tennessee in 1943.

THE AMERICANS
"INVADE" THE UNITED KINGDOM

As early as the autumn of 1940, amidst the raging aerial battle, the American government sent its very first observers to the United Kingdom. A thirty-man *special observers group* led by General Chaney established itself in London in May 1941. Although in civilian dress, to protect the American principle of neutrality, they were nevertheless entrusted with an overtly military mission aimed at studying the potential difficulties that would be encountered by arriving troops should the United States join the conflict. Furthermore, the *Magnet* plan, which consisted in sending an initial 100,000-man contingent, had already been approved. Our "observers" were consequently in search of potential camp locations, airfield sites and port facilities in Northern Ireland and Scotland.

The vanguard of the US Army landed in Northern Ireland in January 1942.

◀ GIs manoeuvring in the English countryside.

January 1942: the first Americans land in Northern Ireland

Barely seven weeks after Pearl Harbor, four thousand men from the 34th US Infantry Division, still donning their Great War uniforms, landed in Belfast to be welcomed by representatives from His Majesty's government and a horde of journalists. A vast communication campaign had been specially launched for the occasion. Private Milburn H. Henke, from Hutchison, Minnesota, was chosen to personify "the first American to set foot on European soil". To the clattering sound of the cameras, five hundred exhausted troops, who had landed ten minutes previously, paraded behind the regimental band on the nearby quayside, their expressions sending a chill through the assembly that was as cold as the wintry climate. The press was tactful enough not to broadcast the event.

Over the following months, other units in turn headed for Northern Ireland. In May 1942, only 32,000 US Army soldiers had been dispatched across the Atlantic. In

Private Milburn H. Henke, "the first American to set foot on European soil".

addition, the air and ground crews from General Eaker's 8th Bomber Command had also been engaged by the Allies in aerial attacks against the Reich. The RAF had consequently and immediately conceded eight airfields for use by the Americans, whilst launching a vast programme to develop a further thirty sites in order to ultimately

American camp in Northern Ireland.

Assembling a *Nissen Hut*.

welcome General Carl Spaatz' entire 8th US Air Force. The first *B-17s* left the Maine coastline to reach Prestwick, in Scotland, on the 1st of July, after stopping over in Iceland. On the 17th of August 1942, they entered into action by bombing the Rouen-Sotteville railway line.

A few camps had been evacuated to make room for the American troops. But others would need to be rapidly built. The adopted solution consisted in making massive use of *Nissen Huts*, which were to become both part of the landscape and of the GIs' day-to-day life. These semi-circular corrugated steel constructions were of varying dimensions; placed on a concrete base, they were both simple and quick to assemble. Dating back from World War I, they owed their name to their designer, Major Nissen, from the Royal Engineers. These shelters fulfilled a number of purposes: quarters, canteens, mess, offices, briefing rooms for pilots, ammunitions stores, field hospitals, latrines...

In the spring of 1942, the American contingent posted in the United Kingdom remained but symbolic. However, this did not prevent General Marshall, along with Harry Hopkins, President Roosevelt's personal adviser, from travelling to London in April and from presenting the British with several potential plans for American intervention in Europe The *Yankees* were keen to get rid of the German enemy as fast as they could, before turning their efforts on Japan, as expected by the large majority of public opinion. Without an inkling, they presented their proposals which met with a lukewarm welcome from the Allies.

Strategic discord between the Americans and the British

Marshall pulled several plans out of his briefcase. Operation *Roundup* planned to mobilise a total of forty-eight divisions (nine of them armoured), supported by around six thousand planes, and required seven thousand ships. The assault, to be launched between Le Havre and Boulogne, would be led by a wave of at least six divisions, progressively reinforced by 100,000 men every week. To satisfy these needs, the *Bolero* plan involved massive shipments of American troops and equipment towards the United Kingdom. Yet, for the time being, its implementation remained but theory. The German submarines haunted the Atlantic waters, causing considerable losses among convoys heading for the United Kingdom. As Hitler jubilantly declared, the ocean formed Nazi Europe's first line of defence and it was holding strong.

Given the sheer scale of *Roundup*, it was impossible to implement before the spring of 1943. But would the Russian front hold out that long? There was no guarantee, for the German offensive had resumed with a vengeance in the spring of 1942. Subsequently, the Americans were quick to put forward a different landing project, possibly in the Cotentin peninsula and using available troops, in order - in the case of emergency - to alleviate the pressure exerted on the Red Army by the *Wehrmacht*; the plan was codenamed *Sledgehammer*. General Alan Brooke, Chief of the Imperial General Staff, was stupefied, and wrote "The Americans have not begun to realise all the implications of this plan. It was not possible to take Marshall's 'castle in the air' too seriously. The plans are fraught with the gravest dangers. The prospects of success are small and dependent on a mass of unknowns whilst the chances of disaster are great and dependent on a mass of well-established facts."

As for Churchill, he approved the *Roundup* plan, nevertheless stressing that the spring of 1943 appeared a somewhat premature date; in contrast, he clearly expressed his hostility to the *Sledgehammer* plan, which he deemed to be a "hazardous" operation. Led only by a handful of divisions - essentially British, since the GIs posted in Europe were, as yet, in too small numbers - the plan would offer no real support to the Soviets. Hence,

July 1942, King George and Queen Elizabeth visit the American troops based in Northern Ireland.

Roosevelt and Churchill reunited in Casablanca on the 24th of January 1943.

over several months of heated negotiations, the British struggled to convince their impetuous allies to abandon *Sledgehammer*. Yet there was very little leeway. "We either play our cards, or we put them back in the pack," the Americans were quick to threaten; Roosevelt himself talked of, "packing up his bags"; in other words, if nothing was to be undertaken in Europe in 1942, their best bet was to wage war against Japan.

In July 1942, Churchill finally put an end to the stalemate by proposing to replace a direct attack against the formidable *Fortress Europe* with a landing operation in North Africa, where the Vichy troops - we could always hope - would put up but weak resistance. Operation *Torch* was launched without delay on the Moroccan and Algerian coasts on the 8th of November 1942. It was led essentially by American troops who had been brought in convoys from England or direct from the United States.

After this successful mission, the debate between the Allies became increasingly heated. As did many other American officers, General Wedemeyer took a severe tone, "The British were masters in negotiations. What I witnessed was the British power of diplomatic finesse in its finest hour, a power that had been developed over centuries of successful international intrigue." The Secretary of War, Harry Stimson's conclusion was crystal clear, "We cannot reasonably hope to cross the English Channel and do battle with the Germans. The Prime Minister and the Chief of the Imperial General Staff are frankly opposed to this project."

In truth, there was a clash between two strategic positions. The American officers, who had been trained according to Napoleonic theories at West Point Academy, endorsed the principle of a "strong to strong" attack. They firmly believed that the key objective remained a direct attack on Germany, in order to hasten its final defeat: in other words, thanks to a cross-Channel landing operation, as close as possible to the frontiers of the Reich. The British, who had already been offered an opportunity to defy the Germans - rarely to their advantage - in France, Greece and

German propaganda poster making fun of the Allies' slow progress in Italy.

During the Trident Conference, held in Washington in May 1943, plans were developed to launch an assault early May 1944. In August, the Quadrant Conference in Quebec opted for the coast alongside the Bay of Seine, deemed more propitious than the Pas-de-Calais. Indeed, the short distance that separated the English shores from the latter rendered it far too predictable for the Germans. Consequently, the Atlantic Wall in this zone had been fortified to a far greater extent than anywhere else. The strategy also involved an element of surprise, by attacking the Normandy beaches which - although at a greater distance - were considered by the enemy to be less at threat; they were consequently insufficiently defended.

The time had come to revive the *Bolero* plan - all the more so since the Allies had taken a considerable advantage in the Atlantic. Since mid-1943, German submarines had suffered heavy losses. The Allied convoys, in the company of their powerful escorts, could now freely ship and deliver a profusion of vehicles, tanks,

Libya, took on a more cautious stance. They advocated a "peripheral" strategy, occasionally referred to as the "bullfighting strategy". The concept involved exhausting the enemy via a series of peripheral attacks, before delivering the final blow.

Whether they liked it or not, the Americans were finally forced to resign themselves to following their allies in their proposals for Mediterranean intervention: the landing operation in Sicily in July 1943, followed by southern Italy in September. Yet the Americans now weighed heavier in the coalition balance and their voice was stronger. In January 1943, during the Casablanca Conference, the British were coerced into making a major concession by formally promising to put the cross-Channel landing back on the table. The *Overlord* plan, which was no more and no less than a revival of the general outline of *Roundup*, was now in the making. The operation remained to be planned and a precise date and location to be established. Such was the mission entrusted to the military staff led by the British General Morgan.

August 1943, reunited in Quebec for the Quadrant Conference, William Mackenzie King (Canadian Prime Minister), Franklin D. Roosevelt (President of the United States) and Winston Churchill (British Prime Minister) chose the Normandy beaches for their assault against Hitler's Nazi Europe.

The Queen Mary with thousands of American soldiers on board.

guns and ammunition to British ports, for them to be transported and stored in mass in warehouses scattered across the verdant English countryside. The monthly tonnage transported in the spring of 1944 was sixteen times more than it had been a year earlier.

Troops essentially travelled in large converted cruise ships. Among them, two of the Cunard Line's flagships, the *Queen Mary* and the *Queen Elizabeth*, were now decked with camouflage. Their extremely high speed meant that they were literally invulnerable to attack from the German *U-Boots*. The *Queen Mary* alone made fifteen return trips from New York to Gourock in Scotland with an average of 11,000 to 12,000 soldiers on board - sometimes even 15,000, without counting its thousand crew members. For a ship designed to comfortably welcome 2,000 passengers in times of peace, one can but imagine how they must have been packed together as far as the steerage, the gangway and even on the deck.

The "Yankees" discover "Old England".

As from late 1943, American troops arrived in the United Kingdom in ever-increasing numbers: from 100,000 to 150,000 every month, and even more than 200,000 in April 1944. Immediately prior to the landing operation, a total of 1,670,000 men – 427,000 of them from the US Air Force – were based in the UK, compared to only 300,000 in May 1943.

When he landed in Liverpool, just like his buddies, Private Vernon Tart from the 6th Engineer Brigade discovered the reality of a country at war, "There was a delegation who gave a short welcome speech and a small band playing, and after that was over we marched through the streets of Liverpool to the railroad station. This was my first view of any war damage or anything and I was fascinated, looking to the left and right at the ruins of buildings

In the spring of 1944, tens of thousands of GIs landed in the United Kingdom.

American equipment camps occupied the British countryside.

and the rubble in the streets, block after block. This was as a result of the Blitz, of course. Everything was under blackout, so that is how we travelled across Britain."

The centre of gravity of the American camps was progressively moved towards the centre and, in particular, the south of England, over a zone stretching from Hampshire to Cornwall. Camps, equipment depots and ammunition swathed the English countryside as far as the eye could see. The 8th Air Force's airfields alone covered thousands of hectares, literally saturating the counties of Norfolk and Suffolk. The equally cumbersome 9th Air Force set up camp further south. To facilitate transport, several hundred miles of railway line were built, whilst 20,000 wagons and a thousand locomotives were imported from the United States. In a country where space was scarce, congestion was a genuine threat, "In crowded England we could not fire a gun without moving someone out of the way of where the bullet might go," a staff officer ironically claimed. An amusing gag was quite popular in 1944, "If all of those barrage balloons hadn't permanently been in the British sky to hold it up, it would've fallen into the sea a long time ago."

John, who was but a schoolboy at the time, can remember this Yankee outbreak in his, otherwise quiet, village, "Our backwater which British soldiers had garrisoned so sparsely for four years, overflowed almost overnight with GIs. The American presence had swollen that spring to almost all pervading proportions, so that there seemed more Americans than natives in the district. How different they looked from our own jumble-sale champions, beautifully clothed in smooth khaki, as fine in cut and quality as a British officer's and armed with glistening, modern, automatic weapons. More striking still were the number, size and elegance of the vehicles in which they paraded about the countryside in stately convoy. The British Army's transport was a sad collection of underpowered makeshifts, whose dun paint flaked from their tinpot bodywork. The Americans travelled in magnificent, gleaming, olive-green, pressed-steel, four-wheel-drive juggernauts."

So what welcome would be extended to the GIs in the United Kingdom? The War Department was well aware that Nazi propaganda had, for many months, been striving to set the two Anglo-Saxon allies at loggerheads by trying to convince the British that they were, in fact, fighting to defend the interests of American plutocracy. It was therefore vital to control the attitude of the troops who were to land in a country were the vast majority of people were totally oblivious to the truth.

When they arrived in England, all American soldiers were provided with a small booklet entitled, *Instructions for American servicemen in Britain*. Over and above purely practical information on the country itself, the book paid particular attention to the British nature and to local customs. "British are like the Americans in many ways, but not in all ways. You will quickly discover differences like driving on the left side of the road, and having money based on an "impossible" accounting system, and drinking warm beer. The British don't know how to make a good cup of coffee. You don't know how to make a good cup of tea. It's an even swap. The British make much of Sunday. All the shops are closed, most of the restaurants are closed, and in the small towns there is not much to do. You had better follow the example of the British and try to spend Sunday afternoon in the country. The British are reserved, not unfriendly. So if Britons sit in trains or busses without striking up conversation with you, it doesn't mean they are being haughty and unfriendly. They don't speak to you because they don't want to appear intrusive or rude. They are not given to back-slapping and they are shy about showing their affection. But once they get to like you they make the best friends in the world."

As Churchill jokingly used to say, "Britain and America are two nations divided by a common language." The GIs' attention was drawn to differences in accent and pronunciation and, in particular, to the meaning of certain words or expressions. For example, "*homely*" means "simple, unpretentious" for a Brit, yet "ugly, unattractive" for an American. Such confusion could, indeed, have led to somewhat embarrassing situations!

Then followed a long list of what to do and, especially, what not to do; for example, in a pub, if you want to play

Encounter between an American woman from the Women's Army Corps (WAC) and a British "Bobby".

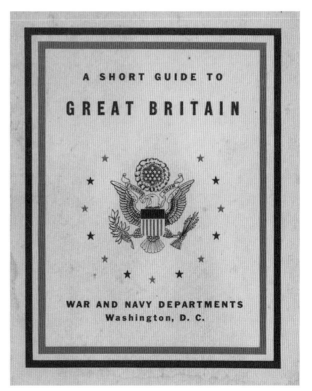

The guidebook that was given to Americans on their arrival in the United Kingdom.

At the Dove Inn, a pub in Burton Bradstock, in Dorset.

darts, wait until you are asked and don't walk away if you lose. If you are invited by a family for a meal, don't eat too much because food is rationed in Britain. Never remind the British that they have lost the first "rounds" in the war. For whilst it is impolite to criticise one's host, it is militarily stupid to criticise one's allies. Last but not least, never try to "steal" a British soldier's girlfriend or be seen in public with a woman whose husband has gone to the front. Hence this sardonic remark by Lieutenant Ingersoll, "it was hard to tell what relations might have been had both parties been left to their own devices."

All efforts were made by the American government to maintain a comfortable and familiar environment for their soldiers posted in the UK. In their wake, pinball machines, juke-boxes and Coca-Cola also crossed the Atlantic. The American Red Cross multiplied its rounds across the nation, distributing good coffee and the doughnuts the boys were so keen on. The GIs could watch "their" films and listen to "their" radio stations that played the latest releases by Duke Ellington and Glenn Miller. Every day, for just 2 cents, they could buy the American armed forces' newspaper, *The Stars and Stripes*, printed in London by The *Times*.

Yet the Americans were far from living in a closed environment. Throughout the countryside, contact with the local population was essentially made in pubs, those quintessential focal points of village conviviality. Many a tongue was loosened over a few pints of beer; some

The Burton Bradstock smithy.

losing their traditional inhibitions, others forgetting the precious advice they had been given. They talked about the weather, politics, the harvest. But it was essentially an excellent way to forge links with families likely to invite for dinner. Attentive to maintaining good relations with the local population, the American Army had generously distributed, among its men, food supplements that were sure to delight their British hosts. Officers were, in turn, regularly invited for tea by the local ladies.

Sport was also an excellent method for bringing people together. Yet cultural differences meant that improvements remained to be made on both sides, as Lieutenant Colonel Nathaniel Hoskot, from the 101st Airborne, posted near Nottingham, reminds us, "We used to play them at baseball on Saturdays and cricket on Sundays. We weren't very good at cricket and they weren't very good at baseball. It was a lot of fun. The people were delightful to us. The relations between the Americans and the British couldn't have been nicer." So was it a love match or a marriage of convenience? Ralph Ingersoll humorously relates, "A friendly old lady I used to call on in a nearby farmhouse summed her side of it up for me by saying, "Well, they grumble about this and that that your boys do, but I won't have any of it. Better to have them here, than the Germans any time, I always say."

Pinball machines crossed the Atlantic.

The Americans arrived with their Coca-Cola.

Initiation to baseball.

"Overpaid, oversexed and over here"

Despite generally cordial relations, the Americans were nevertheless the subject of a certain degree of criticism. As a Bristol journalist daringly wrote, "they are foreigners. Only a small percentage have any British forbears. They are all young in spirit as well as in body, and the mistakes that they make are likely to spring from too quick enthusiasm and too little background. Though we may be spiritually far more civilized, materially they have the advantage. They know the value of comfort, we don't."

And denigration didn't stop there. The expression "overpaid, oversexed and over here" was commonplace. "Over here" referred to the massive influx of GIs since late 1943, but was also very probably due to the impression that the Americans behaved as if they were on conquered territory. Yet no one went as far as talking of occupation.

"Overpaid"? Well paid without a doubt, since a private's pay was around three times more than that of the equivalent British "Tommy". A sergeant earned as much as a captain in the British Army. A difference that was very likely to generate a somewhat unhealthy atmosphere among men who were called upon to fight side by side. The risk had been calculated in the small instruction manual which recommended that American troops refrain from conspicuously spending money to avoid offending anyone. "They are more likely to feel that you haven't learned the common-

Mrs Hale, whose husband is a soldier, serving tea and refreshments to passing GIs.

sense virtues of thrift." Was this advice taken? Apparently not, according to General Bradley, "By the spring of 1944 the hospitable towns of southwest England were thronged with American troops. They filled the cobblestoned streets of Devonshire villages, drained the local pubs of beer, and made an affectionate union of our British alliance. Indeed, nowhere was amity courted with a greater diligence than in the homes of British fathers with pretty unmarried daughters. The Yankee invasion had come to England well heeled with American dollars. A substantial share of this wealth was invested in local courting."

"Oversexed"? In prudish old England, the Americans were undoubtedly blameworthy on that front! However, these men were alone and far from home; the quest for a soul mate was perfectly understandable, as Ralph Ingersoll endeavoured to explain "The real combination was between our young soldiers and the young English girls, particularly among farm and factory work. This was almost a case of spontaneous social combustion, so satisfactory did each seem to the other. The English girl is brought up to respect her men folk and to consider their pleasure her law. The American boys were bowled over to meet girls who were instinctively polite and obedient, inexpensive to entertain and anxious to please. On her side, the English girl was initiated into the charm of being with boys who, however rough or ignorant, had been brought up to put a woman's wishes before their own – whether it was in a matter of choosing which movie to go to or who would carry the heavy bundles home."

However, their intentions were sometimes expressed far more abruptly. "*Ok, Baby, let's go.*" (which could be interpreted as, "Ok baby, let's get serious.") was a phrase uttered to many a young British girl. Many a

Flirting during the harvest in Hertfordshire.

A GI with his girlfriend in Hyde Park.

rather taken aback passer-by was asked, "So what do you guys say when you mean sex?" However, our GIs needed to slow things down, as the anthropologist, Margaret Mead, analysed in an article published in 1944 in *Army Talks*, "When boys and girls do go to the same school in Britain, they act as if they were still going to separate schools. To an American eye, the absence of flirting and back chat among secondary school boys and girls is astonishing. Of course, this is very confusing to British girls who haven't had any practise in wisecracking. Some of them are insulted by the speed and assurance of the American's approach and turn chilly and unapproachable, and make him feel that Britain is a cold – and then he will add – little country." One English girl remembers their frequently "excessive" behaviour, "They knocked on house doors without the slightest apprehension; they even declared their love to police women whilst they were controlling the traffic; with no sense of judgment whatsoever, they accosted women of all ages as if they were prostitutes. The GIs finally forced those of us who were unwilling to accept their company to always, in winter as in summer, carry an umbrella which we used for self defence."

Despite all, many an "encounter", be it occasional or long-lasting, was made. Whilst some 80,000 Americans returned home after the war arm-in-arm with a British girl, the number of illegitimate births during the conflict was to escalate and the GIs' contribution was far from negligible.

The Americans import the "racial debate" into Britain

More deep-rooted discord was quick to emerge on the question of racial segregation, one of the American Army's other importations. As early as April 1942, General Channey had tried to convince Washington not to send any black soldiers to Ireland. However his requests were in vain, the War Department fully intending to scrupulously respect Roosevelt's orders with regard to quotas. The British Cabinet proved to be no more gracious when it asked for "coloured troops to be kept to a minimum".

The affair was soon to be entrusted to Major General Eisenhower, appointed Commanding General for the US Army's European Theatre of Operations in June 1942. He very rapidly grasped where the problem was, "To most English people, including the village girls,

July 1942, the first black soldiers arrive in Northern Ireland.

the negro soldier is just another man. Our own white soldiers, seeing a girl walk down the street with a negro, frequently see themselves as protectors of the weaker sex and believe it necessary to intervene even to the extent of using force, to let her know what she's doing." Indeed, clashes and scuffles were almost always for the same reason: it was almost inconceivable for the white GIs, who essentially originated from southern States, not to react when facing a situation that, back home, would - at the very least - lead to a good hiding. Eisenhower fully intended to abide by his decrees and by the principle that was largely shared across America, "Equal, but separated". As such, he reasserted the fact that no difference in treatment between blacks and whites was to be tolerated. They were all to be afforded the same rights. So, in principal, there was no discrimination; however, strict separation between races was to be applied - hence endorsing a policy of racial segregation. All efforts were to be made to avoid contact, hence avoiding unrest. In major towns and cities, army-run leisure facilities (clubs, cinemas...) were either reserved for whites or for blacks. In small towns and villages, leave was granted either to one, or the other, but never simultaneously.

So, how would the British authorities react to the application of imported racial segregation within their own territory? The War Office was keen, first and foremost, to maintain its excellent links with its American allies. It even considered discreetly advising British soldiers - women in particular - to avoid mixing with blacks. It also went as far as proposing that the troop be "educated", by explaining the racial policy in force in the United States and by adding that the best bet was to respect "American custom". The Home Office appeared to seek inspiration in Pontius Pilate. Although stating that the British police was not in charge of enforcing segregative measures in public places, it washed its hands of the rest. The Foreign Office was more attentive to the liberal movement and

This poster deals with the Nazi propaganda that strove to divide British and American soldiers.

Black GIs explaining to a British policeman how their submachine gun works.

Black and white couple dancing at *Frisco's International Club* in Piccadilly, London; the type of scene many white GIs could barely tolerate and which often led to brawls.

At the jukebox.

to the organisations that strove to defend blacks in the United States. The Colonial Office in turn feared the negative repercussions that the American racial policy ("a genuine stick of dynamite") might have on its own black soldiers in the United Kingdom and beyond, throughout the entire Empire. Churchill finally approved the War Office's position, "It is a host's duty not to embarrass his guests." He nevertheless added that his attitude towards his colonial troops would be different from that of the Americans.

However, quite a different viewpoint predominated in the public opinion. In 1943, a survey revealed that the American Army's segregation policy was welcomed with hostility by the vast majority of the population. A large share of the press took its own stand, particularly following a number of death sentences pronounced by court martial subsequent to rapes attributed to blacks, often based on dubious witness reports. The American military staff's public relations officer lost his temper, "These articles are far more harmful than Goebbels' propaganda, for they present us as an uncivilised nation, come to invade the United Kingdom."

The *Bolero* plan was to bring increasing numbers of black troops to the United Kingdom (130,000 in May 1944) and scuffles with GIs were frequent; it is interesting to note that civilians often intervened in favour of the former. Back in the United States, southerners began to worry about the ramifications this warm welcome extended to the blacks by the British might generate. They were particularly concerned about the risk of black militants utilising the situation to further support their claims after the war. In the spring of 1944, the US Army's postal control department examined outgoing mail from soldiers - both black and white - with a fine-tooth comb, to observe that 90% of letters broaching the subject of racial relationships did so in an extremely negative way. The final report, dated 29th May, concluded, "If the landing doesn't come soon, we can expect trouble."

"Ike" takes control of operation *Overlord*

Teheran, November 1943, the first of the conferences to be held between the "Big Three". *Overlord* was obviously at the heart of the debate. Joseph Stalin was evidently satisfied; Roosevelt and Churchill had just delivered the news he had been awaiting for so long: the opening of a second front in France in the early days of May 1944. The idea to launch a support landing operation in Provence, simultaneous to the Normandy landings was also back on the agenda. The American strategists believed it to be a standard pincer movement, likely to drive the enemy even faster out of France and to accelerate the final assault against the Reich. Stalin was immediately won over by this proposition. In contrast, Churchill expressed little enthusiasm, concerned that operation *Anvil* may monopolise efforts to the detriment of the Italian front which, in his opinion, was progressing far too slowly; outnumbered, he finally adopted the project.

Yet, the master of the Kremlin remained uneasy on one point. No Commander in Chief had, as yet, been named for *Overlord*. Churchill suggested the responsibility be entrusted to an American general, since the US forces engaged in the combat would be in greater numbers than the British troops. Roosevelt agreed and promised to rapidly appoint someone. Many predictions were in favour of General Marshall. However, the President was reluctant to lose his Chief of Staff.

Reluctance that was to favour Dwight D. Eisenhower. "Ike" was a strapping, bald, Texas-born lad, with a calm and placid nature - more of an administrator than a genuine warrior - and almost unknown to the general public when Marshall, well aware of his capabilities, had appointed him Supreme Commander of the Allied Force in charge of the landings in North Africa in 1942. In December 1943, following his successful operations in Tunisia, then in Sicily and Italy, Eisenhower received the perilous honour of becoming Supreme Allied Commander in charge of *Overlord*.

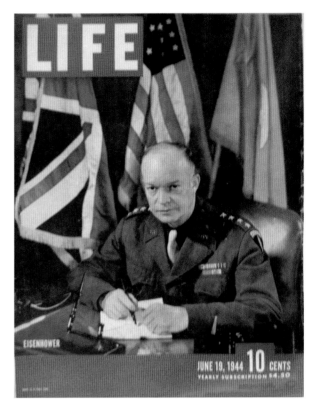

Eisenhower on the cover of *Life* magazine.

Overlord's military staff. From left to right: Montgomery, Ramsay, Eisenhower, Leigh-Mallory, Tedder and Bedell Smith.

A born organiser, he was behind the successful accomplishment of one of History's most ambitious military operations. A skilled politician and an astute diplomat, he was sure to reconcile with both benevolence and tenacity, the often contradictory military plans of the ten different nationalities under his command. Profoundly humane, he was sure always to show concern for what was to become of the men he would lead to the final victory in 1945.

Eisenhower arrived in London on the 14th of January 1944. A few days later, he established his headquarters in Bushey Park, a charming property on the outskirts of the city. Alongside Eisenhower, the SHAEF (Supreme Headquarter Allied Expeditionary Forces) was progressively set up. His second in command was Air Chief Marshal Tedder, a Scot whose aptitude had impressed Eisenhower in both North Africa and Italy. His Chief of Staff was his ever-loyal Bedell Smith, "efficiency personified". The naval forces were placed under the orders of Admiral Ramsay,

who had demonstrated brilliant command during the Dunkirk evacuation in 1940. For this new mission, he was to be in charge of operation *Neptune*, the landing operation itself, the initial phase of operation *Overlord*. The Battle of Britain veteran, Air Chief Marshal Leigh-Mallory was appointed Commander-in-Chief of the Air Force. General Montgomery took command of ground forces, in the form of the 21st Army Group; under "Monty's" orders, General Dempsey was in command of the British 2nd Army and General Bradley was in command of the US First Army.

Eisenhower and Montgomery discovered the plans developed be General Morgan and approved in August 1943. They immediately agreed that the landing zone - stretching from Grandcamp to Courseulles - was too tight and the number of divisions scheduled to intervene on D-Day insufficient. Above all, they were dubious as to the changes of rapidly taking control of Cherbourg, whose port was a vital strategic component, without a direct landing on the Cotentin peninsula. The project was consequently given an in-depth review. The assault would be launched over a far larger front, including five beaches instead of three, from Ouistreham, at the mouth of the River Orne, to Varreville, on the east coast of the Cotentin. The Allies engaged armed forces equivalent to six infantry divisions, whose flanks were protected by three airborne divisions: two in the Cotentin, the other in the British zone, between the rivers Orne and Dives. Their proposed amendments were endorsed by the Allied chiefs of staff.

The problem they now faced was to find the necessary ships and barges to transport the extra divisions. After a long moment's hesitation, Eisenhower had no choice but to resign himself to postponing the Provence landing, in order to requisition the necessary landing craft. The remainder would come from an ultimate effort by Allied shipyards. To achieve this, the landing was postponed one month, from early May to early June 1944.

Poster encouraging the increased production of landing barges.

EIGHTH AIR FORCE

The 8th US Air Force

With around 200,000 men and 2,700 planes, including 1,800 *B-17* and *B-24* heavy bombers, the 8th Air Force was a genuine army in its own right.

As from the spring of 1943, along with the RAF's Bomber Command, it was actively involved in the large-scale strategic attack on the Third Reich - the British troops operating by night and the Americans by day.

Their common aim was to destroy the enemy's industrial potential, to undermine the population and to dupe the *Luftwaffe*. In just one year, the 8th Air Force's four-engine planes made 60,000 flights, dropping 100,000 tonnes of bombs, essentially over Germany.

However, this type of mission proved to be particularly hazardous and the chances of survival were limited. The risks were such that the military staff decided that the crews who had survived twenty-five missions could return to the United States. One of them was the crew of the legendary *Memphis Belle* which, in 1944, became the hero of William Wyler's eponymous film and the pride of America's aviation.

Subsequent to the dramatic losses sustained during the raid on the ball bearing plants in Schweinfurt in August 1943, bombers were thereafter escorted by long-range fighter planes.

Throughout the duration of the war, the 8th Air Force was to lose over 5,500 planes and 50,000 airmen. A shattering toll.

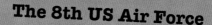

DIRECTION NORMANDY!

The spring of 1944 had come. The launch of operation *Overlord*, which had been postponed till early June, was but a few weeks away. The date for D-Day had been decided upon based on several criteria. The Germans were expecting a high-tide attack; consequently, they had riddled the upper shoreline with formidable obstacles to both barges and men. In contrast, a low-tide attack would mean covering a long distance totally exposed. The choice was therefore to land at mid rising tide. In addition, the airborne troops' mission required a full moon. Finally, the naval and air forces, charged with annihilating the German defences immediately prior to H-Hour, were to enter into action at the very first light of dawn, to ensure they correctly identify their targets. These three conditions: mid rising tide, at dawn and after a full moon night are only reunited a few days each month. The chosen date was the 5th of June, with a potential postponement to the 6th or 7th. Revved up and ready to go, the massive Allied war machine was gathered together in England and preparing to head for the Normandy beaches.

◀ Early June 1944: men from the 1st Infantry Division aboard an LCT (Landing Craft Tank).

The American generals reunited with General Eisenhower, Commander in Chief of *Overlord*. Front row, from left to right: *Generals Simpsons, Patton, Spaatz, Eisenhower, Bradley, Hodges* and *Gerow*.

The crew of one of the 9th Air Force's *B-26 Marauders*.

Air Force. On the 17th of April, Eisenhower obtained the placement of heavy bombers, which had to date been operating in Reich territory, under his direct control. The priority was now to use them over France. This transfer was nevertheless to meet with resistance both on the part of Air Chief Marshal Harris, Commander in Chief of the RAF Bomber Command, and of General Spaatz, Commander of the US Strategic Air Forces in Europe. Both were convinced that they could drive Germany to surrender thanks to aerial bombardments alone. Eisenhower put his foot down, even threatening to resign before finally winning over the Allied staff. He was granted two tactical air forces, the RAF 2nd Tactical Air Force and

Bombs over France

Yet prior to the attack, the German defensive system required to be weakened and its capacity for immediate reaction paralysed. This mission was entrusted to the

Bombardments over a plane engine plant in Courbevoie, on the outskirts of Paris.

the 9th US Air force, transferred to England from North Africa in October 1943 and both equipped with mid-range fighters and bombers.

Of all of the bombs to be dropped over France by the Allies throughout the entire duration of the war, 80% were scheduled for the year of 1944 alone! Civilian losses among the French population were likely to be particularly high. SHAEF experts had estimated at least 80,000 deaths. In London, General de Gaulle was moved by the situation, as was Churchill, "These bombings are likely to generate much hatred against the Allies. We trust that post-war France will remain our friend."The French Resistance in turn proposed substituting bombings with sabotage operations, which they judged to be equally efficient and more likely to spare civilian lives. Yet Eisenhower, with Roosevelt's support, proved to be totally inflexible, "The weight of the argument that has been brought against the bombing of transportation centres in occupied territories is heavy indeed; but I and my military advisers have become convinced that the bombing of these centres will increase our chances for success in the critical battle... I personally believe that estimates of probable casualties have been grossly exaggerated."

The debate had been brought to a close.

The first aim of the *Transport* plan was to dismember the railway network. Whilst convoys were systematically gunned, bombs struck railway stations, marshalling yards, repair workshops... A thousand locomotives were put out of action, countless wagons destroyed, considerably slowing down rail traffic. Sights were then set on the fortifications that comprised the Atlantic Wall, the coastal radar stations and the V1 and V2 secret weapons launch bases, located in France's Nord and Normandy regions. Ammunition and fuel depots were also victim to the aerial attacks. Airfields were strategic targets, in an aim to drive the *Luftwaffe* squadrons eastwards and to desert the Channel coast. In May, the bombardment plan entered its final phase with

Collaborationist propaganda poster condemning the Allied aerial bombings over France.

attacks on road and rail bridges, in an attempt to isolate north-western France. From the 1st of April to the 5th of June, around 200,000 tonnes of bombs were launched over the country by the Allies.

The definite number of French civilians killed during these preliminary bombings was never precisely and officially announced, but was very probably in the region of some tens of thousands: 450 victims in Lille, 460 in Noisy-le-Sec, 670 in Paris-la-Chapelle, 800 in Rouen and Sotteville, 500 in Avignon, 700 in Lyon, 1,100 in Saint-Étienne, 1,700 in Marseille... Collaborationist groups were, of course, to seize this heaven-sent opportunity to denounce what they referred to in the press or in posters as the "libéra-tueurs"(a play on the words "liberators"and "killers").

L'Amérique en Guerre

LE 26 AVRIL 1944   No. 99

★ ★ ★ ★ ★ ★ ★

MESSAGE AU PEUPLE DE FRANCE

Les équipages de l'armée américaine de l'air combattent pour votre libération

Les bombardements alliés ont atteint ces jours derniers une puissance destructrice accrue.

Nous attaquons l'ennemi partout où il est. En Allemagne d'abord ; dans les Balkans, de concert avec l'armée soviétique ; en France et en Belgique.

Partout où des voies ferrées servent au transport de troupes allemandes, de munitions allemandes, de ravitaillement allemand, nous frappons.

Nous savons que

vous subissez l'occupation allemande

vous subissez la police de Vichy

vous subissez la milice de Darnand.

Nous savons que depuis quatre ans l'ennemi vous inflige l'oppression morale et physique, le mensonge, la contrainte, la faim.

Nous vous disons: nous nous fions à votre compréhension pour tout entreprendre afin de vous écarter, dans toute la mesure du possible, des centres ferroviaires, des gares de triage, des embranchements, des dépôts de locomotives, des ateliers de réparations.

La destruction systématique des voies de communications de l'ennemi est une nécessité militaire.

C'est un gage de votre libération.

" Ils savent tout cela," dites-vous, " et ils nous bombardent."

De même qu'en 1914-18 les territoires français occupés étaient inévitablement atteints par des obus français, de même aujourd'hui le sol de France reçoit des bombes alliées.

Nous savons que ces bombardements ajoutent aux souffrances de certains d'entre vous. Nous ne prétendons pas ignorer cela. Il serait impudique de notre part de prétendre alléger ces souffrances en vous affirmant notre sympathie.

Victoires alliées en Extrême-Orient

Au cours de la semaine écoulée trois faits principaux ont marqué l'évolution de la guerre en Extrême-Orient.

En Nouvelle-Guinée, par une attaque qui a pris les Japonais complètement au dépourvu, les forces du Général MacArthur viennent de débarquer près de Hollandia, où elles ont coupé de leurs bases de ravitaillement 60.000 Japonais appartenant à la 18ème Armée. 80.000 autres appartenant aux 8ème et 17ème Armées se trouvaient déjà dans une situation semblable depuis la victoire alliée des Iles de l'Amirauté. Sur 250.000 hommes massés vers Tokyo en vue d'une offensive en direction de l'Australie c'est donc 140.000 qui se trouvent encerclés, tandis que les autres sont sur la défensive.

L'attaque massive menée par l'escadre Somerville contre les bases japonaises de Sumatra constitue une nouvelle et éclatante preuve de la supériorité aérienne et navale alliée. L'escadre Somerville où figurent des navires de guerre français, aussi bien qu'américains, britanniques et hollandais, a dû parcourir à travers le golfe du Bengale plus de 1.800 kms. Sadang, qui fut un des deux objectifs visés, se trouve à l'extrême nord de Sumatra et fait pratiquement partie des défenses extérieures de Singapour. Voilà qui donne une idée précise de l'audace et du mordant alliés. L'escadre comprenait des cuirassés, des croiseurs, des destroyers et des sous-marins escortant plusieurs porte-avions. Les brillants résultats obtenus montrent l'extraordinaire cohésion qui existe maintenant entre les forces alliées. Les deux objectifs ont été ravagés, des docks détruits, des réservoirs de pétrole incendiés, 22 avions nippons dont 6 grands appareils de transport ont été détruits au sol, 2 destroyers et 1 escorteur coulés, 2 cargos gravement ava-

(Suite à la page 4.)

LES ALLEMANDS ORGANISENT LE CHAOS PARTOUT

Les Allemands n'improvisent jamais rien: pas même leur défaite.

Dès maintenant ils s'ingénient à organiser en Europe et singulièrement en France, le chaos qui, à leur gré, devra suivre la libération.

D'une part ils annoncent ou font annoncer par certains de leurs agents—Doriot, Déat, Darnand—des mesures d'ordre, c'est à dire de terreur, aux premiers jours du débarquement. D'autre part ils affectent de déplorer le désordre que feront alors régner les "terroristes," c'est-à-dire les patriotes.

Leurs inquiétudes hypocrites sont vaines. Les nazis devraient bien savoir qu'au moment venu, les Français ne feront aucun geste inutile qui les exposerait à de sanglantes représailles. Loin de tomber dans les "pièges de l'ennemi, les Français—qui savent défendre leurs appareils de radio contre les réquisitions—conscients du rôle précis qu'ils auront à jouer, sauront attendre les instructions précises du Commandement Suprême Allié, transmises par les Radios alliées.

BOMBARDEMENTS ALLIES A TRAVERS L'EUROPE

Londres, 25 avril.—Jour et nuit, à travers toute l'Europe, les bombardiers américains et britanniques frappent, avec une force sans cesse croissante, les objectifs allemands.

La semaine passée est caractérisée par la plus puissante attaque jamais dirigée contre les lignes de communications de l'ennemi, tant à l'ouest, en Belgique et dans les régions au Nord de la France, qu'au sud-est de l'Europe, de concert avec les offensives russes—les Alliés bombardent les arrières allemands et les voies ferrées des Balkans.

Les bombardements les plus puissants qui aient jamais été entrepris ont été effectués sur l'ensemble du réseau ferroviaire allemand: En Belgique, Charleroi, Namur, Malines, Gand, Hasselt, Ottignies, Courtrai, ont été attaquées ; en France, les nœuds de communications de Juvisy, Noisy-le-Sec, la Chapelle, Villeneuve-Saint Georges, Lille, Laon, Lens et les voies ferrées qui aboutissent à la côte, ont été pilonnés. L'objectif est précis:

(Suite à la page 3)

Le front russe de Sébastopol à la Baltique

Moscou, 25 avril.—De la Crimée à la Baltique c'est, brusquement, le calme. Calme relatif, d'ailleurs : on se bat aux deux extrémités du front : à Sébastopol, où les Russes viennent d'amener de l'artillerie de siège, et, à l'extrême nord, autour de Narva, où une série de contre-attaques allemandes ont échoué. Ces engagements, toutefois, ne sauraient se comparer aux gigantesques batailles des semaines

(Suite à la page 2)

L'armée allemande, au cours de sa retraite en Russie, subit des pertes terribles en hommes. Beaucoup en plus nombreux sont ceux qui préfèrent se rendre et qui, épuisés, s'acheminent en longues colonnes vers la captivité.

USF 108   **Apporté au Peuple Français par l'Armée de l'Air Américaine**

L'Amérique en Guerre, a newspaper that was regularly dropped over France by the US Air Force.

Final training exercises

While the aviation was delivering its first blows, ground troops posted in England were relentlessly preparing for the attack, multiplying their training exercises. Private William Smith from the 29th Infantry Division, kept somewhat bitter memories of the period, "The training on landing craft was as realistic as they could make it. They used live ammunition, which was fired over your head. Occasionally they fired a live artillery shell over your head so you could get used to the sound of artillery, and as you crossed the beach they would detonate dynamite that had been buried in the sand beforehand. I recall one landing we made real early in the morning when it was pitch black. I mean, you couldn't see your hand in front of your face. The sailor pulled up to the beach, let the ramp down and off we went. Next thing I know, there was water up to my mouth. How I ever got ashore and didn't lose my rifle I'll never know. As I recall, I think half of the people that came off that landing craft that morning lost rifles, packs, web belts, the whole bit. That was one miserable day.

After training in Scotland we were sent to a little town on the southwest coast of England. Our training there consisted of field training, marches, lectures, pretty much that sort of thing. Most of the marches were forced marches, double-time marches. We'd run for five minutes, walk for five minutes, or walk for five minutes, run for ten minutes. It was, always run and walk, we never did just walk. Just a short time into them your boots would get to feeling like they weighed a ton. The canteen beating on one hip would have you really tee'd off. A commando knife on the other hip, bouncing up and down, had you tee'd off. The hand grenade bouncing on your belly didn't help any. The rifle sling digging into your shoulder and the helmet on your head bouncing up and down, beating your brains out. It's amazing what a guy will go through for his country."

Large-scale manoeuvres were organised, each time with increasing numbers of troops, planes and ships, in order to perfect assault techniques and to test coordination between the Army, the Navy and the Air Force. Early May, the V Corps that was to land on *Omaha Beach* was subjected to operation *Fabius*, which was conducted in relatively acceptable conditions. In contrast, operation *Tiger*, led the same week by the VII Corps, was to meet with total disaster. Due to topographical similarities with the Normandy coast, Slapton Sands in Devon was the chosen site for the operation. Late 1943, some

Landing exercise on the beach at Slapton Sands in the spring of 1944.

A team from the Signal Corps at work on a British beach.

3,000 inhabitants were evacuated from the sector to leave sufficient leeway for the landing exercises. On the second day of this "rehearsal", precisely on the morning of the 28th of April, whilst nine large LST transport vessels loaded with equipment and troops made their way to their target, several German speed boats suddenly appeared out of nowhere and began to blast sprays of torpedo fire. Two of the LSTs sunk and a third suffered serious damage. Certain soldiers and seamen were killed outright. Many others plunged into the chilly waters. Some of them had not correctly fastened their life jackets and immediately sunk to the sea bed. The vast majority drowned, submerged by the weight of their packs. Rescue ships were in insufficient numbers and the sea was soon covered with drifting bodies. The death toll was horrendous: 638 men had perished or were unaccounted for.

Survivors received strict orders to keep the Slapton Sands affair under wraps, officially in order not to demoralise their fellow troops. However, if truth be told, the military staff were extremely anxious. They feared that the bodies of a dozen soldiers, who had the secret landing plans in their possession, may fall into enemy hands. They consequently launched a frenzied and macabre hunt. Finally, all of the "important" bodies were recovered.

Without necessarily meeting with the same catastrophic fate, operation *Eagle*, conducted mid-May by paratroopers, was far from reassuring, despite over two years' training. Dropping operations were extremely inaccurate, as they already had been for the 82nd Airborne during the Sicily landings in July 1943. This time, the vast majority of the troops from the 101st Airborne found themselves over 10 miles astray from their targets, whereas many planes had been forced to retreat back to base without dropping a single paratrooper. Finally, many had jumped at too low altitude: fractures, sprains and strains could be counted in hundreds. Airborne troop commanders sought solace as best they could, in the traditional belief that a disastrous "dress rehearsal" often heralds a great "première".

Paratrooper in training.

Escalating tension

On the 15th of May, an ultimate meeting was held in St. Paul's School in London, the headquarters of the 21st Army Group. Overlord's entire military staff attended, in the presence of King George VI and Winston Churchill, together with a number of Army and Air Force admirals and generals. Among them, Admiral Deyo, Commander of the bombing force in charge of the *Utah Beach* sector, described the scene: The room was hushed and the tension palpable. It seemed to most of us that the proper meshing of so many gears would need nothing less than divine guidance. A failure at one point could throw the momentum out of balance and result in chaos. The first to rise and

Early June: amphibious DUKW truck (under camouflage nets) drivers tried to take their mind off their worries as best they could.

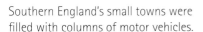

Southern England's small towns were filled with columns of motor vehicles.

The day before the landings, black and white identification stripes were painted on the wings and cabins of Allied planes.

Aboard a *half-track* just a few hours before embarkation. The soldier on the bonnet is revising his French thanks to a small textbook provided to GIs.

break the silence was the Supreme Commander himself. It had been said that his smile was worth twenty divisions. That day it was worth more. He spoke for ten minutes. Before the warmth of his quiet confidence the mists of doubt dissolved. When he had finished the tension was gone. Not often has one man been called upon to accept so great a burden of responsibility. But here was one at peace with his soul."

Since late 1943, Allied troops had been progressively moved to the south-west of England. In April 1944, they were brought even closer to their embarkation sites, to be grouped together in vast assembly zones that included a multitude of perfectly camouflaged camps totally isolated from the outside world. Sergeant Slaughter from the 116th Infantry Regiment related his surprising stay in the Blandford camp in Dorset, "we were fed the best répétition food we'd ever had in the army – steak and pork chops with all the trimmings, topped off with lemon meringue pie, were items on a typical menu. The officers became friendlier and it seemed that the men were a bit kinder to each other. We were treated royally we could sleep late, we had recreation, played football and baseball and boxed and had tremendous movies every night. We were also issued with brand new equipment and the new weapons had to be test fired and zeroed in on the firing range. Unlimited amounts of ammo were given to each of us for practice firing. We sharpened our bayonets, honed them finely and got ready for one of the biggest adventures of our life. Just prior to D-Day a German plane flew Over and dropped some bombs and the 29th Division had casualties there in the marshalling area. We were shown what our objective would be on D-Day. We were told we would land on *Dog Green* sector of *Omaha Beach*, in front of the Vierville draw. We were shown a sand-table mock-up of what the landing area would look like. They told us we would have twenty-one pillboxes in our area but that only one or two would actually be manned. The troops guarding the area were

A battalion from the 1st Infantry Division approaching the port.

old or were Russian or Polish nationals conscripted into the German army and that they would not fight very forcefully and that we shouldn't have any trouble just going in and marching across the beach."

For security reasons, barbed wiring prevented soldiers from leaving and civilians from entering the camp. Furthermore, 2,000 counterespionage agents were on the lookout in the surrounding countryside. But precautions didn't stop there! All efforts needed to be made to avoid leaks in the enemy's direction. Eisenhower imposed drastic demands on Churchill, "Establish a surveillance cordon around the British Isles, monitor all incoming traffic, censor all communications - including diplomatic ones - by all necessary means, stop all air and sea traffic departing from Great Britain

that is not under our direct control." He even - although with much difficulty - obtained from the Prime Minister the strict control of all movements towards the south of England.

Whilst every effort was made to obscure the preparations in the south-west of the country, the Allies also contrived to deliberately offer the Germans proof of intense Allied activity in the south-east, directly opposite the Pas-de-Calais coast, via the disinformation campaign entitled operation "Fortitude." Such was the aim of the totally fictitious military manoeuvres deployed by a genuine phantom army, but with an unquestionably prestigious commander, General Patton, for whom this somewhat inglorious mission was due punishment for having slapped a depressive soldier in the face in Sicily in 1943.

Ralph Ingersoll related the last, both exquisite and frightening, weeks before the assault, "The vehicles of the assault columns jammed the road sides. They were squeezed in together wherever there was the shade of a tree for cover, and crouched down under camouflage netting wherever there wasn't. During rehearsals, each vehicle made this passage round-trip; for the real thing it would be a one-way journey down the outbound net. Coming back, there would be only the ambulances returning with wounded. To meet the ambulances, the whole paraphernalia of field medicine now moved in the clearing stations, the ward tents, the operating rooms under canvas, the graves registration units. All day long the troops on maneuvers passed and repassed them, tidying up, laying out their scalpels and their bandages, and getting ready, waiting for calamity. Back at the hospitals there were the railhead companies bringing in supplies, the ordnance dumps, the repair pools, the sweet smelling bakeries and the signal battalions with

the big coils of copper wire that would one day unwind across France. It was all there, the whole great army of invasion, packed in as tight as the link wheels and cogs in a Swiss watch. It was all."

From the 30th of May to the 2nd of June, the assault troops progressively left their camps and headed for their departure ports. Private George McIntyre climbed into a transport truck, along with his buddies from the 4th Engineer Battalion, and headed for the unknown, "We had written our final notes to the folks at home, at least until we hit the coast of France. Of course, we knew that the letters would not be mailed until the invasion was well under way. Our convoy was long and there were many stops. Along with the regular equipment of the combat soldier, we were given an extra carton of cigarettes and a French-English phrase book. To pass away the time, we practiced our French on each other. We laughed and joked outwardly, but an undercurrent of fear could be felt. At last we reached

Assault troops converging towards their embarkation ports.

the crest of a long hill and looking off into the distance we could see the English Channel. From chance civilians we met we learned that the town we were entering was Dartmouth. As we approached, an informal reception committee of children and dogs met us. As we reached the first street of the city, some of the older people joined the parade. Others watched from doorways and windows, or gathered in groups to offer encouragement as we marched along. We were walking on smooth-worn cobblestone streets. Judging by the sounds, we were getting very close to the harbor. Here we found field kitchens. The meal was excellent, macaroni, cheese, peas, carrots, mashed potatoes, bread, butter and coffee. For dessert we had fruit salad. One of the fellows near me griped because there was no ice cream, but I think he was just sounding off. A comic, yelled, 'Eat hearty, me mates, for tomorrow it's K Rations.' In fact, none of us was absolutely sure that the present preparation was the real thing, or just another dry run. A fraction of our mind hoped it was another dry run, but we also knew that D-Day had to come."

Sergeant Haas, from the 467th Antiaircraft Artillery Battalion, was already waiting on the Weymouth docks, "There were religious services. I can remember being at a mass for the Jewish boys with a Catholic priest holding mass on one side and a Protestant minister holding a service for the Protestant boys on the other. It was really strange – everyone praying in different religions and denominations, each watching the other. Right next to us in the marshalling area was a Ranger battalion. We could see them. For some strange reason they were kept in a separate area. What I mean by separate is that I think there was a fence between us, a wire fence. I think they sort of meant to keep us apart. But still, you know, you get to talking. They said they had a suicide mission coming up. We heard that they would have to scale a cliff, which seemed like suicide to me. As I recall, a young boy – he looked to me to be about seventeen

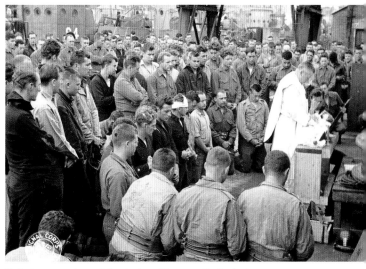

Religious service celebrated on Weymouth docks by Captain Waters, a Catholic chaplain.

or eighteen – was with them and these men, these tough-looking guys, took care of him like a father would his son. I often wondered what happened to that young fellow. I know many of them were killed."

On *USS Augusta*, the chaplain gave boarding soldiers a sheet of paper, upon which the 8th verse of psalm 121 had been printed, "The LORD will watch over your coming and going both now and forevermore." Below it, under the title, "Our aim", he had copied article 6 of the Atlantic Charter, "After the final destruction of the Nazi tyranny, we hope to see established a peace which will afford to all nations the means of dwelling in safety within their own boundaries, and which will afford assurance that all the men in all lands may live out their lives in freedom from fear, want and oppression."

War correspondents soon came to join the assault troops. Ernest Hemmingway, the most famous of them all, made a remarkable appearance on the deck of *USS Ancon*, generating great excitement among the ship's crew, "He came on board with a bandage round his head through which some blood had already soaked through. He looked very heroic and warlike, "Lieutenant Elsey recalls," but the gossip was that he'd gotten drunk the night before and fallen down."

"OK, let's go!"

Eisenhower left London on the 2nd of June to establish his advanced command post near Portsmouth, in the immediate vicinity of a splendid Georgian-style property - Southwick House - which was occupied by Admiral Ramsay, Commander in Chief of operation *Neptune*, and his services. In keeping with his rudimentary way of life, Ike decided to settle in a simple caravan, which had been pitched in a nearby wood.

By the 3rd of June, embarkation operations were close to complete. The weather looked promising and, based on forecasts, Eisenhower sent a reassuring cable message to General Marshall, back in Washington, "We have almost every chance of meeting with the best possible conditions. Only a marked deterioration in the weather could hinder our plans." Yet, the very same evening, Group Captain Stagg, chief meteorological officer, came

GIs being transferred on barges to an LSI (Landing Ship Infantry) for their Channel crossing.

with bad news. The situation had taken a turn for the worse. At 4 a.m. on the morning of the 4th of June, the SHAEF staff, reunited in the Southwick House library, was hanging on Stagg's every word. Tension was at its peak. The forecast for the following day was poor: low cloud, force 5 to 6 winds and choppy seas; no aerial support was possible and both troop landings and naval bombing adjustments would be particularly problematic. In these conditions, the operation would be more than perilous. Although Montgomery was, nevertheless, in favour of maintaining the scheduled date, Tedder and Leigh-Mallory were opposed, whilst Ramsay remained undecided. Eisenhower was to settle the affair: the landing was postponed for at least 24 hours. If there was no change, the operation would need to be delayed by a fortnight, which would generate insurmountable problems. In the meantime, the ships that had already cast off from the most distant ports were urgently called back to dock. Consequently, a thirty-eight-ship convoy, which was on its way to *Utah Beach* with the 4th US Division on board, was forced to take a homeward U-turn from the high seas.

As forecast, on the evening of the 4th of June, a violent storm swept through the south of England. "At three-thirty the next morning," Eisenhower recalled, "our little camp was shaking and shuddering under a wind of almost hurricane proportions and the accompanying rain

seemed to be traveling in horizontal streaks. The mile-long trip through muddy roads to the naval headquarters was anything but a cheerful one, since it seemed impossible that in such conditions there was any reason for even discussing the situation." Yet, at the start of the meeting, Stagg made an astonishing declaration, "By the following morning a period of relatively good weather, heretofore completely unexpected, would ensue, lasting probably thirty-six hours. The long-term prediction was not good. The prospect was not bright because of the possibility that we might land the first several waves successfully and then find later build-up impracticable." As he paced up and down the room,

Paratroops listening to their final brief before jumping.

Time to board.

GIs packed inside the hold of an LCI.

saw so many men packed into such a small space. I'll never forget Captain Smith's opening words as long as I live, 'Well men, this is it! Tomorrow morning at six o'clock, by order of General Eisenhower, the invasion of France begins. We are to hit the beaches of Normandy. I want every man to check his equipment and keep it nearby. Remember, your rifle is your army wife, so take it to bed with you. Sleep in your clothes and be ready to move out.' We realized that there wouldn't be much sleep that night, but we went back to our quarters to round up our equipment. There were important decisions to make regarding the personal belongings each of us would take, for these had to be cut down to a minimum. I had previously decided what I would take with me: just my prayer book, my rosary, a few choice snapshots of the folks at home, writing paper, a pencil and a small penknife. These items, along with the $4 in French money the army had allowed us, were placed in a waterproof bag. I was about five minutes deciding which pocket I would carry the bag in. I finally decided on the top pocket of my fatigue jacket, probably influenced by the fact that the prayer book might deflect a bullet.

the Commander in Chief asked for each and every staff member's opinion before taking what was probably the most difficult decision of his entire existence, "OK, let's go! "It was 4.15 a.m. on the 5th of June 1944, "Without a further word", Eisenhower added, "each went off to his respective post of duty to flash out to his command the messages that would set the whole host in motion." Upon his return to his caravan, he drafted a short release that was to be broadcast should the operation fail, "Our landings in the Cherbourg-Havre area have failed to gain a satisfactory foothold and I have withdrawn the troops. My decision to attack at this time and place was based upon the best information available. The troops, the air and the Navy did all that bravery and devotion could do. If any blame or fault attaches to the attempt it is mine alone." He was to find this sombre message, forgotten in the depths of one of his pockets, several weeks after the successful landings.

On the morning of the 5th of June, all units had received their orders. "At ten o'clock by my watch we were summoned to the crew's quarters for a briefing," Private McIntyre, who had boarded LST no47 recalled, "I never

Private Charles Blackledge reading the bible his mother had given him.

Eisenhower pays a visit to paratroopers from the 101st Airborne Division before they leave for Normandy.

Naturally we all thought of the morrow. Where would we be if we were still alive? One boy said he would dig in on the beach and stay there indefinitely. At the other end of the conjecture was a boy who would be making love to a French girl in Paris by sundown. Personally, I prayed: didn't use a prayer from a book, or even one I made up myself. I just remembered something Joe Louis, the heavyweight champion, had uttered when questioned about the outcome of the war. If I remember correctly, he said, 'We're on God's side and we can't lose'. "

Admiral Ramsay's plan could be put into action. The convoys cast off, one by one, amidst a choppy sea, to reach the agreed assembly point to the south of the Isle of Wight and codenamed "Z" zone. The area was soon to be nicknamed *Piccadilly Circus* due to the incredible concentration of ships there, reminiscent of the famous and busy London square. Around 5,300 vessels were preparing to cross the English Channel. They were led by thirty fleets of minesweepers, sent to secure ten 1,300 to 4,000-feet channels - two for each beach - marked out by illuminated beacons. Behind them, the warships that comprised the two bombing forces, one American (the Western Task Force), the other British (the Eastern Task Force), including a total of seven battleships, two monitors, twenty-three cruisers and one hundred and three destroyers, the majority of which belonged to the Royal Navy. Endless streams of infantry and armoured transport ships, most of them supplied by the United States, were to follow, all abiding by their strictly established schedules. They were escorted on their flanks by swarms of destroyers, frigates, corvettes and patrol boats, all ready to intervene in the case of a German attack. Finally came hundreds of auxiliary ships, merchant navy cargo ships and sixty or so old boats - on their last journey; they were to be sunk offshore to form breakwaters, referred to as *Gooseberries*.

Late afternoon, Eisenhower left Portsmouth and headed for Newbury, to the west of London, from where the 101st Airborne was to take off. He showed particular concern for the fate that awaited the paratroopers. A week earlier, Air Chief Marshal Leigh-Mallory had informed him of reinforcements among German troops posted in the Cotentin peninsula, precisely where they were to be dropped, and his estimation of the number of potential casualties had been particularly alarming: 70%! Heavy-hearted, but refusing to compromise the chances of success on *Utah Beach* and, ultimately, the capture of Cherbourg, the Commander in Chief, confirmed his orders, authorising but a slight displacement of the *Drop Zone*. On site, he adopted

a highly familiar tone with his men, who had already blackened their faces to melt into the dark backdrop, "No need to worry,"he explained," you have the best commanders and the best weapons. "To which one soldier replied," Hell, we ain't worried. It's the Krauts that ought ot be worrying now. "Another yelled to the entire company," Look out Hitler, we're coming! "Ike remained static at the extremity of the runway until the very last C-47 had taken off, simply uttering, "Well, it's on."

In the meantime, night had fallen and the Allied convoys were advancing towards the Normandy coastline. The sea was rough and the crossing was far from a pleasure cruise. Lieutenant Bodell had boarded a US Navy *Landing Craft Tank*, that was laboriously advancing at 4 to 5 knots, "We had the misfortune to have a British 'lettered craft' behind us which had the ability to go

Loading LSTs in Brixham harbour (Devon).

ahead twice as fast as the Americans, but lacked the backing power that we had. We would pound along, the whole boat bending and buckling; then the one ahead would slow down. We would go into full reverse to keep from riding up its stern, then the Britisher would start to climb ours. To avoid collision, we would go full speed ahead with full right rudder, and sheer off towards the other column. The vessels of different columns would close to about five feet or less, usually crashing together then separating with one going full speed at right angles to the course of the convoy."

On another boat, Ralph Ingersoll was intrigued by the behaviour of one young officer, "A little lieutenant from Brooklyn had a waking fantasy. He used to lean on the rail next to me and say, "You don't suppose there has been an armistice and nobody has told us, do you? Gee, it would be funny if it were all over and we didn't know

it, wouldn't it?" Every few hours you would see him kicking this idea around with someone."

Aboard *USS Bayfield*, on its way to *Utah Beach*, Rear Admiral Moon, Commander of Assault Force "U", had boarded a host of high-ranking officers, among whom General Barton, Commander of the 4th Infantry Division and his second in command, General "Teddy" Roosevelt. As the ship approached the Cotentin coastline, all of these officers gathered on the deck with their staff and broke into song with *Onward Christian Soldiers* to continue with the old Northerners' hymn from the American Civil War: *Battle Hymn of the Republic*. A young ensign, who had heard them sing, couldn't help notice how appropriate one of the verses were, "Comme Dieu est mort pour rendre les hommes saints, / Mourrons pour rendre les hommes libres." - As He died to make men holy, let us die to make men free.

A GIs last message to his girlfriend.

As per the plans established by the *Overlord* staff, the Americans were assigned the western half of the assault front. At dawn, they landed on *Utah Beach* and *Omaha Beach*, whilst striving to capture the dangerous artillery battery at Pointe du Hoc, located between the two. Yet, before doing so, the paratroopers were to make the first move in this epic adventure. Their role consisted in securing the inland sector at the base of the Cotentin peninsula, hence preventing any German counterattack on *Utah Beach*, where the infantrymen were to land at dawn. The mission incumbent upon the 82nd Airborne, also known as the *All American*, was to take control of the Sainte-Mère-Église road junction, on the RN13 trunk road, and to establish a bridgehead to the west of the River Merderet. The 101st Airborne, referred to as the *Screaming Eagles*, was in turn in charge of controlling the beach exits and of advancing southwards as far as the River Douves, on the road to Carentan.

Aboard their *C-47* transport planes, the men from the 101st Airborne approach the Cotentin coast.

◀ One of the very rare colour photographs taken on D-Day.
Sappers from the 1st Engineer Special Brigade on *Utah Beach*.

The paras jump over the Cotentin peninsula

At around 1 a.m. eight hundred *C-47* planes, flying in close formation, began their approach towards the west coast of the Cotentin peninsula. Aboard each one of them, a stick of twenty paratroopers, heavily laden with their 90 to 110 lbs-worth of gear. In anticipation of the fierce combat they would be engaging in over several days, they had been provided with Benzedrine, in order to better withstand the effects of tiredness. Some of them, although this was not common practice, had contracted life insurance before heading into unknown territory.

Pilots had been given precise instructions. Paratroopers were to be dropped at a speed of 95 mph and at an altitude of 650 feet. Yet many of them had no experience of real combat. It was their first wartime mission and they were particularly nervous. They were very soon to be confronted with violent barrage fire from the FLAK, the German anti-aircraft defence. Jack Schlegel remembered

Many paratroopers were captured by the Germans and imprisoned in a camp near Saint-Lô.

this terrifying welcome, "As we approached our area to jump of tracer bullets cut through the length of the fuselage of the *C-47* causing the men sitting on either side to pull their feet in closer. No one was hit, but it got their attention fast so that everyone was fully alert for the next surprise – a direct hit on the left engine. Immediately, Lt John Evans yelled, 'Stand up and Hook up!' I didn't take any urging for the paratroopers to obey that order, as the plane was struggling to remain airborne. No sooner were we in place when a third hit took off part of the right wing. The plane tilted down and to the right. Lt Evans yelled, 'GO!' and led the way. That was the last time anyone ever saw or heard from Evans. I recall that I was the twenty-fourth man and last to leave the plane, and remember how the plane was going down. I moved as fast as I could to get out and, after baling out, saw the plane go up in a bail of fire."

Many young airmen literally panicked behind their plane's instrument panels. Others swerved or accelerated violently to avoid enemy projectiles. In doing so, they flew beyond their drop zones, often haphazardly dropping their sticks several miles from their targets. Furthermore, their excessive speed was to result in the paratroopers being largely dispersed across the countryside. Pilots flew too low, leaving them just a few seconds before they hit the ground, at the risk of many a broken bone. Others rose too high, up to

Paratroopers ready to jump.

Several gliders crash landed.

2,000 feet, which meant they ran another risk, that of being pursued by German gunfire over an interminable descent.

Georges Rosie from 101st Airborne's 506th Regiment recalled, "Through broken clouds and a bright moon we headed for the coast. Over the Channel we could see hundreds of boats starting towards the south. About 1.00 a. m. on June 6, one of the guys yelled, 'There she is boys.' We all knew what it was – the coast of France. About nine minutes to the drop zone. Flak and machine-gun tracers could be seen to the right and left. About that moment a plane on our right blew up, hit the ground in a large ball of fire – 18 to 20 men wiped out. Welcome to the real war.

The red light in the door came on. We stood up and hooked up. Then came the green light and we were out the door. Quite a struggle because of all our equipment. Someone fell down and had to be helped up and out the door. I remember landing in the middle of a road. I finally got out of my harness and could hear some soldiers coming down the road. I started up a hedgerow. I could hear the boots getting closer and closer. In about a minute 35 or 40 Germans came marching past. I could

have reached out and touched them. Being alone behind enemy lines is a unique, indescribable feeling. You just feel so helpless, so alone that there is nothing in your life you can relate it to.

After a while I ran into John Gibson and Charles Lee. It was as if I had found a long-lost brother. It was the greatest feeling in the world."

Major General Maxwell Taylor, commander of the 101st Airborne, found himself in a rather delicate position, somewhere to the south of Sainte-Marie-du-Mont. He was terribly alone and was to stay so for many long and anxious minutes. The vast majority of his men had been dispersed across a large quadrilateral stretching from Sainte-Mère-Église to the coast. Around a third of them had even found themselves well beyond this zone. Consequently, when - as he turned a hedge - the general stumbled on a Private from the 501st Regiment, the two men fell into each other's arms in an enthusiastic embrace. They later came across the Commander of Division Artillery, Brigadier General McAuliffe, followed by a group of forty paratroopers led by Lieutenant Colonel Ewell and, finally, another group essentially comprised of officers from Taylor's staff.

Patrol at the foot of the Sainte-Mère-Église church spire hunting out a sniper.

Sainte-Mère-Église under American control.

Although reduced to only a hundred men, as opposed to the mission's scheduled 1,200, the detachment headed for Pouppeville, in order to secure the first exit from Utah Beach. The small troop started marching, led by two generals, an aide, two colonels, a major, several captains and eight lieutenants. Taylor was later to joke, "Never were so few led by so many."

The 82nd Airborne's drop, under Major General Ridgway's command, had been less catastrophic, without for as much being perfect - far from it. One stick found itself uncomfortably amidst the staff of the German 91st Division in Picauville. The centre of Sainte-Mère-Église had been the theatre of intense agitation since the very early hours.

Some of the village's inhabitants, wakened by an alarm, had gathered in the village square and were trying to extinguish the - very probably accidental - fire that raged in a nearby house.

Shortly after 1 a.m., a handful of paratroopers began to fall out of the sky unexpectedly amidst a scene of total confusion. They belonged to the 101st Airborne and had been dropped there by mistake. A few of them were shot down by the German garrison, already on the alert; others succeeded in sneaking away unnoticed.

Their respite was short-lived. A little after 1.40 a.m., the C-47s transporting a battalion from the 82nd Airborne's 505th Regiment arrived above their target. Ken Russell from Tennessee was, at the time, just a young 17 year-old lad, "As we came in, there was a building on fire. The fire gave light for miles around. The pilot dropped us in the middle of the town of Ste-Mere-Église. I knew we were in trouble, and it was so horrifying, because most of our stick were killed. They didn't even hit the ground. Coming down, one fellow had a Gammon grenade on his hip. I looked to my right, and I saw the guy, and instantaneously, I looked around and there was just an empty parachute coming down. He was blown away. The heat drew the nylon chutes toward the fire, and the air to feed the fire was actually drawing us into it. I saw one trooper, John Holsbeck, land in the flames. I heard him scream one time before he was engulfed, and he didn't scream any more.

I finally hit the roof of the church and a couple of my suspension lines went around the belfry and I slid on the roof. Luckily, I wasn't stuck on the side facing the square, but on opposite side in a narrow street. I was hanging on the edge of the roof. Steele was hanging there too, not far away from me, canopy and shroudlines wrapped around a gargoyle. Sergeant Ray carne down and missed the edge of the church, but he hit in front of it. A Nazi soldier shot Ray in the stomach and called on Steele and me. But, while he was dying in agony, Ray got his 45 out and shot him in the back of the head.

I finally got my knife out of my boot and cut myself loose from my parachute. I fell to the ground, hurting my back in the process. Bullets still kept coming from all directions. I made a dash across the square and it seemed to me the all German Army was shooting at me. Next to the church were three telephone poles. Our platoon leader, Lt. Cadish, hit the first one and was killed instantly. Talapa hung dead from the second. June 6 was his 21st birthday; he lived it about one hour! On the third pole was my buddy H.T. Bryant. It was like they were crucified there."

Shortly after 4 a.m., the 505th's 3rd battalion, led by Lieutenant Colonel Edward Krause, surrounded the village of Sainte-Mère, which was to become the very first mainland French village to be liberated by the Americans. The trunk road linking Carentan and Cherbourg had been blocked. To the west of the village, the 507th and 508th Regiments were supposed to establish themselves on either bank of the River Merderet and across the surrounding marshes. Yet, they were unaware that they had been flooded by the Germans. An extremely unpleasant surprise awaited Private Thomas Porcella, just like many other

The body of a paratrooper from the 82nd Airborne, drowned in the Merderet marshes.

paratroopers, "I had the shock of my life. I plunged into water. When my feet touched the bottom I straightened and kicked up for air. The water was almost above my nose. I stood on my toes and gasped for another breath of air. My heart was beating so rapidly that I thought it would burst. I pleaded, 'Oh God, please, don't let me down'. Below the water in went and tried to remove the leg straps. They were too tight and wouldn't unsnap. Needing more air, I jumped up and as soon as my head was above the water. I began splashing around. I started to pray, standing on my toes, my heart beating faster. After a few seconds I calmed down and decided to cut the straps. 'God, my only chance is the knife'. Going down in the water again, I slipped it between my leg and the strap, working back and forth in an upward motion. Nothing happened. In a panic, I thought my heart would burst from fright. 'Why can't I cut the strap? My knife is razor sharp'. As I was gasping for air I kept saying Hail Mary's. It seemed an eternity before I realized I had the blade upside down. Taking another gulp of air I was finally free of the chute. But the weight

The wreck of the glider flown by General Pratt, second in command of the 101st Airborne and who was killed in the accident. The body of his co-pilot can be seen in the foreground.

of the musette bag and land mine was still holding me down. With my knife I cut loose the land mine and the musette bag. I unfastened the chin strap of the helmet and let it fall into the water. My eyes strained to see a landmark, but I could see nothing in the darkness. I was cold and began to shiver."

All of Porcella's buddies were sadly not as fortunate. Many perished in the Merderet marshes, without having been given a chance to fight. In the meantime, Ridgway's men had successfully taken control of the river's east bank, but had as yet failed to cross the Fière and Chef-du-Pont bridges to establish a link with the groups that had been dropped to the west of the river and who had landed amidst the enemy lines and were totally exposed to incessant attack.

Lost in the dark of the night, the American paratroopers endeavoured to join forces, whilst striving to dodge the patrols that were hot on their heels. The Germans fought tooth and nail, but with no genuine battle plan; confounded by the surprise attack and the dispersion of their enemy, which was finally to prevent any general counterattack. Fighting was amidst total confusion.

Gunfire came from all directions. It was a deadly game of hide-and-seek in the labyrinthine Normandy hedgerows. Who's behind this one? Friend? Foe? To identify each other, the men from the 101st let out incessant clicks and clacks with the famous metal "crickets" they had been supplied with. La Fière, Les Forges, Les Droueries, Pouppeville… so many peaceful hamlets had brusquely become the theatre of sporadic, yet merciless confrontation. While rushing back from Rennes to his command post in Picauville, General Wilhelm Falley, Chief of the German 91st Division, came face-to-face with an American patrol and was shot down. When informed, Ridgway curtly concluded, "Given the situation we were in, the death of a division commander did not amuse me at all."

Around 13,500 paratroopers were engaged in combat in the Cotentin peninsula in the early hours of the 6th of June. They were to be sent reinforcements, in the form of both men and equipment (jeeps, guns, antitank guns…), transported by several waves of gliders. The first wave arrived at 4 a.m. After having been towed across the English Channel by *C-47s*, a hundred *Waco* gliders were then left to fend for themselves. They flew in circles in order to find a landing zone amidst the dense Normandy bocage, which proved to be a tricky manoeuvre. Captain Harold Shebeck recalled, "Machine-gun, artillery and small-arms fire was now coming up from barns, houses and German firing positions in scattered locations. In the glider we tried to make ourselves as small as possible, elbows close to the body, knees pulled up to chest and head bowed down. Now it was time for our pilot to cut loose from our tow plane. The pilot was desperately trying to slow the speed of the glider, which was now about 50 or 60 miles per hour. We came across the top of a hedgerow, knocked the wheels off the glider, crash-landed, and came to a stop about 4 miles inland from *Utah Beach*. Miraculously, no one was hurt. Not long after our landing, I approached a smashed glider in which I saw the pilot slumped dead over the controls. No one else was around. The fields were often smaller then they appeared on the photos and the sand-box models. The hedgerows which surrounded most of the fields in Normandy were often much higher than they appeared in the photographs, in some cases 20ft high. The result was that the pilots misjudged the height as they came in for a landing, and this caused a great many crashes, including ours." Losses were countless. Among them, Brigadier General Don Pratt, Second in Command of the 101st Airborne, whose glider struck a tree near the village of Hiesville, breaking his neck; he was the first high-ranking officer killed in Normandy.

The paratroopers sustained heavy losses. Without for as much reaching Air Chief Marshal Leigh-Mallory's sombre forecast, they were nevertheless high, with estimations in the region of 3,700 killed, wounded or missing. Many of those unaccounted for had fallen into enemy hands; others escaped capture, but were to remain totally isolated for several days before managing to join their own lines.

The beach assault

Deceived by the storm that continued to rage in the English Channel and oblivious to the lull that was in store, the Germans had fooled themselves into a perilously false sense of security. The *Kriegsmarine*'s customary high sea patrols had been cancelled,

as had the *Luftwaffe*'s aerial reconnaissance missions. To add insult to injury, radars had been destroyed by aerial bombardments over the previous weeks and the immense Allied armada of some 5,000 ships had crossed the Channel unnoticed. "We achieved a degree of tactical surprise for which we had hardly dared to hope," Eisenhower had declared. To which General Bradley added, "In this capricious turn of the weather we had found a Trojan horse."

In the midst of the night, the landing forces took position several miles off *Utah Beach* and *Omaha Beach*. Alongside the LSIs (*Landing Ship Infantry*) and LSTs (*Landing Ship Tanks*), packed with men and equipment, vast warships, battleships and cruisers were ready and waiting to discharge their powerful gunfire on the German defences. Among them, three battleships, *USS Texas*, *USS Arkansas* and *USS Nevada*, the latter having been refloated since Pearl Harbor. The attack was to

Soldiers on the deck of a troop transport ship, waiting to board their assault barges. Their rifles were protected with plastic covers.

Assault unit boarding an LCVP.

be launched at 6.30 a.m., at mid rising tide, before the waves had reached the obstacles that had been scattered on the beaches under Rommel's orders.

Three to four hours prior to H-Hour, the men that were to lead the first wave of assault left their troop transport vessels to board the LCAs (*Landing Craft Assault*) or LCVPs (*Landing Craft Vehicle and Personnel*) that would take them to the beaches, around 6 miles from there. Private Bruce Bradley was among them, "We were told we were expendable in the first wave. I remember nobody responded to those chilling words. We were also cautioned to loosen our helmet straps as if we lost our grip on the rope ladders going down the side of the ship, we could plunge down with force enough to break our necks when the water hit the helmet rim. The sea was rough and it was dark. The navy guys had remarked that they were glad they were navy at this point. I'm sure they were. We got V for Victory signs from them as they helped us over the side. Victory didn't seem possible at the time, to me. Survival, maybe."

The already laden barges were required to turn in circles until they were all ready to line up before preparing to launch the attack. Under heavy swell. Strong waves crushed against the frail embarkations. Pumps failed to evacuate all of the incoming water and the troops were soon obliged to use their helmets to empty their craft. Soaked by the sea spray, frozen to the bone, many also suffered from severe seasickness, despite their standard issue pills.

At around 5.40 a.m., approximately 3 miles from the coast, the LCTs (*Landing Craft Tank*) began to launch the amphibious tanks. Off *Omaha Beach*, most of the tanks from the 741st battalion were submerged by the huge waves and sunk almost instantaneously. A few minutes later, the warships opened their deadly fire in the direction of the shoreline. At 6 a.m., the 8th US Air Force's heavy bombers in turn moved into action, relaying the RAF's Bomber Command planes that had copiously inundated the Atlantic Wall defences throughout the night.

Aboard their LCVP, Bruce Bradley and his buddies could now perceive the shoreline, "Making the run into shore, the sky was intermittently lit by explosions, some of them of tremendous force. Bombs, shells from the battleships standing out to sea, rockets whooshing overhead, ack-ack from German positions and tracers were coming and going. An awesome display. As we drew closer to the beach we could see the shape of the land. Also geysers of sea water were coming from shell fire, aimed at us. We had to keep our heads down."

In the meantime, a duel had been engaged between Admiral Kirk's Western Task Force ships and the Atlantic Wall coastal artillery batteries. The Saint-Marcouf/ Crisbecq battery, located on the Cotentin peninsula, was the most formidable of them all with its powerful 210mm guns. At around 6.30 a.m., it succeeded a bull's-eye hit on the destroyer *USS Corry*. With a mortal blow under the waterline, the engine room was quickly engulfed in water; the ship was evacuated, soon to disappear from view. Although the German coastal defence's only noteworthy success on the 6th of June, it cost the lives of twenty-four American seamen.

The *USS Nevada*'s guns open fire on the Azeville artillery battery.

Utah Beach, a providential error in navigation

Utah Beach, on the Cotentin peninsula's eastern coastline, was the sector assigned to General Collins' VII Army Corps. The 8th Regiment from General Barton's 4th Division had been entrusted with the mission of leading the assault.

Captain George Mayberry was one of the troops that comprised the first wave of assault, "The landing craft drove onto the shore at 6.30 in the morning, within a minute of the time of H-Hour. I jumped off into four feet of water. Never before in my life had I wanted so badly to run, but I could only wade slowly forward. It was approximately 100 yards to the edge of the shore and it took me two minutes to reach the shallow water. Those two minutes were extremely long. Even on the beach I couldn't run as my uniform was sodden and heavy and my legs were numb and cramped. Heavy shells commenced exploding on the beach, as well as sporadic mortar fire from a short distance inland. A soldier just ahead of me was blown to pieces by a direct hit. The instant it happened, something small hit me in the stomach – It was the man's thumb."

Despite his 57 years and his failing health, General "Teddy" Roosevelt, the son of an early 20th century US President and second in command of the 4th division, had insisted in accompanying his

A 4th Division medical unit landing on *Utah Beach*.

A relatively trouble-free
landing on Utah Beach.

In the vicinity of *Utah Beach*, wounded 4th Division and airborne troops were gathered together.

men on their baptism of fire, "The kids will be reassured to know I'm with them." He reunited his officers on the very beach, "Listen guys, you landed around 2,000 yards south of the planned spot. But so what! The war starts here!" For due to the wind and strong coastal currents, the landing barges had drifted to finally land on the beach in La Madeleine - a hamlet in the village of Sainte-Marie-du-Mont - instead of on the Varreville dunes. Rarely had an error in navigation proved to be so auspicious. Indeed, the GIs, supported by amphibious tanks, were to find themselves face to face with a perfectly mediocre enemy battalion. What's more, the defences that comprised the Atlantic Wall in this zone were far less dangerous than those they expected to meet with further north. The German fortifications here had been given a seriously rough time after extremely accurate bombardments by the 9th Air Force's *B-26 Marauders* and put up but feeble resistance. Captain Mayberry added, "General was waving his cane and bellowing at everybody to get moving across the dunes. We kept moving as fast as possible. Some enemy rifleman began firing at me, so I picked myself up and began to run forward over the top of the dunes. Facing me were five of the enemy. I shot the one with his hand raised to hurl a grenade, the rest threw down

their rifles and put up their hands. I handed them over to a wounded corporal and went forward again." The beach was rapidly cleared of its obstacles by men from the 1st Engineer Special Brigade and the Beach Battalions. The vast majority of troops were able to land without major hindrance, despite sporadic gunfire from the Saint-Marcouf/Crisbecq battery, the only capable of hitting *Utah Beach*. By the evening of the 6th of June, the 4th Division had progressed approximately 6 miles inland, having made its first contact with the parachutists from the 101st Airborne in Pouppeville just before midday. Losses sustained throughout the day remained modest, including fifty dead and one hundred and fifty wounded. No comparison with the carnage, over those very same hours, less than twenty miles from there, on *Omaha Beach*.

The incredible attack on Pointe du Hoc

Located not far from *Omaha Beach*, Pointe du Hoc was to become the theatre of one of D-Day's most incredible feats. On this rocky headland, whose sheer cliffs plunge down to the sea 100 feet below, the Germans had established a formidable heavy artillery battery with six 155mm guns capable of spanning the nearby beaches:

Utah to the west and *Omaha* to the east. The position had, of course, been copiously bombed over the weeks prior to the landings. Yet how could the Allies be sure that the guns had been put out of action? A particularly dangerous mission was consequently entrusted to Lieutenant Colonel Rudder's 2nd Rangers Battalion: to arrive from the sea, climb up the cliff and capture the position. On his return to the site ten years later, he confided in a journalist, "Can you tell me just how we managed to do that? It was pure madness at the time, and still would be today!"

Things got off to a relatively bad start for the small fleet, comprised of twelve LCAs and four DUKW amphibious trucks transporting the 225 Rangers, had mistakenly headed for Pointe de la Percée. They made a U-turn, losing several embarkations on their way, to finally reach their target at around 7.10 a.m. as opposed to the scheduled arrival time of 6.30 a.m.

First Sergeant Leonard Lomell was one of the battalion's D Company, in charge of neutralising the three guns located on the headland's western zone, "300 yards

offshore, we were under fire from the german soldiers from cliff tops, determined to drive us back into the sea. They were waiting to cut our ropes, drop grenades on us and shoot us off the ropes.

When the ramp of the LCA went down I was the first one to step out. As I was getting off, I was shot in my right side, but the bullet only went through muscle, so I was able to keep going. But I stepped in a shell crater which I couldn't see, water over my head. The other guys pulled me up, cold and wet, and we started our assault of the cliffs. We fired hooks, with ropes attached, onto the cliffs, and up we went as fast as we could climb. We could not shoot back or defend ourselves very well while climbing. We were seriously outnumbered but we prevailed. There had been twenty-two of us in our LCA and we were all up the cliff within 15 minutes.

We continued to have more combat with the Germans. Enemy fire was coming from everywhere. We moved on very quickly to avoid machine-gun fire, as well as flat trajectory anti-aircraft machine-gun fire, too, which was becoming more and more of a serious problem. We

Rock fall at the foot of the Pointe du Hoc cliff, caused by bombing and naval artillery fire.

Rangers in combat in the craters that covered the headland plateau.

charged, yelled, jumping from crater to crater. We didn't stop. We played it just like a football game, charging hard and low. This fortress had underground tunnels, troop quarters etc. and the Germans popped up often firing their weapons from where we least expected. Ten of the original 22 Rangers in my boot team had been killed or were badly wounded. Our first objective, three guns in positions number four, five and six were not there. There were no big guns anywhere on the Pointe, only telephone poles or something similar sticking out of the bombed out encasements."

Indeed, upon Field Marshal Rommel's orders, the guns had been dismantled and removed from their open platforms after the Allied bombings on the 15th of April had destroyed one of them. However Lommel and Sergeant Jack Kuhn were to waste no time in unearthing them via an inland reconnaissance mission, whilst the battle continued on the cliff top.

"Jack and I saw markings in a sunken road that looked like something heavy had been over it. We started leapfrogging down this sunken farm road, between high hedgerows. It led to a little swale, or draw in an apple orchard. There was netting with camouflage over the five big 155mm guns and their ammunitions.

It was pure luck. They were located a little over a mile from where we had landed, in firing position, pointed at *Utah Beach*. There was nobody at the emplacement. We put thermite grenades in each traversing and recoil mechanism. Then Jack and I decided to get out of there on the double. The guns were rendered completely inoperable by 8.30 a.m."

Rudder and his men had accomplished their mission. However, given the turn of events on *Omaha* five miles away, the reinforcements that were supposed to relieve them around midday were still a long way off. By this time, the Rangers were surrounded on the tip of the headland, facing fierce German counterattack.

A Ranger's helmet, placed on a *K-Gun* driven into the ground, very probably to mark a temporary grave.

Omaha: the road to hell

From Arromanches to Grandcamp, the Calvados coastline forms a long line of steep cliffs. The only indentation in this impassable barrier is in the form of a 4 to 5-mile depression before the villages of Vierville, Saint-Laurent and Colleville, overlooking a vast beach strewn with obstacles. The upper part of the depression is bordered by a promenade to the west, whereas to the east, a pebbled levee rises several feet high. Above, a ledge is surmounted by an arresting embankment that steeply slopes up to the plateau.

There was no heavy artillery battery in the vicinity of *Omaha*. The closest, located 6 miles away as the crow flies, were at Pointe du Hoc to the west and Longues to the east. Nevertheless, the Germans had made the most of the terrain by setting up a series of fifteen "resistance nests" (*Widerstandsnester*) overlooking the shoreline and covering the valleys that lead to the plateau. Designed for close coastal defence, each of these fortifications included solid concrete casemates that housed mid-calibre guns, machine guns or mortars whose crossfire raked the entire beach.

Such was the zone chosen by the Allies to comprise one of the assault beaches on the morning of D-Day, under the codename *Omaha Beach*. It appeared perfectly evident that landing here would not be devoid of major risk. However, it was the only way to ensure the

Men from the 1st Division aboard an LCVP approaching *Omaha* with the first wave of assault.

H-Hour - 6.30 a.m.

was carrying. I tried to pull the release straps on my assault jacket, but I couldn't move. Lieutenant Gearing grabbed my jacket and, using his bayonet, cut the straps. I was all right now. I could swim. We counted heads. One was missing: Padley, our radio operator." After waiting for hours, Barnes and his fellow soldiers were finally rescued by an empty barge on its way back to the high seas to find themselves back on board the troop transport vessel they had left at 4 a.m.

necessary continuity between *Gold Beach* (British 50th Division) and *Utah Beach*. Well aware of the danger, the Allies had decided to reduce the German defences to a minimum via aerial and naval bombing. General Gerow's V Corps, which comprised two divisions, had received the perilous mission of setting foot on *Omaha*. The assault front had been divided into several sub-sectors, respectively codenamed *Charlie, Dog, Easy* and *Fox*, the first two being assigned to the 116th Regiment (29th Division) and the two others to the 16th Regiment (1st Division).

The men from General Gerhardt's 29th Division, who had arrived in England in 1942, had never fought before. Their baptism of fire was to prove horrifying. Under a deluge of enemy fire, the 116th Regiment's A Company led the assault before Vierville, in the *Dog Green* sector, with support on its right flank from a company of Rangers. A mile from the shoreline, an LCA sunk, plunging the heavily laden men it transported into the sea. Private Barnes was among them, "I was going under. I turned to grab the man behind me. I climbed on his back and pulled myself up in a panic. Our heads bobbed up above the water. We could still see some other boats moving off to the shore. I was unable keep my head above the surface with all the equipment I

The company's other barges continued their route. Corporal Gilbert Murdoch was aboard one of them, "As the coxswain of the assault craft thought he had reached the beach, he stopped engines and had the ramp lowered. The lieutenant ran off down the middle of the ramp and was immediately killed by machine-gun fire. Rodriguez, who was a private, ran off at the right side and was immediately cut in half by the machine guns. I jumped off from the left side and found myself in about nine feet of water. The coxswain of the landing

Aboard their ship, next to a 20mm gun, US Navy sailors watch a huge explosion on the beach.

In the *Fox Green* sector, a wounded soldier receives a plasma transfusion; his head is resting on a lifebelt.

was now coming forward at me, full speed with the ramp down, to try and get over the sandbar. The ramp hit me and knocked me under the water. I grabbed the one-inch hawser line which I used as a bumper and the landing craft hit the beach with me still hanging on to it. As soon as I got the strength to get up, I realized I could hardly see because I was wearing glasses and my glasses were coated with salt. I started to move forward, creeping and crawling, and I realized that my rifle wouldn't fire because the sand had cemented the operating rod. I came across one of our riflemen, wounded, a man named McSkimming. He was wounded in the arm and he asked me to give him a shot of morphine, which I did. We wished each other luck and I moved on. I finally came to one of the underwater obstacles which, since we landed at high tide, was out of the water. There were two people there. George Roach said all the officers were dead, all the noncoms were dead and that as far as he could see he and I, as Pfcs, were the senior men on the beach. There were thirteen of us alive out of 205."

Almost completely annihilated, the A Company was undoubtedly the one to pay the greatest price in human lives on the morning of the 6th of June. Among the many victims, twenty-one boys from Bedford, a small village in Virginia, from where thirty-five of the company's men originated. In the neighbouring *Charlie* sector, the Rangers who were being transported by two LCAs had met with similar fate. The first was struck full force by shellfire from an antitank gun and twelve men were lost. A machine gun concentrated its fire on the second, killing or wounding fifteen of their buddies. The survivors painstakingly made their way to the foot of the cliff, sustaining further losses. Only thirty-five of sixty-four men remained.

The F Company reached land opposite the entrance to the Moulins valley, a position that had been solidly fortified by the Germans. The company was welcomed with brutal hostility. Warner Hamlett was to experience this dramatic confrontation, along with his fellow soldiers, "Thousands of obstacles with mines attached lined the beach. Many assault craft stopped far short of the beach, in fear of hitting mines. As the men jumped into the water, it was often over their heads. Heavy equipment caused them to be pulled down into the rough water. Constant 88 artillery machine-gun fire and rifle fire criss-crossed the beach, mowing down helpless soldiers who couldn't find cover or fire their sand-clogged rifles. I saw Lieutenant Hillshure go down on his knees as a shell exploded. He fell into the hole caused by the explosion and died there on the beach. Private Gillingham, a young soldier, fell in beside me, white with fear. He seemed to be begging for help with his eyes. His look was that of a child asking what to do. I heard a shell coming and dove into the sand, face down. Shrapnel rose over my head and hit all around me, blowing me three or four feet. My rifle was ripped from my hand and my helmet went twenty-five or thirty feet in front of me. When I started to jump up and run, a sharp pain hit my spine from my neck to my lower back. The shell that injured me took Gillingham's chin off, including the bone, except for a small piece of flesh. Bill Hawkes and I gave him his morphine shot. We stayed with him for approximately thirty minutes until he died. The entire time, he remained conscious and aware that he was

The 1st Infantry Division's 16th Regiment attacking the *Easy Red* sector.

dying. He groaned in pain but was unable to speak".

The barges that were transporting the E Company had drifted considerably eastwards and had landed their men opposite the *Easy Red* and *Fox Green* sectors, which had in fact been assigned to the 1st Division. "What I found is difficult to describe. I can only call it disorganized chaos" Private Harry Parley recalled. "Along the beach I could see burning wreckage, damaged landing craft and, of course, men trying to get off the beach. I realized that we had landed in the wrong beach sector and that many of the people around me were from other units and were strangers to me. What's more, the terrain before us was not what I had been trained to encounter. All disorganized, all trying to stay alive."

The 16th Infantry Regiment was the 1st Division's spearhead, General Huebner's famous *Big Red One* - the US Army's most prestigious unit and the most seasoned after having fought in North Africa and Sicily. Yet it was equally put to the test on *Easy Red* and *Fox Green*. The barges that were transporting the I Company drifted as far

as Port-en-Bessin, before turning back. In the meantime, their buddies were going through sheer hell on *Fox Green*. More than half of the men from the E Company were killed or wounded, either in the waters or on the sand. The F Company lost a good half of its troops before it even reached the shelter of the pebbled embankment at the top of the beach. Only two officers were unscathed. The men, extenuated, wounded or in a state of shock had no other solution but to take refuge, huddled under the sheer cliff that soared above Colleville's eastern extremity. Despite having lost thirty men, the L Company was the only one to efficiently make its way to the foot of the rock face. In the *Easy Red* sector, leaping from beach obstacles to wrecked tanks, the photographer Robert Capa captured the scene, roll after roll. Dramatic instants where men faced with death struggled helplessly in the cold waters of this 6th of June 1944. Only a handful of his pictures survived, but they were to travel the world over. Lost amidst the dead, the wounded and the charred equipment, Sergeant Plick thought to himself, "We've lost."

LCIs transporting reinforcements to Saint-Laurent-sur-Mer.

Medical teams working on the beaches were particularly vulnerable in these perilous conditions. Under enemy fire, the many wounded were evacuated by landing barges or Coast Guard rescue ships. They were transferred to specially equipped ships where surgical teams procured first aid before their transfer into British hospitals.

Whilst the GIs were pinned to the spot, after sustaining huge losses, the first troops from the second wave of assault were within sight of *Omaha*, just half an hour after the first wave. The fourteen companies engaged in the assault were to land every ten minutes as from 7 a.m. An extremely unpleasant surprise awaited them.

Sergeant Slaughter was a member of the 116th Infantry Division's D Company, whose sections were scattered across the shoreline before Vierville, between *Dog Green* and *Dog Red*, "About 200 or 300 yards from shore we encountered artillery fire. Near misses sent water skyward and then it rained back on us. My thinking, as we approached the beach, was that if the boat didn't hurry up and get us in I would die from seasickness.

At this point, death is not so dreadful. Thinking I was immune to seasickness, earlier I had given my 'puke bag' to a buddy who had already filled his. Minus the paper bag, I used the first thing at hand, my helmet. British coxswain said he had to lower the ramp and for us to quickly disembark. I heard Sergeant Norfleet counter, 'These men have heavy equipment and you will take them all the way in.' The coxswain begged, 'But we'll all be killed!' Norfleet unholstered his .45 Colt pistol, put it to the sailor's head and ordered, 'ALL THE WAY IN!' The craft proceeded as far as it could go.

We knew then that this was not going to be a walk-in. No one thought that the enemy was going to give us this kind of opposition on the water's edge. We expected A and B companies to have the beach secured by the time we landed. This turned boys into men. Some would be very brave men, others would soon be dead men. Some wet their britches, others cried unashamedly. As we approached the beach the ramp was lowered. Mortar and artillery shells exploded on land and in the water. Unseen snipers were shooting down at individuals, causing screams from those being hit. The water was turning red from the blood. The noise from artillery fire, the rapid-fire rattle from nearby MG42S, and naval gunfire was deafening. The smell of cordite was something that would forever become fixed in our minds, always associated with death and destruction. There were dead men in the water and there were live men as well. The Germans couldn't tell which was which. All were coming in with the tide. I don't know how long we were in the water before the move was made, but I would guess close to an hour. While lying on the sand behind one of the log poles, I watched a GI get shot trying to cross the beach, running from my right to left. An enemy gunner shot him and he screamed for a medic. One of the aid men moved quickly to help him and he was shot too. I'll never forget seeing that medic lying next to that wounded GI and both of them screaming. They both died within minutes."

One after another, each and every section that set foot on *Omaha* met with the same ordeal. The deadly hostilities continued inexorably. Aboard an LCVP that was approaching the *Fox Red* sector shortly after 8 a.m., John McVane, an NBC correspondent in Europe, could but observe what appeared to be total disaster, "Certain barges had sunk even before the shoreline was in view. We encountered floating debris or men held up by their lifebelts. Columns of black smoke rose up as high as the clouds. Whilst the beach should have been relatively clear and the men well inland, it was black with soldiers strewn across on the ground. I had no way of knowing if they were dead or alive. Things had surely turned out badly for they were not moving, apart from a few who were wriggling on their bellies trying to reach the pebbled embankment. The dead were floating here and there, as survivors swam to the shore amidst the obstacles. We felt like rats, caught in a trap. Everyone could see that something had gone wrong!"

Yet the finest details of the plan of attack had been painstakingly put together. It had, unfortunately, been thwarted by a series of imponderables. First of all, against all expectations, the enemy defences were intact. The 8th US Air Force's *B-24 Liberators* had received orders to bomb the German coastal strong points in the *Omaha* sector as of 6 a.m. They were to fail miserably, as General Bradley was later to concede, "The 13,000 bombs dropped by these heavies had cascaded harmlessly into the hedgerows three miles behind the coast. In bombing through the overcast, air had deliberately delayed its drop to lessen the danger of spill-over on craft approaching the shore. This margin for safety had undermined the effectiveness of the heavy air mission." The results obtained by the naval artillery were hardly more conclusive. The casemates that housed guns and machine guns, with their embrasures obliquely aimed at the beach and protected from high-seas attack by thick flanking walls were - if truth be told - extremely difficult to neutralise. What's more, Germany's mediocre 709th Division, in charge of defending the coast from Caen to Grandcamp, had largely been relieved in the *Omaha* sector by a far superior unit, the 352nd Division, whose transfer from the Saint-Lô region to the coast in April 1944 appeared to have escaped the attention of the Allied strategists.

Exhausted and wounded soldiers from the 1st and 29th Divisions taking shelter under the cliff at Colleville's eastern extremity.

Evacuating the wounded

The dramatic circumstances on *Omaha Beach* had singularly complicated the evacuation of the many wounded, who were given initial care, directly on the beaches, by medical teams working in extremely perilous conditions.
The Americans had no specific hospital ships in Normandy, in contrast with the British who offered them use of two of their own ships - the *Naushon* off *Omaha* and the *Lady Connaught* off *Utah Beach* – but only as from the 7th of June.
The very first wounded troops were transported for first aid to specially equipped LST ships where surgical teams, medical equipment, plasma and medication awaited them.
They were taken to the LSTs, under sustained enemy fire, by landing barges (LCT, LCM or LCVP), or by Coast Guard rescue boats.
A total of 863 wounded troops were evacuated from *Omaha* to England on the day of the 6th of June alone; they were admitted to hospitals in Southampton, Portsmouth, Weymouth and Brixham.

The situation out at sea was often as catastrophic as it was on the beaches. An LCI-85 in distress after being hit by a mine, then shellfire. On board, fifteen or so dead troops and thirty wounded.

The crew of a wrecked LCI being recovered by a Coast Guard rescue ship.

Under direct shellfire, their *Landing Craft* and pneumatic dinghies charged with explosives were blown to shreds, generating absolute carnage all around them. Most of their bulldozers were lost or destroyed before being given a chance to clear corridors through the beaches. The Engineer units' losses were phenomenal, with 1,300 men killed, wounded or lost to sight, representing 40% of their troops. Despite their great heroism, they had only succeeded in partly fulfilling their mission. Many barges exploded or became impaled on the traps set by Rommel.

The infantry was to be given vital support by amphibious tanks. Most of the 741st Battalion's thirty-two tanks launched to cover the 16th Regiment sunk; only two made their own way to the beach and three others were landed directly on the shore by an LCT barge. This prudent solution - in view of sea conditions - was adopted for the 743rd Division before Vierville; however, it did not prevent the fearsome German 88mm guns from causing considerable damage.

Strong north-westerly winds added further turmoil to the coastal currents, carrying the majority of the waves of assault off course, some of them almost a mile east of their intended landing points. Hence the extreme confusion that reigned on the beaches, with huge gaps in the assault zone alongside stretches of sand packed with entangled units, totally disorientated by the absence of their expected landmarks. Amidst the resulting chaos, severe losses among officers were also to paralyse the continuation of operations. Many surviving troops had lost their commanders, their priority now being to save their skins rather than to reassemble to continue their assault further inland.

With these conditions reunited, the first waves of American assault found themselves face to face with unyielding opposition. The Engineer units, reinforced by several US Navy Beach Battalions in charge of clearing the beaches by opening breaches through the obstacles, were the first to bear the cost. Laden with their heavy equipment and demolition material, the sappers were among the first prime targets for the German snipers.

Barges laden with wounded soldiers relentlessly shuttled to and from the shore and the troop transport vessels. The Coast Guards' small rescue Cutters scoured the seas to recover the many castaways whose embarkations had sunk before even reaching the shore, along with crews from instantaneously submerged amphibious tanks, and even a few pilots whose planes had been shot down by the FLAK.

Aboard the heavy cruiser *USS Augusta*, the US First Army's commander, General Bradley, was anxious, "As the morning lengthened, my worries deepened over the alarming and fragmentary reports we picked up on the navy net. From these messages we could piece together only an incoherent account of sinkings, swampings, heavy enemy fire, and chaos on the beaches.

When V Corps reported at noon that the situation was 'still critical' on all four beach exits, I reluctantly contemplated the diversion of *Omaha* follow-up forces to *Utah* and the British beaches."

The situation was nevertheless to improve by late morning. Deprived of reinforcements, the German defenders began to yield under the virtually point-blank gunfire from Allied destroyers that had now approached the shoreline as close as they could. Back on the beaches, a few energetic officers managed to round up their ranks and urge them forwards at all costs. Among them, in the *Dog White* sector, General Cotta, second in command of the 29th Division and Colonel Canham, commander of the 116th Regiment, who refused evacuation despite wounds and a slinged arm. On *Easy Red*, Colonel Taylor, commander of the 16th Regiment, then cried out what was to become a famous quote, "There are only two kinds of people who are staying on this beach: those who are dead and those who are going to die. Now let's get the hell out of here!" A few subalterns, whose names did not necessarily go down in History, were also to play a capital role in salvaging the situation.

Having given up on the idea of forcing their way through the valleys that were riddled with antitank walls and largely covered by intense enemy fire, small groups of GIs began to filter their way between them by climbing up the embankment. In a thrust of energy and courage,

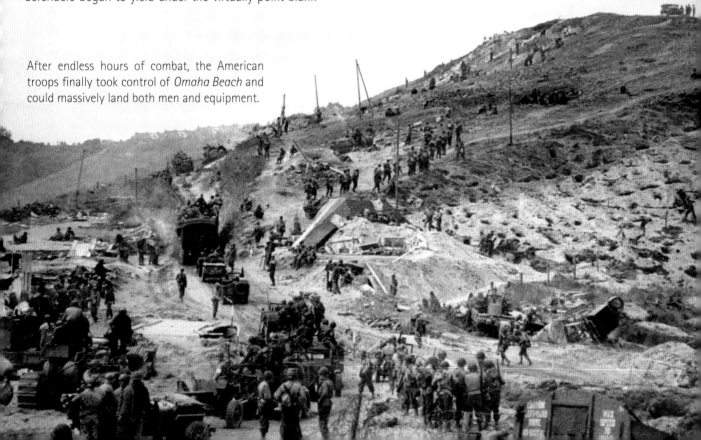

After endless hours of combat, the American troops finally took control of *Omaha Beach* and could massively land both men and equipment.

Counting and identifying the dead on the evening of the 6th of June.

inch by inch, they gradually got the better of several of the German defences, to finally reach the plateau, several hours after the assault had begun. The reporter John McVane was a distant witness to this change in the course of events, "Infantrymen set out on the assault when a sergeant or a lieutenant decided it was better to be killed standing than grovelling. I saw men stand up, advance towards the embankment and climb up it. In swaying lines, they crossed mines and barbed wire, each of them meandering his own way through. I saw some of them fall and others disappear amidst the explosions. Yet the line continued to move forward, towards the top of the escarpment. I could see the black outline of a few of those tiny silhouettes against the grey sky; they had reached the ridge. Some of our men had penetrated inland, and it was fantastic!"

In small formations, the GIs captured the German defences from the rear, advancing laboriously under sniper fire, but nevertheless progressing and gradually reassembling. Whilst the village of Vierville was liberated at around 11 a.m., the defenders put up much fiercer resistance in Saint-Laurent and Colleville. Fighting continued throughout the afternoon. Men and material continued to be unloaded on the beach, by now somewhat crowded due to insufficient inland clearance. The first tanks were late to reach the plateau, only at around 8 p.m. By nightfall, the Americans were in control of a narrow bridgehead that rarely exceeded two miles in depth and that still comprised several pockets of resistance. The villages of Colleville and Saint-Laurent were consequently only liberated on the morning of the 7th of June. The D-Day objectives were far from achieved; great quantities of material and equipment had been lost and, of course, human losses were particularly severe: 1,800 dead or unaccounted for and 2,300 wounded. But the most important aim had been accomplished: the assault had not been repelled. Yet, if there is one site where the D-Day Landings could well have failed, it is undoubtedly "Bloody Omaha".

In the evening, the bodies that were strewn across the shoreline were hastily offered temporary graves. James Tucker, a non-commissioned officer from the 299th Engineer Combat Battalion, was among those in charge of this macabre task, "Part of our crew began clearing the beach of bodies but there was no place to put them. Orders came down to dig a temporary mass grave. I had one of my dozers do it. The driver kept going back and forth until he had a big enough trench. The chaplain and I gathered men to collect the bodies. They all got sick leaving only the chaplain and I to finish. Then the bodies were stacked in there, like cordwood and covered over with sand. I understand it was the first American graveyard in Normandy WWII."

Religious service in front of the temporary cemetery on Vierville beach.

The 8th and 9th US Air Forces in action

Never before had such an impressive aerial armada been reunited. Indeed, in addition to transport craft, Eisenhower had at his disposal some eleven thousand planes, including six thousand fighter planes and bombers belonging to the 8th and 9th US Air Forces. The *Luftwaffe* appeared somewhat powerless against such aerial supremacy. Massive Allied bombardments over Germany had pushed many fighter squadrons into retreat across the Rhine in order to protect the Reich. In the spring, attack on airfields in north-western France had further confused and weakened its defensive potential. Field Marshal Hugo Sperrle, commander of *Luftflotte 3*, was to content himself with just a thousand planes - some of which were not even in a state to fly - scattered across France, Belgium and the Netherlands. This blatant inequity between the aerial forces within the assault zone was to prove one of the essential ingredients for the Allied victory in Normandy. Their aerial superiority was manifest as from the 6th of June: 14,700 Allied flights were recorded on that one day, compared to just five hundred on the German side.

In principle, the bridgehead - with its swarms of ships out in the high seas and extremely vulnerable quantities

A *B-26 Marauder* flies above *Sword Beach* on its way back from a bombing mission.

of men and material strewn across the beaches - was the ideal target for the *Luftwaffe*. Yet, it was a target that appeared out of reach: eight hundred 8th Air Force fighter planes occupied the skies in turns from dawn to dusk, forming an aerial screen that stretched from the Mont-Saint-Michel bay to Dieppe. Their key mission consisted in intercepting any enemy plane that attempted to reach the bridgehead. Protection above the beaches themselves was offered by six *Spitfire* squadrons flying at low altitude, in turn covered by three American *P-47 Thunderbolt* squadrons flying above them.

Over and above protecting the landing forces, the Allied aviation had been entrusted with another crucial task: to slow down to a minimum the arrival of any enemy reinforcements on the front. Essentially assigned to the Normandy sector, the 8th and 9th US Air Forces' formidable *P-47 Thunderbolt* fighter bombers accomplished several simultaneous missions the same day, relentlessly multiplying their ground attacks.

The *8th Air Force's* heavy bombers were, in turn, assigned to cutting major road links leading to the bridgehead, by reducing a certain number of important junctions to ruins. The arrival of the German armoured reinforcements was particularly feared. A blanket of low cloud rendered the mission extremely difficult for planes that are accustomed to flying at higher altitude. Even before the landings, Generals Spaatz and Doolittle had clearly informed *Overlord's* staff of their reservations on the suitability of a strategic fleet for such tactical missions. They had even persevered by clearly stating that the destruction of towns devoid of military installations - and the consequent programmed death of a share of their inhabitants - was something they considered particularly "unpleasant". Yet Eisenhower decided otherwise. At best, they obtained the distribution - at 6.30 a.m. - of leaflets alerting the populations in target towns of the imminent danger, hence allowing them sufficient time to evacuate. Unfortunately, the aerial distribution of these leaflets was extremely inaccurate and was virtually ineffective.

The first mission, scheduled for 9 a.m., turned into a total fiasco due to the cloudy conditions: planes simply returned to England with their bombs. At 1.30 p.m., 73 *B-24s* entered the skies above Caen, with the bridges over the River Orne as targets. The result was disastrous: no bridge was hit and one hundred and fifty tonnes of bombs struck the town, between the river and the castle, totally devastating the town centre and killing around five hundred civilians. A second attempt was launched at 4.30 p.m., this time by the 9th Air Force's *B-26 Marauders*, meeting with little more success.

These failed missions, along with the *Panzerdivisionnen's* steady progression towards Normandy were to intensify anxiety amidst the Allied command. A new large-scale mission was launched at around 8 p.m. by 736 *B-24s* and *B-17s*. The clouds had begun to disperse in certain zones. A third of the planes failed to identify their targets: Argentan, Falaise and Thury-Harcourt were - at least momentarily - spared from destruction. In contrast, 1,568 tonnes of bombs were dropped over Saint-Lô, Coutances, Vire, Condé-sur-Noireau, Flers, Pont-l'Évêque and Lisieux, reducing most of these towns to ruins and killing a thousand of their inhabitants. Yet these were considered insufficient results and, on the night of the 6th to the 7th of June, a new massive bombing campaign was launched, this time by the RAF's Bomber Command and with just as many victims.

The small town of Littry, bombed by a 9th Air Force A-20 Havoc.

The United States learns of the landings

Radio Berlin was efficiently fast to announce, as early as 6.30 a.m. on the very morning, an "enemy attack between Le Havre and Cherbourg," news that was fast to reach Allied agencies. It was 0.30 a.m. on the east coast of the United States and, in New York, the information was captured by the radio channel CBS's teleprinters and cautiously relayed, "We are interrupting this program to bring you a special bulletin. A bulletin has just been received from the London office of the Associated Press which quotes the German Transocean News Agency as asserting that the invasion of Western Europe has begun. This report - and we stress it is of enemy origin with absolutely no confirmation from Allied source - says that American landings were made this morning on the shores of north-western France. We will now leave you with your usual program."

At 3.32 a.m. precisely - 9.32 a.m. London time - the landing operation was officially confirmed by release n°1 issued by the SHAEF and read

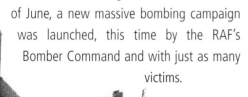

Vire, after the bombings on the 6th and 7th of June.

at the microphone by the press director himself, "Under the command of general Eisenhower, allied naval forces, supported by strong air forces, began landing allied armies this morning on the northern coast of France." The *Office of War Information* immediately broadcast this brief release across the globe. In the midst of the night, telephones began to ring in sleepy households, "Up you get Al, switch on your radio and listen: the invasion's started."

The American press in its entirety, from the most illustrious daily broadsheets to the humblest of local papers, was fast to spread the news of the event. As early as 6. a.m. on the very morning of the 6th of June, the *New York Times* issued a special edition. The headline, initially on the subject of the capture of Rome two days previously, had been hastily replaced: "Great invasion is under way." On the airwaves, whilst awaiting further news, radio commentators relentlessly repeated the same information, much to the dismay of eagerly impatient listeners. However, a few reports had indeed reached London and the United States the very same morning, recorded by the war correspondents who had accompanied the landing troops on the beaches. Yet nothing was to transpire of the battle itself. Faces lit up when the 10 o'clock news bulletin - 4 p.m. in Europe - reported the Allied troops' progression 6 miles inland.

The Normandy landings hit the headlines in the American press.

A group of demonstrators on its way to the patriotic gathering in Madison Square.

Each and every American felt more or less concerned about what was happening over there, thousands of miles from home. Many had worked hard for long years to manufacture the equipment or the weapons the *boys* now held in their hands; others had purchased the war bonds that had enabled them to be produced. It was as if the combat that had just begun was, to an extent, their own. Andrew Higgins, whose New Orleans shipyards had produced thousands of assault barges, was proud to remind his workforce, "The first landings on the Continent were made by the Allies in our boats." Only a few rare families had no family member, friend or neighbour who had crossed the Atlantic and was,

perhaps at this very instant, defying the enemy. However, accurate information updates were painfully lacking, despite great expectations among the population. A disquieting medley of enthusiasm and apprehension reigned, as newspapers sold like hotcakes. Most of them reproduced a map of the north-west of France to enable their readers, generally unfamiliar with European geography, to locate Normandy.

In New York, passers-by stopped and gathered in front of department store windows where loud speakers broadcast radio programmes. Religious services were held throughout the day, both in St Patrick's Cathedral and in the synagogue on 33rd Street. In Madison Square,

Chicago

a massive demonstration reunited tens of thousands of participants brandishing banners and flags, as the fanfare blasted out patriotic songs. Fiorello La Guardia, the Mayor of New York, together with personalities and representatives of various religious confessions, bellowed to the crowd, one after another.

The same fever had struck the entire country. President Roosevelt spoke on the radio to appeal for divine protection and to urge his compatriots to have faith in victory for democracy and civilisation. The Star Spangled Banner was flown from many windows. Blood donors rushed in crowds to hospitals. Church bells were pealing

Crowds gathered at the foot of the *New York Times* building to watch the latest news on an illuminated panel.

out. In Philadelphia, the Mayor had the venerable *Liberty Bell* symbolically tapped several times; this glorious symbol of American Independence had not rung since 1835. In Marietta, in Georgia, police cars drove round residential districts with their sirens howling, to alert the population. Patriotic fervour was even to name a baby girl - born in Dallas, Texas on the 6th of June 1944 - "Invasia", whilst another girl, born in Norfolk, Virginia was named "Dee Day"...

All ordinary activities had been interrupted. In Colombus, Ohio, upon orders from the Mayor, factory sirens wailed, calling the population into prayer. The entire city was ground to a halt for five minutes, buses and trucks stopped in the middle of the street, as did pedestrians on the pavements. From coast to coast, baseball matches were cancelled, as were all other sporting events. In Mobile, in Alabama, not a single glass of alcohol was served throughout the day. In Reno, Nevada, gambling was suspended in clubs, whereas the activity that had gained the city fame - ultra-quick on the trot divorces - was to plummet by 90%. Broadway's usual shows were cancelled, whereas Wall Street suspended its listings for a short while, before resuming with a massive increase in values. The Statue of Liberty - the very symbol of Franco-American friendship - which had been plunged into total darkness every night since Pearl Harbor, was exceptionally illuminated for fifteen minutes.

As the entire United States population awaited further information on the advancement of military operations amidst great agitation, this historic 6th of June was coming to a close in France. By the evening of D-Day, the Americans had landed 81,000 men, i.e. a little over half of the entire Allied forces engaged in Normandy. With 8,000 killed, missing and wounded - compared to 2,500 in the British and Canadian ranks - they had paid a horrendous price, essentially due to heavy losses among the paratroopers from the V Corps before *Omaha*.

Upon the announcement of the landings, labourers in an Illinois factory stopped working to pray.

Buy More War Bonds and Stamps

WINNER R. HOE & CO., INC. AWARD — NATIONAL WAR POSTER COMPETITION
HELD UNDER AUSPICES OF ARTISTS FOR VICTORY, INC.—COUNCIL FOR DEMOCRACY—MUSEUM OF MODERN ART

On the 6th of June, the Allies had succeeded in establishing a foothold in Normandy. However, the road to Berlin was, as yet, far from wide open. The Germans were preparing to vigorously defend their "Fortress Europe". The Battle of Normandy had begun; it was to last almost three months. Montgomery had given strict orders: to consolidate the positions that had been secured on D-Day and to wait for sufficient reinforcements to arrive before launching any large-scale operation.

The Americans' key objective was to take control of Cherbourg and its port. However, before doing so, they needed to fill the gap between their two army corps; a dangerously wide 13-mile breach caused by the difficulties encountered on *Omaha* on D-Day.

A long column of prisoners of war heading for their internment camp along the RN13 trunk road on the outskirts of the town.

◄ This photograph, taken in June 1944 near Saint-Sauveur-le-Vicomte, was published on the front cover of *Life* Magazine, transforming Lieutenant Kelso C. Horne from the 82nd Airborne into the symbol of the American Second World War soldier.

Spectacular turnaround on *Omaha Beach*

General Gerow's V Corps, who had been given a rough time on the morning of the 6th of June, succeeded in creating a spectacular turnaround over the following days. The engineers cleared the shoreline of the cumbersome piles of debris and wrecks, enlarging exit routes to prepare for the arrival of reinforcements. The 2nd Infantry Division, also known as the "Indian Head", landed on the 7th of June, closely followed by the first units from the 2nd Armoured Division. In the enemy ranks, the German 352nd and 709th Divisions had undeniably inflicted a costly ordeal on the Americans on *Omaha Beach*. Yet they had also suffered bitterly from the day's combat and their capacity to resist was now severely weakened.

In addition, the Allies were at a considerable advantage for their warships were still anchored off the coast, ready to offer support to the infantry. Their battleships and cruisers were armed with powerful guns, capable of firing up to 10 miles inland, some even further. Their target coordinates and firing corrections were provided either by aerial reconnaissance or by ground observers who had landed with the assault troops.

The 29th Division left Vierville and headed, first of all, towards the mouth of the River Vire. On the morning of the 8th of June, they freed Lieutenant Colonel Rudder's

The small town of Isigny was ravaged by naval artillery fire on the 8th of June, to be liberated the next day.

A 1st Infantry Division antitank unit in a defensive position in Caumont-L'Éventé, the most advanced American position in the Bessin.

A Signal Corps team installing a telephone line in Trévières, a village that suffered greatly from naval artillery fire and the hostilities that led to its liberation.

Rangers, who had been surrounded for 2 days with only 90 men still fit for combat. The division continued to hug the coast, taking control of Grandcamp and the Maisy artillery battery after bitter hand-to-hand fighting with its garrison. On the dawn of the 9th of June, the 29th Division entered the ruins of Isigny. Continuing its progression, the division succeeded in establishing a bridgehead on the left bank of the Vire.

At the opposite extremity of the V Corps' sectors, the collapse of the German 716th Division's left flank had enabled the 1st Division to liaise with British troops near Bayeux. On the 9th of June, they reached the River Drôme, captured Balleroy on the 11th, to reach Caumont-l'Éventé two days later, some 20 miles inland; they had just achieved the most impressive Allied progression on the Normandy front.

Amidst Gerow's plan of attack, the 2nd Division's advance proved to be more problematic. After making good progression towards Trévières, Gerow's men took control of the town on the evening of the 9th, after intense fighting. Their adversary, the German 352nd Division - worn out by its relentless resistance on *Omaha* - now barely boasted 2,500 men fit for combat, out of a total of 8,000, and was forced into retreat; the road was clear and the Americans rapidly progressed to the Cerisy forest which they cleared.

In the meantime, the 29th Division had turned off southwards, crossed the River Elle and was charging towards Saint-Lô, progressing a further 10 miles in just one day. However, German resistance had toughened in the vicinity of the town and Bradley ordered General Gerhardt to halt his troops' advance, "He could take Saint-Lô without breaking the back of his 29th. I wouldn't object. But I doubt very much that he could. Sure, Saint-Lô would make good news and give the correspondents something to write about. But we're not going to spend a division just to take a place name. We can get along very nicely without Saint-Lô at this time." Capturing Cherbourg was the utmost priority. The same instructions were given to General Corlett's XIX Corps, also in combat in the sector as from the 15th of June.

A gruelling war of positions then followed. Lieutenant Colonel Snetzer, in charge of the 2nd Engineer Battalion, was to support the 2nd Division - engaged in combat before Hill 192, located a few miles to the east of Saint-Lô and in the hands of the German 3rd Parachute Division. Snetzer's men, unaccustomed to combat, were put to the test. He jotted down events, day by day, in his notebook, "June 18: This infantry work is really rough, hard, dirty, and deadly. Thank God we don't have to do this every day for a living. It is a hell of an existence, lying in a slit trench trying to save your hide.

June 19: Continued to hold positions. Miserable cold rain all day. Wet and muddy everywhere. No blankets. No raincoats. Just mud. June 20: Received heavy mortar fire on A Company. Lieutenants Lepper and Wright killed. Sixteen other casualties in the company. June 21: More of the same. Rain, mud, cold, mortar fire, and more casualties. June 23: Captain Huthnance killed by mortar fire this morning on Hill 192. Really giving us hell. No advance has been made for a week."

From *Utah Beach* to Cherbourg

The situation for the paratroopers in the Cotentin peninsula was starting to improve, all the more so since the Germans had partly evacuated the drop zone in an attempt to encircle it in a new line of defence. The junction was made with the 4th Division on the 7th of June. It was high time. Ralph Ingersoll was among the detachment that joined General Ridgway's command

14th June: two Allied officers giving war correspondents a breakdown of the situation during a press conference.

post to the west of Sainte-Mère-Église, "When we came all the way around the field to the farmhouse, we saw that a high stone wall enclosed it. Inside the wall there was a sight to make you stop and shake your head. The big muddy yard was carpeted with several hundred german soldiers and officers in various states of disrepair, lying down or sitting up silently. They lay like gray green water in a sump, quite still. Around them, sat a circle of muddy desperadoes with pistols and Tommy guns pointed at the pool of Germans. It was quite a tableau. The boys who were guarding the Germans were all wounded or hurt, which was why they were sitting down. But each had at least one good arias in which he held his gun. I went past the pool of prisoners to the house. But inside the house there was only another nightmare. There was a big room with a stove set in the wall on one side but all the other furniture cleared out of it. On the floor, from wall to wall, packed solid, arms and legs over one another and intertwined, there were badly wounded paratroopers. They were not silent and the room was alive with the kind of sound that animals make when they are hurt. Amongst the wreckage there climbed carefully two French women, a mother and a daughter."

Along the banks of the Merderet, paratroopers from the 82nd Division were struggling their way, foot by foot, through the marshlands to rescue their buddies from the 507th Regiment, still isolated on the opposite bank. Although the Americans had succeeded in taking control of the La Fière and Chef-du-Pont bridges, they were at a standstill, unable to clear the "causeways" that surmounted the flooded prairies. On the contrary, for three long days they were to be subjected to intense artillery fire and to challenge fierce German counterattacks in an attempt to regain possession of the two bridges. The 9th of June was to mark the victorious breakthrough, under showers of bullets, that was to enable the paratroopers to cross the La Fière bridge and to establish a solid foothold in Cauquigny, to the west of the Merderet. The following day, the 90th Infantry

As they advanced through the Cotentin, the Americans discovered a number of V1 launch bases, along with the impressive V2 rocket launch base in Brix-Sottevast, still under construction. In this picture, Eisenhower and Bradley pay a visit to the site.

Division, landed a few days previously on *Utah Beach*, was free to cross the river and to clear Lieutenant Colonel Timmes and his men from a critical position where they had been encircled by the Germans for five days.

Yet all of the paratroopers were not so fortunate. Some of them found themselves totally isolated, amidst the very core of the enemy lines. Such was the fate of some 170 men, lost several miles to the south of Carentan, who sought refuge in the small village of Graignes, where the local population had rallied round to welcome them and to offer them supplies. Yet despite the mayor's advice to be careful, the paratroopers - who were keen to engage in battle - multiplied surprise attacks in the surrounding area, which was only to arouse the Germans' attention. The village was attacked on the

11th of June by a powerful 17th SS Panzergrenadier Division column, whose frontline units had just arrived in Normandy. Despite staunch resistance, the paratroopers were finally forced into retreat, leaving behind thirty of their men, killed during the hostilities. The SS, now in control of the village, shot down two women and two priests, and executed eight of the severely wounded troops along with the medical captain who had chosen to stay with them.

Whilst Ridgway's men held the western front, General

The Saint-Marcouf/Crisbecq coastal artillery battery – equipped with three powerful 210 mm guns, two of which were housed in casemates - fell into American hands on the 12th of June after several days of bitter combat.

Collins' VII Corps launched a double attack in both northerly and southerly directions. The 4th Division was to progress along the coastline towards Cherbourg and, in the process, to put several coastal batteries out of firing action in order to facilitate the landing operations on *Utah Beach*. After having successfully repelled an Allied assault two days earlier, the Azeville battery was finally captured on the 9th of June thanks to flamethrowers. The Crisbecq-Saint/Marcouf battery was to put up heroic resistance. Its initially 400-man garrison had driven back the first attack by the 22nd US Regiment, forced into retreat. A second attempt was made the following day, backed by powerful artillery fire. The Americans surrounded the position and engaged in hand-to-hand combat. However, fire support from the Azeville battery accompanied by a vigorous counterattack was to halt the Allied offensive. A further attempt on the 9th of June was also to fail. Crisbecq still held strong! However, on the night of the 11th to the 12th, upon orders from its

superiors, the *Oberleutnant* Ohmsen evacuated the position along with its surviving defenders. Only the dead and the severely wounded were left behind and the battery was effortlessly taken in the morning. Quinéville fell on the evening of the 14th.

However, on the RN13 trunk road, the Americans failed to recapture Montebourg. From the 9th of June onwards, each and every one of their assaults was fended off by accurate artillery fire. Many of the inhabitants had taken refuge in basements or in the abbey, as the small town was ravaged by heavy naval shellfire, yet in vain, for the German defence was unyielding. A week of merciless conflict and the prospect of deadly street combat led General Barton, who had already lost many of his men, to renounce any further head-on attacks. The most direct route to Cherbourg appeared to be blocked.

Carentan, to the south, was still in enemy hands and formed a dangerously entrenched "pocket" between the *Utah* and *Omaha* bridgeheads. Bradley gave Collins quite

The Germans put up steadfast resistance for over two weeks in Montebourg, 90% of which was destroyed.

Carentan was liberated on the 12th of June by parachutists from the 101st Airborne.

categorical orders, " We've got to join up with Gerow just as quickly as possible. If it becomes necessary to save time, put 500 or even 1,000 tons of air on Carentan and take the city apart. Then rush it and you'll get in." The task was assigned to General Taylor's 101st Airborne Division. Exposed, the division was to cross the only route towards the town - a causeway across the Douves marshes - and to take control of four bridges before reaching its target. The assault was launched on the night of the 9th to the 10th of June. The men progressed for two days, at a cost of heavy losses and under unremitting gunfire from Colonel von der Heydte's paratroopers who were deeply entrenched in farmyards and behind the hedges. However, in the meantime, other troops had crossed the river near Brévands, further north, and were preparing a pincer movement against the Germans. Faced with this threat of encirclement, the occupant evacuated Carentan on the evening of the 11th of June.

On the morning of the 12th, the men from the 101st Division entered the town, severely ravaged by the night's bombings. Yet the battle was not over. At dawn the next day, a violent counterattack was launched by grenadiers from the *17th SS Panzergrenadier* Division and their

Saint-Sauveur-le-Vicomte, liberated on the 16th of June by the 82nd Airborne, finally in the hands of the American troops.

assault guns. They progressed along the Périers route to reach the outskirts of the town. Devoid of heavy weapons, General Taylor's men struggled to hold them in check. Thankfully, by late morning, the combined efforts of fighter bombers and reinforcements in the form of a detachment of 2nd Armoured Division tanks, were to ruthlessly stop the assailants in their tracks. This counterattack by the paratroopers and armoured units drove the enemy into retreat, leaving behind a long line of charred vehicles and scores of dead bodies. This success was to offer the Allies a continuous bridgehead six to twenty miles in depth and stretching over sixty miles of coastline from Quinéville to the east of the mouth of the Orne.

General Bradley had said, "If we're lucky it'll take us ten days to seize Cherbourg, thirty if we're unlucky."

And it was finally to take twenty. For the Allies, it was a strategic target, essential to the overall success of *Overlord*. They needed a large deep-water port to unload the necessary men and supplies to secure - well beyond the Battle of Normandy - the reconquest of Europe. The port was to welcome, in particular, *Liberty Ships*

18th June: an enthusiastic welcome was extended to men from the 9th Infantry Division by the inhabitants of Barneville.

herd by instinct in fear and confusion. Within a few days this shock ordinarily wears off, the division overcomes its baptismal panic, and troops respond normally to assured and intelligent command. Where possible we made an effort to relieve the severity of that shock by conditioning each new unit in a 'quiet' sector before committing it to attack. But when the 90th came ashore on the heels of the 4th Division across *Utah Beach*, there were no 'quiet' sectors."

The fact that Collins dismissed the division's commander, McKelvie, to replace him with General Landrum, was not enough. He could but resolve to purely and simply relieving the division, calling the 82nd Airborne to the front line. Henceforth, progression was considerably accelerated. Despite the fatigue they had accumulated since D-Day, the paratroopers were once more placed in

direct from the United States.

Mid-June, since the RN13 route was blocked by the stopper at Montebourg, General Bradley dispatched Collins' VII Corps westwards with the Cotentin's opposite coast as their target. The aim of the manoeuvre was perfectly clear: to slash the enemy lines and to isolate the north of the peninsula and Cherbourg in a net that would then simply need to be closed. The 90th Division was entrusted with the mission. However, despite their nickname - the *Tough Ombres*, the troops, a share of whom were from Texas and Oklahoma, had no combat experience.

The 90th Division set off from the narrow bridgehead to the west of the Merderet, so laboriously established by the paratroopers, and headed off on the offensive for Pont-l'Abbé, Gourbesville and Orglandes. However, not only were they incapable of any further advance, certain units even broke up. It was a bitter defeat, much to Bradley's dismay, "For three days the division floundered in its starting attack. For the first few days in combat most new divisions suffer a disorder resulting from acute mental shock. Until troops can acclimate themselves to the agony of the wounded and the finality of death, they

The ruins of the church of Saint-Malo in Valognes. The town was bombed several times by *9th US Air Force* medium-range bombers over the days that followed the D-Day Landings.

the vanguard and reconquered Saint-Sauveur-le-Vicomte on the 16th of June. On their right flank, General Eddy's 9th Division, comprised of veterans from North Africa and Sicily, charged through Sainte-Colombe, Néhou, Saint-Maurice, overwhelming the enemy to finally reach Barneville on the night of the 17th to 18th of June. The peninsula was cut in two. Rommel ordered for some of his troops to withdraw southwards. Certain units even managed to cross the, as yet, narrow American lines. However, around 40,000 Germans were now surrounded.

On the 19th of June, at 5 a.m., the VII Corps' general assault resumed, this time in a northerly direction. Its advance was largely facilitated by the general withdrawal of enemy ranks within the defensive perimeter round Cherbourg. Three divisions led the advance: the 9th

Division towards La Hague, General Wyche's 79th Division in the centre and the 4th Division to the east; the latter finally took over Montebourg which, although abandoned by its defenders, had been virtually wiped out. Valognes was taken without resistance on the night of the 20th to the 21st. Heavily bombed from the 6th to the 10th of June, "Normandy's little Versailles", the pride of 18th century Cotentin nobility, was no more than a deserted and devastated city.

Alas, the storm that had been raging in the English Channel since the 19th of June was soon to adversely affect the American progression. Despite the airlift provided by *C-47s*, ammunition stocks were dangerously low. Bradley implemented a reduction by one third of bullet and shell consumption; a measure his units were quite unfamiliar with.

The assault on defences on the outskirts of Cherbourg.

Street by street, the GIs gradually took control of the town centre. Rue Dom-Pedro.

29th June: surrender of the Fort de l'Ouest artillery battery on the natural harbour promenade after several days of resistance.

Reconquering Cherbourg

Despite all of these difficulties, the VII Corps reached the outskirts of Cherbourg on the 21st of June. Some 30,000 German soldiers, under General von Schlieben's command, had recoiled within the fortress. Formidable... impregnable even against any seaward attack, its inland borders were nevertheless far more vulnerable, despite a multitude of fortified strong points comprising a double line of defence of a depth of over six miles. Hitler, imperturbable, had given strict orders, "We must defend the port and the town to the very last man."

An initial ultimatum demanding that the Germans surrender had been ignored; the attack was consequently launched on the 22nd of June at around midday, after violent aerial bombardments. Despite steadfast defence, the Americans overwhelmed the enemy positions, one after another, continuing their methodical advance: the 4th Division via Tourlaville, the 9th via Equeurdreville and the 79th in the centre. Little by little, the noose was tightening. The Corps' commander, General Collins, relentlessly covered the front, hounding his officers, scolding his men, urging each and every one to accelerate. Indeed, his nickname of Lightning Joe, earned in the Guadalcanal jungle, proved to be quite appropriate. "One

of the most outstanding field commanders in Europe, without doubt also the most aggressive," Bradley said of him. In the meantime, in Cherbourg, the German Rear Admiral Hennecke persisted in his plans to sabotage the port. Under no circumstances were its facilities to fall, intact, into Allied hands. The Fuehrer, visibly satisfied, conveyed his personal congratulations to the admiral for such "exemplary destruction".

Several sections of the first defensive curtain had been broken through by the 23rd of June. The following day, the Americans occupied the heights overlooking Cherbourg. The city streets were the theatre of fighting on the 25th. Ernie Pyle, a war correspondent, was a frontline witness along with the photographer Robert Capa. They both joined an infantry company in charge of clearance operations, "The shells stopped, and finally the order to start was given. The men went forward one at a time. They crouched and ran, ape-like, across this dangerous space. The lieutenant kept yelling at them as they started, "Spread it out now. Do you want to draw fire on yourselves? Don't bunch up like that. Keep five yards apart. Spread it out, dammit. There is an almost irresistible pull to get close to somebody when you are in danger. The soldiers hugged the walls, crouching all the time. The city around us was still full of sound and fury.

Now and then a wall would have a round hole through it, and the windows had all been knocked out by concussion, and shattered glass littered the pavements. Gnarled telephone wire was lying everywhere. Lonely doors and shutters banged noisily back and forth. The men didn't talk among themselves. They just went. They weren't heroic figures as they moved forward one at a time, a few seconds apart. You think of attackers as being savage and bold. These men were hesitant and cautious. They were really the hunters, but they looked like the hunted. There was a confused excitement and a grim anxiety in their faces. They seemed terribly pathetic to me. They weren't warriors. They were American boys who by mere chance of fate had wound up with guns in their hands, sneaking up a death-laden street in a strange and shattered city in a faraway country in a driving rain. They were afraid, but it was beyond their power to quit. They had no choice. They were good boys. And even though they weren't warriors born to kill, they won their battles. That's the point."

The vestiges of four years of German occupation remained on Place Napoléon.

Admiral Kirk, commander of the American naval forces, had accepted that his fleet offer support to General Bradley's infantrymen. On the morning of the 25th of June, Rear Admiral Deyo's Task Force had taken position off Cherbourg. The fortress it faced comprised ten artillery batteries, heavily armed with 150mm and 240mm guns, established over a 15-mile stretch of coastline. A spectacular battle began at around midday. A battle that was to rage for three long hours. The batteries' accurate gunfire offered fierce resistance against the 3,000 shells fired by the Allied fleet. Ships, riddled with several salvos, multiplied manoeuvres to avoid them. Three destroyers and a cruiser were nevertheless hit. The battleship *USS Texas* was also struck; however it retaliated with a bulls-eye shot on one of the Hamburg battery's most dangerous casemates, equipped with 240mm guns. After three hours of sustained gunfire, the fleet retreated.

Yet, concurrently, the American infantry was advancing. On the 26th, the GIs entered all quarters of the town centre. The last pockets of resistance capitulated. In the afternoon, Fort du Roule had just fallen as General von Schlieben and Admiral Hennecke left their underground command posts and surrendered. The Allies still needed to take control of the arsenal, a few fortified strong points and the entrenched camp in La Hague, whose defenders were to hold out a few days before finally surrendering to the 79th Division, which took a further 10,000 German prisoners.

To appropriately praise the event - and perhaps to enhance his own reputation in the process - Collins obliged the defeated to sign a capitulation act, in due form, inside his command post at the Château de Servigny, in Yvetot-Bocage. Although a relatively uncommon procedure, it was quite comprehensible immediately after the Americans' very first major victory on French soil. The capture of Cherbourg was, of course, to hit the headlines back in the United States.

27th June: official ceremony on the town hall steps. General Collins, commander of the VII Corps, speaking to the congregation. Beside him: Paul Renault - Mayor of Cherbourg; behind him (from right to left), Generals Taylor (101st Airborne), Eddy (9th Division), Ridgway (82nd Airborne), Barton (4th Division) and Wyche (79th Division).

On the 27th of June, Cherbourg was both liberated and jubilant. The joy among the local population far exceeded anything the GIs had seen to date. Although the port had suffered greatly, the town was more or less intact. Its inhabitants had not been subjected to the same ordeal as many of their fellow Norman citizens. The crowd cheered Collins and his generals, as they stood on the steps of the Town Hall. When the Mayor of Cherbourg very movingly thanked him on behalf of his fellow citizens, Collins replied in French, "The paratroopers from this army corps were the first troops to set foot on the Cotentin peninsula. It therefore appeared fitting that the French tricolour I am presenting to the town of Cherbourg, in honour of this occasion, be made from the silk of the very parachutes of those who, on the morning of the 6th of June, descended in torrents to mark the end of the German tyranny."

As they fraternised enthusiastically with the locals, the troops indulged in a few hours of pleasure, as General Bradley watched with amusement, "Among the troops in Normandy, Cherbourg's strategic worth was soon overshadowed by the wealth of its booty and it was there that the term 'liberate' came into popular use in the army. Von Schlieben's forces had thoughtfully stocked their underground shelters for a prolonged campaign. Their soldiers' hearts rebelled at the sacrilege of destroying or spilling good wine and brandy. As a result we fell heir not only to a transatlantic port but to a massive underground wine cellar as well. Word of the prize leaked out even before the fighting ended and the scroungers scurried into position for a claims race into those caves. Here was a problem for which the school at Leavenworth had not prepared me."

29th June: patriotic demonstration around a bandstand in front of the town hall.

The port of Cherbourg in a sorry state

During the siege, the Germans had multiplied destruction and sabotage operations in the port of Cherbourg in order to delay as best they could any future use by the Americans. Over and above riddling the anchorage with mines, their plan consisted in blocking up the docks and channels by cunningly placing wrecks and debris in highly sensitive locations: ships of all sizes, but also cranes, trucks and miscellaneous objects... Consequently, a few heavy tonnage cargo ships were laid on their sides, preventing any access to the commercial port or the transatlantic dock.

Similarly, several quays and buildings had been blown up, as had arsenal facilities, railway lines, locks and even the venerable swing bridge at the entrance to the trading dock.

The pride of the town - the marine terminal inaugurated in 1933 - had suffered appalling damage. All that remained was an indescribable heap of rubble. Its docks, hitherto accustomed to welcoming vast transatlantic cruise ships, had been dynamited and had partly collapsed into the harbour, along with cranes, walkways and a share of its railway equipment.

A channel leading to the arsenal, blocked by a wreck.

The collapsed swing bridge prevented any access to the trading dock.

The arsenal.

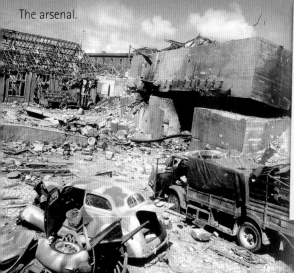

The blown up marine terminal docks.

The brief existence of the *Mulberry "A"*

After D-Day, the outcome of the overall landing operation was to depend on how quickly both camps could gain ground. Each camp needed to reinforce and fast, whilst endeavouring to prevent the enemy from doing the same. For the Allies, transporting men, material and supplies would need to be done across the Channel. Since the choice had been made, in 1943, to land on a coast devoid of major port facilities, the concept of artificial harbours was quick to see the day; all of the elements were to be produced in England, to be transported across the Channel after the invasion fleet, then assembled on site. Two of such harbours were scheduled, *Mulberry "A"* in the American sector before Vierville and Saint-Laurent, and *Mulberry "B"*, in the British sector before Arromanches. Whilst awaiting their installation, lines of old ships - *blockships* - were ballasted with cement and sunk off the landing beaches to form breakwaters, referred to as *Gooseberries*.

These *blockships* were sunk as early as the 7th of June before *Utah* and *Omaha* where, the following day, the Allies unloaded the first concrete *Phoenix* caissons aimed at forming the sea wall that was to protect the inner artificial harbour. Thirty of these caissons were in place by mid-June. Work, conducted by men from US Navy Construction Battalions, nicknamed *Seabees*, made good progress. They were under orders from *US Navy* Captain Dayton Clark. On the 16th of June, although the port was not yet complete, the first floating dock was operational. In barely an hour, an LST could unload a cargo of trucks which was in turn transported to the shore thanks to a floating pontoon. However, on the 18th of June, total traffic via *Utah* and *Omaha* remained slightly under the objectives set for Bradley's 1st Army. Since D-Day, 314,000 men had been landed (against a scheduled 358,000), 40,500 vehicles (instead of 61,000) and 116,000 tonnes of supplies (instead of 159,000), i.e. approximately a quarter less than planned. A delay that was to be dramatically exacerbated by a violent storm in the English Channel as from the 19th of June.

In the morning, force 6 north-easterly gales began to blow, stirring the sea with massive waves. For security reasons, the staff working on the artificial harbour was

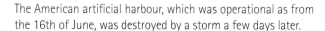

The American artificial harbour, which was operational as from the 16th of June, was destroyed by a storm a few days later.

Floating roadway.

The forgotten artificial harbour: Omaha Beach's Mulberry "A"

Just like in Arromanches, the artificial harbour off *Omaha* was comprised of several elements. Anchored out in the high seas, twenty metallic floating *bombardons*, provided the first line of breakwaters. The sea wall was comprised of fifteen or so sunken old ships, referred to as *blockships*, and forty huge concrete *Phoenix* caissons, of a length of up to 200 feet. Inside the harbour, three *Lobnitz* pierheads were installed on stakes that enabled them to move in time with the tide; they were designed to welcome large troop and equipment transport vessels such as LSIs or LSTs. Floating roadways, each of a length of just over half a mile, then ensured a link to dry land.

Due to the storm that raged from the 19th to the 21st of June 1944, destroying the harbour, very few vestiges of *Mulberry* "A" can be seen today, hence explaining the fact that the facility has virtually fallen into oblivion, in contrast with its illustrious counterpart, *Mulberry* "B" off Arromanches

LST unloading onto one of the artificial harbour docks.

Phoenix caisson surmounted by an anti-aircraft battery.

Lobnitz pierheads.

evacuated. The next day, gusting winds reached peaks of force 8 and the entire structure of the *Omaha* harbour began to crack under the furious elements. By the 21st, it was totally wrecked. The Royal Navy commander Edwards was witness to the disaster, "There where a huge and almost complete harbour once stood, all that remained were wrecks that were a genuine danger to navigation, their steel skeletons jutting out threateningly from the concrete." On the 22nd of June, as the storm was gradually subsiding, all that was left for the Allies to do was inspect the damage: hundreds of barges had been destroyed - more than on D-Day itself - their wrecks strewn across the beach; traffic was brought to a halt for four days. Finally, and most importantly, *Mulberry* "A" was, from now on, totally inoperative.

As such, Admiral Hall, Commander of *Omaha's* naval sector, could but resolve to abandon the operation. Any recoverable elements were used to repair the Arromanches *Mulberry* which had suffered less damage. Certain US Navy officers began to say out loud what many had been thinking for a long time. In his report, the naval expert Captain Lee even stated that the destruction of a port by, "what any seasoned sailor would consider as a mild storm," simply proved the unreliability of the artificial harbours designed by the British.

Henceforth deprived of their *Mulberry*, the Americans were now faced with the challenge of finding other solutions for transporting the valuable men and material

The storm raged through the English Channel from the 19th to the 21st of June.

The floating roadways proved to be particularly vulnerable amidst the storm.

they needed to Normandy. Yet ever-pragmatic and never at a loss, they very quickly adapted to these ill-fated circumstances. Fortunately, they could still take advantage of the shelter provided by the *Gooseberry* which was still in place and which they reinforced.

An LST aground on *Omaha Beach*. It was to wait twelve hours before setting out to sea again. LSTs measured sixty feet in length and could transport a load of up to two thousand tonnes. Two hundred men and officers comprised their crew. They were armed with six 20mm anti-aircraft guns.

Metal *Rhino-ferries* ensured a shuttle service to and from the shore and the high seas.

The question of grounding large LST transport vessels was once more on the agenda. The admiralty had, to date, been opposed to this proposal. Although their flat base and openable stem enabled them to ground at rising tide to unload trucks or tanks directly on the beaches, there were concerns over damaging the rear keel, the rudders and the propellers. Yet the Americans very quickly considered these risks to be low. The only drawback in this technique was that they would need to wait for the next tide, i.e. twelve hours, before being able to sail back out to sea. Consequently, between tides, a shuttle system was set up between the ships anchored out at sea and the coast. Amphibious DUKW trucks proved to be of precious help, along with the *Rhino-ferries*, huge self-propelled metal pontoons measuring 160 feet, two of which sufficed to transport a load equivalent to that of an LST.

Omaha and *Utah* beaches - where the same techniques were applied - were fast to achieve impressive results, this time largely exceeding both expectations and

Intense traffic on *Omaha Beach*. LSTs unloaded hundreds of trucks and other vehicles on the beach.

121

Amphibious DUKW trucks on *Omaha Beach*. ("D" was for the year the model was produced: 1942, "U" for utility (amphibious), "K" all-wheel-drive and "W" double rear axle). These vehicles measured over 30 feet and could carry a load of two tonnes at a speed of 6 mph in water and 50 mph on land.

The Germans were powerless, incapable of curbing the Allies' ever-increasing supremacy. The *Kriegsmarine* had met with total failure. Its submarines and motor torpedo boats had been kept at bay by the Allied aviation and destroyers and were incapable of causing any significant damage to the Channel convoys. In contrast, their naval mines proved to be formidable weapons. On the 15th of June, LST 133 was to fall victim to one of them. It was on its third Channel crossing since the 6th of June, transporting the 113th Artillery Battalion towards *Omaha*. A terrible explosion whipped up its stern at around 8 a.m., killing ten men and

activity at Arromanches. From the 23rd to the 30th of June, 13,110 tonnes of supplies were unloaded every day on *Omaha*, i.e. 15% above target, and 7,328 tonnes on *Utah* (+28%) compared to a daily average of 5,000 tonnes at Arromanches. However, they had not yet compensated for the delays accumulated since the 6th of June and further exacerbated by the storm. But, by the 30th of June, 452,460 soldiers, 70,910 vehicles and 289,827 tonnes of supplies had been unloaded on the two American beaches.

Normandy's inhabitants, now able to approach the coast, discovered a sight that defied all imagination, "In no time our beaches had been transformed into harbours with a constant ebb and flow of hundreds of transport vessels. From their flanks, we could see jeeps, trucks, tanks, ammunition, graders, diggers, trailers, metal beams for bridges, supplies, etc. being unloaded. Hundreds of embarkations shuttled from the coast to the cargo ships. Infantrymen lined the streets in single file alongside tanks that sent up thick clouds of dust. And it all worked, it was all mathematically calculated, just like a precision mechanism."

throwing many others into the sea; the bodies of thirty-three of them were never recovered. The storm that raged from the 19th to the 21st of June had intensified the danger. Minesweepers had been forced to suspend their activity, whilst the German aviation continued to plunge its deadly weapons into the sea.

In the Normandy skies, the *Luftwaffe* was relatively inconspicuous - at least by day - operating by night, launching fairly regular attacks on the beaches, each incursion provoking retaliatory outburst from the Allied anti-aircraft defence. "Everyone seemed to be firing tracers, making crazy patterns that did not focus in the sky because nobody had any idea where the enemy aircraft were. It was fantastic; the decks of hundreds of ships lit with flashes from the muzzles of thousands of guns and the sky was all interlaced cobwebs of sparkling light." Some of these nocturnal attacks hit their targets. Hence, on the 10th of June, off *Utah Beach*, a glide bomb struck the merchant ship *SS Charles Morgan*, killing ten men from a port battalion and wounding as many others. Yet the German aviation's overall achievements were well below those of the Allied Air Forces.

American airfields in Normandy

The A-6 airfield, still under construction, in La Londe-Beuzeville, near Sainte-Mère-Église. It entered into service on the 15th of June.

After D-Day, the 8th and 9th Air Forces continued their missions over a number of Norman towns such as Valognes, Avranches, Périers, Falaise or L'Aigle, always with the same aim of cutting communication links and slowing down the arrival of German reinforcements. Fighter squadrons were in turn assigned the task of offering support to infantrymen and of attacking the enemy columns on the road. Yet, the scope of these planes was relatively limited and their flight time above the battlefield was reduced by the time spent crossing

A *P-38 Lightning* on the emergency runway above *Omaha Beach* (later to become airfield A-21C) a few days after the D-Day Landings.

Airfield A-1 in Saint-Pierre-du-Mont, operational as from the 13th of June. Located on the cliff top, between Pointe du Hoc and *Omaha Beach*, it covered a surface area of three hundred hectares.

the English Channel. Overlord's planners had for a long time intended to establish airfields - as quickly as possible - within the Normandy bridgehead in order to amplify tactical aerial intervention and to obtain optimal coverage of the battle zone.

During the Battle of Normandy, thirty airfields were set up by men from the 9th Engineer Command, all but four of them located in the Cotentin and Bessin. Each of them was assigned with a number, preceded by the letter "A", whereas the letter "B" was used for the twenty British airfields. The first, built under enemy fire in Pouppeville near *Utah Beach*, was completed on the evening of the 6th of June. The second, located in Saint-Laurent – immediately above *Omaha Beach* – was operational on the 9th of June. They consisted of simple Emergency landing strips, devoid of coating and aimed at evacuating the seriously wounded and transporting medical supplies.

Advanced landing grounds, with more sophisticated infrastructures were developed later. The construction of these airfields required, on average, from a week to a fortnight of intense labour for an aviation engineer battalion. The Americans deployed impressive machines throughout the Normandy countryside: from bulldozers to scrapers, much to the amazement of the locals, most of whom had never seen such engines or didn't even know they existed. By late June,

eleven airfields were operational in Saint-Pierre-du-Mont, Cardonville, Beuzeville, Cricqueville, Carentan...

The main runway - sometimes doubled up with an urgent landing strip for planes in distress - was generally around 1,600 yards long and 30 yards wide. In principle, it was only to be used by fighter planes or fighter bombers such as *P-38 Lightnings*, *P-47 Thunderbolts* or *P-51 Mustangs*. Nevertheless, a few airfields, equipped with longer runways and dating from before the war or from the German occupation, such as Lessay and Maupertus near Cherbourg, were suitable for landing twin-engine *B26 Marauders*. Yet these airfields also needed to be equipped with taxi-ways and parking or dispersal zones for planes; camps for ground staff and airmen; hangars for fuel and munitions supplies; a water supply and the installation of an electrical network for the base's lighting and communication and, finally, a link with the nearby road network. Together with their auxiliary facilities, airfields occupied a considerable surface area of up to four to five hundred hectares in some cases.

Fighter groups gradually set up camp on their respective airfields and launched their principle mission: to hound the German reinforcements that were approaching the front via road and rail links. Along with their buddies from the RAF's 2nd Tactical Air Force, pilots from the 9th US Air Force led an infernal ballet that only nightfall and poor weather - alas too frequent in the summer of 1944 - were to hinder.

Annihilating tanks was not the easiest of tasks for onboard guns and machine guns were ineffective on their armoured shells. They could only be destroyed by bombs - however a bulls-eye shot was a rarity -

US Air Force mechanics transporting 12.7mm machine guns and ammunition to equip *P-51 Mustangs*.

or rockets which lacked accuracy. Rail convoys were the easiest targets and their progression was considerably slowed down by the destruction of bridges, via sabotage operations that had begun before the landings, to be actively continued afterwards. Meanwhile, on the roads, truck and light armoured vehicle convoys immediately sustained heavy losses. The Allies' almost total aerial supremacy was to gradually demoralise the German ranks, particularly alarmed when the skies were filled with their terrible fighter bombers, nicknamed "Jabos" (an abbreviation of the German equivalent *Jagdbomber*). An officer from the 17th *SS Panzergrenadier* Division that had left Thouars on the 7th of June recalled, "We were all joyful and impatient to move into action. Our columns meandered their way through the roads that led to the invasion beaches. But something happened that was to leave us all stunned. Bursts of fire gushed forth on the road. Everyone jumped from the cars to hide in the surrounding fields. Several vehicles were already ablaze. Our column was totally broken up and everyone was trying as best he could to escape from the flames. The attack was to end as quickly as it had started. Men began to return to the column; they were pale and trembling and wondered how they had escaped this shower of gunfire. The entire length of the road was strewn with debris and charred material. We stopped our progression and all of the remaining vehicles were hidden from view amidst the trees. No one dared to expose himself. Men started looking at each other. It was our first encounter with the *Jabos.*"

The *Panzer Lehr* had left Nogent-le-Rotrou on the 6th of June to head for Caen, but was - on several occasions - to find itself the target of swarms of *Thunderbolts*.

In just two days, the division lost five tanks, eighty-four half-tracks and one hundred and thirty trucks, forty of which were tank trucks. The Germans consequently strove to camouflage their vehicles under thick layers of foliage. However, their convoys were soon forced to travel almost exclusively under cover of the night - and the summer nights were short - or in poor weather conditions when the Allied planes were pinned to the ground.

During the month of June alone, the 9th Air Force claimed to have added to its tally some 84 road or rail bridges, 122 locomotives, 1,871 rail wagons, 940 vehicles and 46 tanks very probably destroyed or damaged. In contrast, it had also lost 302 planes, including 200 fighter bombers, most of them victim to the particularly efficient German FLAK. Without for as much grinding the German reinforcements to a halt, these tactical aviation operations had nevertheless considerably slowed them down and had imposed upon the enemy genuine difficulties in resupplying with fuel and ammunition.

A *P-47 Thunderbolt* damaged during take-off at the La Londe airfield.

Makeshift control tower.

Runway covered with PSP (*Pierced steel planks*).

A roller being run over a *Hessian mat*.

Installing SMT (*Square mesh track*).

Unrolling *Hessian mats*.

Scrapers in action.

Building hangars.

Construction of the American airfields

The sites chosen for establishing airfields were, first of all, stripped of any mines, undergrowth, trees and hedges, which were razed by bulldozers. Earthwork was then undertaken. The ground surface was levelled out by *scrapers* that scoured the upper soil whilst loading excess debris as they advanced. One single scraper did the work of five hundred men equipped with simple picks, spades and wheelbarrows.

When the often clayey soil in the Cotentin and Bessin proved too loose to support air traffic, it was stabilised with the addition of stone mined in nearby quarries, often specifically opened for the purpose. Once graders had done their job, the soil was compacted and packed down by rollers. Since Normandy is a relatively damp region, great attention was paid to drainage.

The surface of runways was protected with a metallic coating: either *pierced steel planks*, or *square mesh track*, which, after the war, were recovered in huge quantities across the Normandy countryside. A third process, which proved more effective against dust or mud - but also more expensive - consisted in covering the runway with asphalt-impregnated jute, referred to as *Hessian mat*.

Levelling out airfield A-21C in Saint-Laurent-sur-Mer.

Throughout June, the American troops achieved a significant inland advance through Normandy. By the end of the month, they had reconquered a vast share of the Bessin and the Cotentin peninsula and had captured Cherbourg. Their progression contrasted with the poor results obtained by the British and Canadian divisions, still at a standstill on the outskirts of Caen where their offensive efforts were perpetually thwarted by the cordon the formidable German armoured divisions had formed around the town.

Yet on all sides, the darkest month was ahead. Throughout July, both Allied armies were to reach a virtual standstill. Although Montgomery finally succeeded in recapturing Caen, his troops could advance no further to conquer the plain leading to Falaise. In turn, the Americans met with fierce German resistance in the Normandy bocage: for three long weeks, they suffered the terrible ordeal of hedgerow warfare.

A team of medics giving first aid to a wounded soldier on the battlefield.

◀ A soldier from the 79th Infantry Division launching a fragmentation hand grenade over a hedge.

3rd of July: Bradley launches his offensive

After capturing Cherbourg, General Bradley fully indented to rapidly resume his - temporarily suspended - southward offensive. He was perfectly aware of the hurdles his men would face, given the extremely difficult terrain, "Across the neck of the Normandy peninsula, the hedgerows formed a natural line of defense more formidable than any even Rommel could have contrived. For centuries the broad, rich flatlands had been divided and subdivided into tiny pastures whose earthen walls had grown into ramparts. These hedgerows were crowned with a thorny growth of trees and brambles. Their roots had bound the packed earth as steel mesh reinforces concrete. Not even in Tunisia had we found more exasperating defensive terrain. Collins called it no less formidable than the jungles of Guadalcanal. "So how could they avoid becoming entangled in this trap?" It was essential that we break a hole through the enemy's defenses rather than heave him, "Bradley continued," As long as the enemy confined us to the bocage of Normandy, he could exact a prohibitive price for the few miserable yards we might gain." However, in order to launch a genuine "breakthrough", they needed to reach a favourable start line that would offer

The Normandy bocage, a surprise adversary for the GIs.

A terrain "as terrifying as the Guadalcanal jungle" according to General Collins.

access to the road network and enable troops to be deployed. The road leading from Coutances to Saint-Lô was quick to attract the attention of the military staff. First of all, it was located beyond the Cotentin marshes which were unsuitable for launching a large-scale attack. Furthermore, three other roads converged with it - leading to Avranches, Gavray and Villedieu - and were likely to offer armoured divisions an opportunity to rapidly progress southwards towards Brittany. They simply needed to reach the famous RN 172 trunk road, which, late June, was as yet 20 miles or so out of the 1st Army's reach.

On the 3rd of July, the day before America celebrated Independence Day, Bradley launched a general attack involving three army corps - comprising nine divisions - over a 45-mile front stretching from Portbail on the east Cotentin coast to the north of Saint-Lô. However, the second fortnight in June was to mark the reinforcement of German positions in the sector, the enemy having taken advantage of concentrated Allied efforts in Cherbourg. General von Choltitz, commander of the LXXXIV Army Corps, had formed several defensive curtains, the most important of which was located on the "Malhmann Line", named after the commander of the 353rd Infantry Division, in Brittany since June. The men from the 79th Division were quick to grasp what awaited them. One of them recalled: "Meanwhile, the 1st Battalion made another attempt on the afternoon of the 7th to reconnoiter La Haye in force, but the forward elements ran into what the unit journal describes cryptically as 'strong defensive positions' on the outskirts of town. Maybe you remember them - the mine-studded fields strung with checkerboard patterns of piano wire about a foot off the ground and the booby traps set to blow off a leg any tune you tripped the strands, the mortar bursts bracketing you as you tried to high-step over the wire and between the mines, and the trench beyond with the machine-guns you didn't even know were there till they opened up and the men around you began to crumple and fall. They sure were 'strong defensive positions.'" The task the Americans were facing was proving to be far more arduous than expected.

Men from the 29th Infantry Division digging their *foxholes* under the shelter of a hedge.

La Haye-du-Puits, Sainteny, Saint-Lô: one man lost for every yard won

On the 3rd of July, General Middleton's VIII Corps moved off from the south of Saint-Sauveur-le-Vicomte towards Lessay and Coutances. However, on their way, they came face to face with the "Malhmann Line" in the vicinity of La Haye-du-Puits and the solidly fortified hills that surrounded this large town. It took around a week to get the better of it, at a cost of heavy losses. Under torrents of rain and mud, the 82nd Airborne launched its assault on Mont Étenclin and the hill at La Poterie. After a brave struggle, both objectives were attained in a few days. For Ridgway's men, in action since the 6th of June, it was to be the last battle in Normandy. The time had come for them to be relieved and to return to England.

The 90th Division - already shattered by its dramatic defeat at Pont-l'Abbé a few weeks earlier - was less fortunate and was to face a further ordeal before seizing Mont Castre. This steep and wooded hill, ideal as an

Evacuating the wounded from the 82nd *Airborne*; they were grouped together in a barn near La Haye-du-Puits, converted into a first-aid post.

observation post, was defended by fearsome adversaries in the form of *Das Reich* units and a regiment of parachute chasseurs. Several Allied battalions became the targets of accurate and deadly German gunfire; afflicted by such brutal combat, they became disorganised and some of them broke up. Five thousand men were killed, wounded or taken prisoner before the hill finally and permanently fell into American hands on the 11th of July.

General Wyche's 79th Division in turn took control of the Montgardon heights and Mont Doville. However, it struggled for several days outside La Haye-du-Puits, bitterly defended by the German 353rd Division and elements from the 2nd SS Panzer Division *Das Reich*. Repelled several times by German counterattacks, the division finally entered the small town on the 8th of July, but was to endure further combat until nightfall, house by house, before permanently securing what remained. "A mass of shapeless ruins whose only inhabitants were dead German soldiers. What remained of the houses was of a sinister aspect amidst the firelight," an information officer related. Early the next morning, a soldier stopped in front of a building with a sign still hanging on its partly collapsed facade: "A. Céron – Funeral and mortuary monuments" - to which he cried out, "This guy's gonna make a fortune!"

The freshly landed 8th Division left La Haye-du-Puis and headed southwards towards Lessay. General McMahon paid the price of getting off to a hesitant and unconvincing start; he was replaced by General Stroh. On the 14th of July, Bradley ordered for operations to be interrupted due to excessive losses. A total of 10,000 men from the VIII Corps were no longer fit for combat - for an advance of barely six miles, one man had been lost for every yard won!

At the very heart of the American plan of attack, General Collins' VII Corps received orders to seize Périers. The assault troops left Carentan on the morning of the 4th of July. The terrain was particularly hostile. To reach its

14th July 1944 in La Haye-du-Puits after the town's liberation.

The 79th Division preparing to enter la Haye-du-Puits.

target, the unit needed to cross a narrow strip of land between the Gorges and the Graignes marshes. At the opposite extremity of this isthmus, the small village of Sainteny was defended by grenadiers from the 17th *SS Panzergrenadier* Division and a few tanks from the *Das Reich*. A terrible baptism of fire awaited the US 83rd Division. Infantrymen advanced along waterlogged pathways, falling into the mud, some struggling back to their feet...

The Americans seize Sainteny.

others failing. On the 5th, the division lost 1,500 men for an advance of barely 200 yards and six German prisoners. Mercilessly urged on by General Macon, it continued its progression the following day, advancing less than a mile at a cost of 750 new victims from within its ranks. Despite Collins' replacement of the 83rd Division by General Barton's more seasoned 4th Division, the outcome was the same. The Germans even dispatched imprisoned American nurses, sardonically adding, "You'll need them more than we will!" On the 14th of July, when Sainteny was finally taken, the four to five-mile advance had been at a cost of 7,000 GIs no longer fit for combat.

General Corlett, commander of the XIX Corps, was to the east of the front with Saint-Lô as his target. However, his troops were still bogged down to the north of the town, behind the barrier formed by the River Vire. His plan was to thrust forward and to make a forceful surge onto the opposite bank. The assault was to

be led by General Hobbs 30th Division, whose mission was to pave the way for the rest of the XIX Corps. The attack began at dawn on the 7th of July, under a heavy barrage of enemy artillery fire. Two regiments succeeded in crossing the river by surprise between Airel and Saint-Fromond. To the north, the third regiment relatively effortlessly crossed the Vire canal at La Taute. Units then reassembled and took control of Saint-Jean-de-Daye. Yet, German resistance intensified beyond the village.

Engineers building a floating bridge over the River Vire.

Captain Marvin Smith was in command of the 120st Regiment's K Company, «Early in the morning, the company in column advanced down a dirt road in a southerly direction with no opposition. An enemy shell screeched in, killing a soldier. The battle was on. I vividly remember coming upon a destroyed enemy tank with parts of the dead crew scattered about in pieces. I saw a human arm hanging in a tree. An American soldier was sprawled in the middle of a field, apparently dead. Upon examination, I found he was sound asleep instead, exhausted. An enemy machine gun opened up on us, pinning down the leading troops. I watched one of our privates crawl over a hedgerow to move forward. As he reached the top, the machine gun burst fire towards him. He crumbled and lay there, on top.

Bazooka fire against the opposite hedge.

For another day or two we held our position. Finally the order came to move laterally toward the east several miles. We were committed into another offensive action. We passed through a battlefield, and I was shocked at the debris left there: steel helmets, ammunition, rifles, belts, clothes, band-aids, canteens, shoes... Evidence showed they were in a desperate battle, and many were wounded and killed there.

Night came and we were ordered to halt. My runner dug me a foxhole. I was exhausted. The nights were cold and wet. Finally, Lt. Harnden, my second in command, and I fell into the hole together and cuddled to keep warm. I was awakened with much commotion and noise of battle to our front. I heard terrible screaming coming from the enemy side. In a few minutes, we were all awake and watchful. A mortar shell came down silently, with a little swish and hit with a great explosion. When the dust cleared, I found a K company man dead, hit in the temple by a fragment. He had not dug his foxhole as ordered, but was out in the open, cleaning his rifle.

At dawn, I visited battalion headquarters to get orders for the day. We were ordered to attack at 10:00 a.m. We were exhausted from the night's ordeal. How could we even move? But such is war. The attack by K company proceeded on toward the enemy, making

Many were wounded by mortar shell.

what K company men had survived, if any. I found no K company men dead. Or alive! They had all disappeared. They had simply fled the devastated shell fire. They had saved their own lives. K company was soon ordered into yet another field with orders to defend.

We were very tired and we got orders to go to the rear for a shower and rest. We visualized a week or two of rest. After one day, showering and cleaning rifles and equipment, I was bitterly disappointed to get orders that we were to proceed towards the front Lines. We trudged forward back to the front. How much longer could we live?"

On the 8th of July, General Corlett launched the 3rd Armoured Division over the stone bridge at Saint-Fromond which had been hastily repaired by engineers. However, in no time, the narrow bridgehead was the scene of total chaos. The Germans multiplied their counterattacks with recently dispatched tanks from the *Das Reich* and the *Panzer Lehr* divisions. The XIX Corps' assault was brought to a halt by an enemy cordon running from Le Désert to Pont-Hébert. On the 10th of July, the road to Saint-Lô appeared totally blocked and a further 7,000 American soldiers were lost in just a few days.

During the first fortnight of July, the 1st Army had accumulated a dispiriting toll. Its losses - killed, wounded or missing - were in the region of 40,000 men; never had they known such horrific figures since D-Day, to gain but a miserable few miles of enemy ground. Bradley was saddened, "No one disliked more than I did the disagreeable necessity for inching our way through those hedgerows. We could do nothing but belly ahead and swallow those heavy losses." At this rate, "this damn war could go on twenty years!" another general was to retort. According to the Allies' pre-landing forecast, by mid-July the Americans should have been well into Brittany, have recaptured Le Mans and reached the River Loire. Yet, at the same date, they were still at a virtual standstill in the Cotentin

about 200 yards' progress. Heavy enemy artillery fire and small arms fire was concentrating on our lines. We could not move forward at all. I looked around and saw no men. They were retreating on their own! All alone with only my radio operator and runner, we retreated back 200 yards to our previous position.

Much firing of rifles and machine guns was occurring to my right. So, I grabbed my rifle and jumped into a foxhole. To my mind this would be a fight to death. We waited for the enemy to come. There must have been hundreds of shells crashing all around. The noise was terrible. It was devastating. I expected death. When the dust, smoke and debris disappeared, I looked to see

On the 11th of July, a counterattack by the *Panzer Lehr* was to provoke retaliation by the 9th Air Force's *P-47* fighter bombers. Pilots observe the effect of their attacks on a *Panther* tank.

peninsula. Since the British and Canadians were also denied access to Caen, the Allies were haunted with the risk of an interminable war of positions, reminiscent of their Great War ordeal. The shadow of trench warfare was now cast over Normandy. Morale was low, as one soldier recalled, "We were so utterly exhausted that, in the evening, when we drew up the list of the killed and wounded, we were indifferent even to the names of our dearest companions; it was as if we were calling names chosen at random from the telephone directory. All of our traditional values had been abolished and we had a feeling that, if another world did indeed exist beyond those hedges, none of us would ever live long enough to know."

Massive traffic jam for the 3rd Armoured Division on a small road within the narrow Saint-Fromond bridgehead.

The "war of the hedgerows", American power put to the test in the Normandy bocage

The Americans benefited, in principle, from superiority in all domains. Their command of aerial combat was undeniable and they had five times as many tanks as the Germans. By mid-July, they had landed some 700,000 men and were fighting at a ratio of virtually three to one. They were capable, to a far greater extent than their adversaries, of filling the gaps that combat had inflicted on their units. Every day, thousands of vehicles arrived on *Omaha* or *Utah Beach*. From day to day, the American power was reinforced, rendering the imbalance between the opposing forces ever-increasingly blatant. However, the decisive role played by a terrain of which the Germans had developed skilful command, had been somewhat neglected.

Sergeant Bill Davidson, a correspondent for *Yank* magazine, accurately described the very singular nature of the battle in the Normandy bocage, "This is a war of hedgerows, a strangely limited kind of war. Fighting is from field to field and from hedgerow to hedgerow. You don't know whether the field next to you is occupied by friend or foe. You rarely speak of advancing a mile in a single day; you say, instead, 'We advanced eleven

Replacement troops preparing to join the 90th Infantry Division, in great difficulty on the slopes of Mont Castre.

fields'. Normally, no-man's-land is the width of a single field, but sometimes it's the width of a single hedgerow. That happens after a long period of fighting and firing, when both sides are too tired to move and you can hear Jerries talking a few feet away on the other side of the hedge. Sometimes, you hold one end of a field and the enemy holds the other."

Bradley's army's substantial superiority was totally diluted in the bocage. His ultra-mechanised war machine was faltering in this "darned terrain" comprised of an incredible puzzle of enclosed fields, narrow hollow pathways, transformed into a quagmire by persistent rainfall. Tanks had difficulty manoeuvring and became easy targets. If they ventured onto the small narrow roads, they met with antitank guns and the destruction of the lead vehicle was enough to grind the entire column to a halt. If they tried to cross the hedges, they exposed their underside - only flimsily armoured - to gunfire from intrepid gunners armed with *Panzerschreck* or *Panzerfaust* rocket launchers, such as Edwin Schmieger and his fellow paratroopers from the German 3rd Division, "It was so easy that, in the light-heartedness of our youth, we even wrangled over who would fire."

The enemy was cunningly lying in wait, amidst this maze of dense hedges. Its precise positions were almost impossible to identify. "One day," Eisenhower related, "a few of us visited a forward observation tower located on a hill, which took us to a height of about a hundred feet above the surrounding hedgerows. Our vision was so limited that I called upon the air forces to take me in a fighter plane along the battle front in an effort to gain a clear impression of what we were up against. Unfortunately, even from the vantage point of an altitude of several thousand feet there was not much to see that could be classed as helpful."

In these conditions, the artillery was of limited utility. Nevertheless, the American guns unleashed their charges - with a vengeance even - yet, often firing blind with

A Signal Corps unit installing telephone lines.

The US Army's powerful artillery was disabled by its incapacity to reach the German lines without hitting American troops.

inadequate tactical results and running the constant risk of hitting their own ranks. For the same reasons, support from fighter bombers - already limited due to poor weather - was less efficient than usual due to difficulties in accurately identifying targets.

The "war of the hedgerows" was, first and foremost, an infantry battle in which the German troops' experience overshadowed the Americans', around half of whom had never fought before. The average GI was simply a citizen in uniform, not a war professional. Consequently, officers often observed a certain lack of combat enthusiasm and aggressiveness among their troops.

Mortar fire near Saint-Lô forced the occupants of this jeep to seek shelter in the ditch.

Mortars enabled arcing shots that were particularly well-adapted to the war of the hedgerows.

A German non-commissioned officer and Eastern Front veteran somewhat sarcastically declared, "The Americans use their infantry far too cautiously; if they acted like the Russians, they would be in Paris by now."

In this dramatic man-to-man combat, the defender held the stronger position. Each embankment offered a natural entrenchment, each thicket concealed a machine gun and each tree could hide a sniper. It was sheer hell for the GIs. Men fell by dozens, by hundreds; some went astray in this labyrinthine landscape where the short horizon prevented both friend and foe from being identified; others fled, panic-stricken. Gruelling combat, as an American General described, "I doubt if anyone who ever ducked bullets and shells in the hedgerows, waded through the mud on foot, and scrambled over the hedgerows never knowing when he might find himself looking into the muzzle of a german tank gun, will look back on those days with any remembered feeling other than of the deadly unrelenting fatigue and danger. There was so little result to show for so much suffering! Just a few hedgerows gained, each one just like those already behind and those still to take!"

During their preparation, the Allies had everything extremely well planned, up to the quantity of altar wine to take to Normandy. However, curiously, the potential problem caused by the hedges - the existence of which they were perfectly aware of - had been largely underestimated. Consequently, the harsh reality of the Normandy bocage proved to be a very unpleasant surprise for the Americans. "Although back in England, we had occasionally spoken of the hedges, none of us was aware of the problems they were likely to cause us," General Gavin, second in command of the 82nd Airborne admitted. When questioned after the Battle of Normandy, almost all officers admitted that they were ill-prepared for such hostile terrain. An 83rd Division company commander even admitted that his unit, "had never imagined a problem of this kind," adding that training prior to the invasion had, "not in the least paid due consideration to the issue." A few hedge-crossing exercises had been organised in the United States and in England, but they were no comparison to the terrible Normandy hedges.

In contrast, the Germans had set up terrifyingly effective tactical defence against their adversaries. First of all, each

In position behind a hedge, German parachutists waiting for the American assault, armed with MG 34 machine guns.

parcel of land had its own, highly elaborate firing plan. Heavy machine guns were positioned at each far corner of the field, any hostile attacks being caught in their crossfire. Between them, behind the hedge, men with rifles and automatic guns lay in wait, their fingers poised on the trigger. In addition, particularly deadly mortars were adjusted in advance to shower any assailants in the middle of the field. Even when they were forced to retreat, the Germans - who had established an in-depth defensive barrier - simply recoiled into the next, similarly defended, field. The system made the best possible use of the terrain, required few troops and compensated for their considerably inferior numbers.

Dead and wounded by the thousands

From the 6th of June to the 24th of July, the US First Army had suffered a total of 16,293 men fallen in battle. The war of the hedgerows had brought the daily average of killed soldiers to 400 in July, compared to 250 in June. The death toll was particularly dramatic for divisions engaged in battle since the 6th of June: 1,680 deaths for the 90th Division, 1,840 for the 4th Division and 2,000 for the 29th Division.

The Graves Registration platoons were in charge of looking after bodies and preparing their burial. The task consisted in collecting their remains and identifying victims, more often than not thanks to the identification "Dog tags" they wore round their necks. Otherwise,

personal papers, objects or witness reports from fellow soldiers were also of use.

Several temporary cemeteries were opened over the days that followed the landings. On *Omaha*, it was decided that the bodies which had been hastily buried on the beach be transferred to the Saint-Laurent plateau. It was important that freshly arrived troops not be faced with such a demoralising scene. Another cemetery was used in La Cambe, originally intended for victims from the 29th Division. Sainte-Mère-Église welcomed victims from the 4th Division and the 101st Airborne, initially buried in Pouppeville, Saint-Martin-de-Varreville or Hiesville. However, the necessity to create a second, then a third cemetery - in nearby Blosville - soon became apparent. In July a new cemetery was created in Orglandes, where many German soldiers were also buried, as they were in other sites. Early August, around 30,000 bodies from both sides were laid to rest on Norman soil.

In June and July 1944, 103,000 patients were cared for by American medical teams in Normandy. Among them,

The cemetery in Sainte-Mère-Église: an officer from the Graves Registration department preparing a body bag for Private Frederick R. Smith.

96,000 GIs, but also 6,200 Germans and 800 civilians. Whilst hospitals welcomed American soldiers suffering from disease, depression or accidental injury, two-thirds of their patients were men who had been more or less seriously wounded in combat. Their numbers drastically increased during the war of the hedgerows, escalating from 16,500 from the 12th to the 30th of June - i.e. 870 per day - to 37,800 from the 1st to the 25th of July - i.e. 1,500 per day. Engaged in the battle of Saint-Lô, no less than 1,600 soldiers from the 83rd Division were wounded in just three days. Snowed under by this influx, surgeons, nurses and auxiliaries endured particularly arduous and demanding weeks. Each surgical team worked twelve-hour shifts, nonstop, performing an average of twenty operations per day, before being relieved by another team, hence occupying operating theatres on a 24-hour basis.

For a little over 60%, wounds were caused by direct mortar and artillery fire, 27% by firearms and 10% by mines, bombardments or other causes. The vast majority of injuries were to the upper and lower limbs (68%), followed by the abdomen and the thorax (16%) - among which one in four cases was fatal - and the head (11%).

Physical injuries were accompanied by the effects of intense fatigue, triggered by the hostilities which proved as interminable as they were demoralising in the hedgerow hell, and by insufficient time for rest. Exhaustion, fear, the obsessive presence of death and the loss of fellow soldiers were to cause severe neuro-psychiatric disorders which, alone, represented 12% of hospital admissions, rates in less experienced units, such as the 30th, 35th and 83rd Divisions, even reaching 20 to 30%. For the entire 1st Army, these cases were multiplied by four between June and July.

Having learned a lesson from their First World War experience, the American medical services had taken this phenomenon very seriously. Following medical examination, psychiatrists diagnosed the nature of the disorder: in most cases, neurotic anxiety attacks, but also severe shock caused by artillery fire (shell shock), often

Four soldiers from the 29th Division at the grave of one of their fellow soldiers in the La Cambe cemetery.

accompanied by amnesia and, in certain cases, severe psychosis. Ailing troops were granted 72 hours of rest. They were first of all put to sleep for 48 hours thanks to sleeping pills, then given warm meals and attention to their bodily hygiene. If they recovered sufficiently, they were sent back to the front. If not, they were transferred to special camps (*Exhaustion centers*) which had been set up in Sainte-Mère-Église and Bernesq. They were deliberately isolated from other patients in order to avoid contagion, and were cared for by psychiatric teams via individual or group therapy. Treatment was complemented by physical exercise. A total of 62% of soldiers affected with mental disorders were sent back to their companies; others were transferred to non-combat units or sent back to England.

Certain desperate troops suffered from self-inflicted wounds to avoid combat. Those that were identified were isolated and placed under surveillance while an investigation was conducted by a member of the Office of Inspector General, assisted by a psychiatrist. Throughout the Battle of Normandy, 848 cases of self-mutilation were detected, bringing twenty-four of the troops involved before the court martial.

Preparing wooden crosses for *Omaha's* second temporary cemetery, located at the top of the cliff.

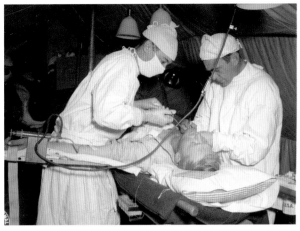

In field hospitals, surgical teams worked in turns night and day.

Over the days that followed the landings, the military hospital system was gradually set up via the development of a relatively complex evacuation chain, within which all of those referred to as *Medics*, regardless of their specific functions, were integrated. *Aid Stations* were set up in the immediate vicinity of the front to receive wounded troops, recovered from the field by teams of nurses and stretcher-bearers who often risked their own lives to do so. Victims were given first aid (sulfa drugs, bandages and - if necessary - blood transfusions, sedatives or morphine

Over the summer of 1944, the American healthcare services established thirty hospitals in the Bessin and Cotentin.

injections...). Depending on their condition, the wounded were treated on site for benign injuries or evacuated by ambulance towards *clearing stations* located a few miles behind the front lines. In these stations, medical teams made their diagnosis, which they noted on an *emergency medical tag* before referring the wounded depending on the seriousness of their condition. In extreme emergency, they were transferred to a *field hospital*, generally located nearby, for surgery. Those who survived their operation (10 to 15% died), remained in hospital until they were fit for transport towards *evacuation hospitals* where other wounded troops had been directly admitted. Equipped with 400 to 750 beds, these structures performed operations of lesser urgency and kept patients requiring to be monitored for an average of ten days before transferring them across the Channel or sending them to the convalescence camp opened late June in La Cambe.

Private Paul Lene was wounded near Saint-Lô.

The first four field hospitals were landed on *Utah Beach* and *Omaha Beach* as early as the 7th and 8th of June - along with their staff, tents and equipment - to become operational just two days later. On the 10th of June, two *evacuation hospitals* were established in Boutteville, near Sainte-Marie-du-Mont. Thanks to the widening of the bridgehead, twenty hospitals of all sorts had been set up by late June. However, the devastating effects of the war of the hedgerows were to oblige the total to be brought to over thirty the following month. Late July, healthcare services and staff in Normandy totalled 35,000 men and women, including 2,500 doctors and 1,100 nurses.

In June, the majority of wounded soldiers had been evacuated to English hospitals. In the medium term, the staff had planned to transfer a dozen general hospitals to the Continent, each of a capacity of 1,000 beds and supplied with all the necessary equipment to ensure comprehensive on-site care for all patients. In principle, they were to be established within existing French hospital buildings. Hence, the 298th General Hospital was set up within the freshly repaired Cherbourg maritime hospital. However, most of the others, in Carentan, Lison, La Haye-du-Puits... were to content themselves with tents or *Nissen* huts.

The hedges rendered the stretcher-bearers' task particularly difficult.

A 35th Division clearing station in the vicinity of Saint-Lô.

Genuine healthcare hubs, reuniting several hospitals, were also established in La Cambe, Le Molay, Lison, Carentan and, later, in Cherbourg and La Haye-du-Puits; they were located in the immediate vicinity of major road or rail links, in order to facilitate transporting the wounded and transferring patients to England. Around 39,000 were evacuated by the sea, most of them directly from the beaches, aboard specially adapted LSTs and, later, via the port of Cherbourg thanks to four hospital ships provided to the Americans by the British. However, air evacuations, deemed preferable by doctors, increased considerably to an average rate of five hundred per day, to finally totalise 26,000 evacuees. As from the 10th of June, they were transported aboard the 9th Air Force's *C-47s* which took off from the Saint-Laurent-sur-Mer airstrip and, later, from the Biniville airfield in the Cotentin, opened late July.

Ships and planes in turn ensured the transport of medical supplies and equipment in the opposite direction. Stretchers, splints, covers, orthopaedic casts and medication were stored in warehouses in Étard, near Trévières, Chef-du-Pont and Cherbourg. Blood and penicillin supplies were the most urgent. Discovered in 1928 by the Scottish scientist Alexander Fleming, penicillin - which had been qualified as a "miracle drug", was to prove its worth during the Second World War,

saving many lives. The American Army launched a mass production campaign in 1943. However, the stocks available in England were dangerously low by July 1944 and an airlift was established between the United States and Normandy, via England.

Although little use was made of blood transfusion during the First World War, it had since progressed slightly. Dr Charles Drew, an American doctor, was behind the creation of the very first blood bank in the United States, managed by the Red Cross. Early 1944, a blood bank was opened in Salisbury, England, provided with enough blood for a fortnight, and constantly resupplied given its short preservation time. In June, 250 pints of blood were flown to Normandy every day. These precious bottles were transported to hospitals in refrigerated trucks. But the war of the hedgerows was to double the required quantities of blood, and

Ambulances boarding wounded troops from an evacuation hospital to drive them to the nearby railway station.

An LST transferring the wounded to the British hospital ship Llandovery Castle in Cherbourg harbour.

An ambulance train leaving the station in Lison to head for Cherbourg.

short-term shortages were feared. Consequently, soldiers posted in Normandy were urged to give blood for their wounded buddies. The idea to establish an airlift with the United States, using long-range *C-57s*, was explored. The service was operational late August.

Among the 96,000 wounded troops cared for by the American healthcare services in June and July 1944, only 2,000 deaths were recorded, i.e. a rate of 2%, which was considerably lower than the rate observed in hospitals during the First World War, hence demonstrating the great progress accomplished in medical techniques and the life-saving role played by antibiotics.

Blood bottles being transferred from a plane to refrigerated trucks.

Air transport for the wounded progressively increased during the Battle of Normandy.

Searching for solutions to break through the bocage trap

Confronted with the harsh reality of the war of the hedgerows, the ever-pragmatic Americans were quick to adapt to the terrain, developing hitherto lacking tactical combinations. Having failed to sufficiently study the specific difficulties the bocage was likely to cause prior to the landing operation, they set to improvising adequate solutions directly on Norman soil.

The lack of coordination between the different services was a recurrent problem in the US Army. In the assaults against the hedges, the infantry suffered from insufficient firing power that only tanks could provide. Armoured units therefore needed to recover their operational potential by charging through the hedges without risking destruction.

In order to clear corridors for them, dynamite was initially considered, by simply placing two heavy charges at a distance of 8 feet at the foot of the embankment. However, that would have required excessive quantities of TNT. Engineers calculated that they would need no less than seventeen tonnes to open one single half-mile

A *Tankdozer* in action.

corridor through the hedges. Transporting explosives to the battlefield was, in itself, both a major problem and a genuine risk. However, they realised that the operation's efficiency could be increased by hollowing out cavities within the hedgerow and by placing far smaller charges. The accomplishment of such a task, armed with spades and shovels was also a laborious and perilous venture for sappers. Hence, the front of the tanks was equipped with solid steel spikes, soon to be nicknamed *Salad Forks*. By simply driving against the obstacle, they were capable of instantly hollowing out the necessary recesses. However, the resulting explosions were likely to alert the enemy.

Other methods were consequently studied to maintain the element of surprise. They quickly realised that *Sherman* tanks equipped with bulldozer blades, *tankdozers*, were capable of breaking up the hedges. However only forty of such tanks were present in Normandy and it would take too long to produce supplementary vehicles. Simpler solutions were consequently sought, "home-made" solutions consisting

This *Stuart* light tank, equipped with a hedge cutter, has just cut its way through its obstacle.

Sergeant Culin's *hedge cutters*

On the 14th of July, General Bradley was called upon urgently by General Gerow, commander of the V Corps, "We've got something that will knock your eyes out." Indeed, not far from Saint-Georges-d'Elle, to the east of Saint-Lô, he was soon to discover rather peculiar tanks, the front of which was equipped with large shears made of sharpened metal beams, forming huge teeth. Thanks to their heavy weight, when launched at around 13 mph, armoured vehicles equipped with these cutters could effortlessly slash their way through the hedges, by cutting them at their base.

Bradley marvelled at the invention, congratulated the man behind it – Curtis G. Culin from the 2nd Armoured Division's 102nd Reconnaissance Squadron, a 29 year-old sergeant from New York - and immediately ordered for large quantities of his *hedge cutters* to be produced.

Extra welding equipment was urgently ordered from England. And the necessary "raw material" was available in huge quantities. *Czech hedgehogs*, those famous steel obstacles laid on the beaches by Rommel, were recovered, cut into sections, welded and attached to the tanks.

Sergeant Culin's *hedge cutter* was kept secret to the very last minute, but had already equipped 500 tanks immediately prior to the launch of operation "*Cobra*".

Curtis Culin

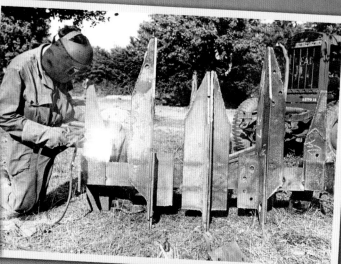

Piper Cub L4 observation plane. This short take-off and landing craft was light, manoeuvrable, silent and perfectly suited to the war of the hedgerows.

in adapting and fixing railway tracks or steel teeth to the front of tanks. Their curious appearance was soon to earn them the nickname of *Rhinoceroses* or *Rhino tanks*. Among the many experimental solutions, the most convincing was undeniably the famous *Hedge Cutter*, designed by Sergeant Culin.

Concurrently, major efforts were deployed to improve the - to date insufficient - radio and telephone communication between armies, an essential ingredient for ensuring the efficient coordination of their operations. Frequencies were harmonised - which had not previously been the case - in order to enable quick contact between the infantry and armoured units. Similarly, links with small observation planes referred to as *Piper Cubs* or *Stinsons*, were reinforced to facilitate the identification of the enemy and to adjust artillery fire.

In the field, behind the front lines, these tactical innovations were initially rehearsed, generally by small groups including an infantry unit, a few tanks and a team of engineers. The continued offensive against Saint-Lô would enable them to be tested against the enemy.

18th of July: the capture of Saint-Lô

Bradley was quick to grasp that he would be unable to reach the Coutances/Saint-Lô line, initially chosen as the departure point for the decisive breakthrough. He consequently decided to opt for a less ambitious alternative: the road that led from the Manche *Préfecture* to Périers. The capture of Saint-Lô remained, nevertheless, an absolute necessity. Given the increasing difficulties encountered to the west of the River Vire, Bradley decided to launch a new attack from the east. On the 11th of July, three divisions were launched over the hills that defended the town, to the north of the Bayeux road.

To the left of the assault force, the 2nd Infantry Division was to take control of Hill 192, bitterly defended by parachutists from General Schimpf's 3rd Division. This mound, located between Saint-André-de-l'Épine and Saint-Georges-d'Elle, was both a prime observation post overlooking the entire region and a genuine threat to the Allied flanks. After intense fighting, the Americans finally took control of the site on the evening of the 11th of July.

A 29th Infantry Division *Weasel* tracked vehicle on its way to Saint-Lô.

Carrefour de la Bascule junction, two American M10 tank destroyers put out of action by the Germans.

The 29th Division, placed in the centre with the 35th Division to its right, was entrusted with the most important mission: to capture Saint-Lô. "The task that awaits us is a darn tough one," General Gerhardt let loose. Nevertheless, positioned immediately behind the front for several weeks, his troops had been given enough time to become accustomed with new combat techniques. The time had come to put them into practice. The tanks advanced to their firing positions behind the hedges, showering the enemy defences with gunfire and machine gunfire, whilst the infantrymen launched their assault. They then reversed to enable engineers to place the explosive charges that would open corridors for them to advance. Whilst continuing to cover the infantrymen, armoured units advanced to the opposite hedge and repeated the manoeuvre.

The Germans witnessed its great efficiency, much to their expense. "This 11th of July has been the most horrendous day of my life," Private Helmut Kaslacka told one of his German colleagues. "At three in the morning, our company's sector was victim to a deluge of heavy artillery and mortar shell, such that one would have thought it was the end of the world. Then the tanks arrived. They were firing from everywhere through the hedges. We received orders to retreat. We could no longer hold our positions."

Yet, everything was not to go exactly according to Gerhardt's men's plans. As it was marching into battle, the 115th Regiment was delayed by an unexpected German counterattack. In contrast, the 116th Regiment made an exceptional two-mile advance in just one day, reaching the Bayeux road. However, progression over the following days was to be seriously hindered

The body of a German soldier in a ditch on the outskirts of Saint-Lô.

An American patrol amidst the ruins of Saint-Lô.

Stuart reconnaissance tank, in Rue du Neubourg.

as the Germans reformed their defensive lines. Sustained artillery fire led to severe losses on both sides. The Americans were reduced to slow, crest by crest progression. On the 14th of July, the weather was so appalling that both sides suspended combat. The 29th Division resumed its assault the next day, obtaining mediocre results with the exception of the 116th Regiment's 2nd Battalion which successfully reached La Madelaine, on the very outskirts of Saint-Lô. However the battalion's flanks were exposed and its position amidst the German lines proved far too perilous. Encircled through the night, it was to remain totally isolated for several long hours and was soon to be short of both food and ammunition. A plane was needed to transport plasma for the wounded. On the 17th of July, the 3rd Battalion re-established the junction, under orders to continue its advance. Major Howie, the battalion's commander, gave instructions and concluded by yelling to his men, "See you soon, in Saint-Lô!" He was mortally wounded by shellfire just a few minutes later. Late in the afternoon, the battalion met with a powerful German counterattack supported by tanks, which the intervention of radio-guided *P-47 Thunderbolts* from the 506th Fighter-bomber Squadron was quick to curb.

On the morning of the 18th of July, the Americans exerted increased pressure on the outskirts of the town. Several German units pulled back. General Gerhardt then decided to thrust forward a combat group, reassembled for two days near Couvains and led by his second in command General Cota. Comprised of reconnaissance units, tanks, infantrymen and engineers, the group was to make shrewd use of both speed and surprise. And that's precisely what it did. Advancing in columns along the Isigny road, its lead elements entered the town at around 6 p.m., facing no keen resistance. The GIs edged their way in small groups and took control of the "capital of the ruins" to meet with scenes of total desolation, "When our troops walked through

Saint-Lô, it was reminiscent of the valley of the shadow of death," noted one war correspondent. "I don't think one single house was still standing. We had pounded it with bombs, shells and machine gunfire until it was reduced to what now remained: the horrible spectre of what once had been a town inhabited by human beings."

The following morning, as the Germans continued to fire shells from their hillside hideaways to the south over what remained of Saint-Lô, Major Howie's body was transported in a jeep and laid before the Sainte-Croix church, covered with the Star-Spangled Banner to symbolise the great sacrifice thousands of soldiers had made to secure the capture of Saint-Lô.

The body of Major Thomas Howie from the 116th Infantry Division, swathed in the American flag and placed before the Sainte-Croix church.

Civilians and soldiers advancing amidst the ruins of the departmental archives.

Ammunition warehouse in the Normandy countryside.

Throughout June, the Americans had taken control of the Cotentin peninsula and a large share of the Bessin. However, July was to prove discouraging. Their progression was considerably slowed down and, by the end of the month, their bridgehead remained disappointingly narrow. It covered a surface of barely 1,400 square miles. Yet, within this confined space, men, vehicles and supplies continued to be unloaded, as according to Allied plans. Hence, by the 24th of July, seventeen American divisions (including four armoured divisions) were ready for action in Normandy, as were fifty 9th Air Force squadrons. In addition to combat troops, the troops from the *Communication Zone* (Com Z), posted to the rear of the battlefield, were in charge of offering logistic support (transport, equipment, food supplies, medical, engineer and signal corps, etc.). Late July, a total of 800,000 GIs crowded the small bridgehead, whereas the local population only totalled 250,000. At the time, the Cotentin and Bessin was home to three times as many Americans as it was to local inhabitants! Even in Cherbourg - where part of the population had been evacuated under German orders - their khaki uniforms were in largely superior numbers. Over the summer of 1944, it was as if this small French province had become the United States' 49th state.

Intense traffic as American convoys travel through Isigny.

Illustrious visitors to the bridgehead

On the 9th of June, General Bradley left the cruiser *USS Augusta* to establish the US 1st Army's command post on dry land, in an orchard near Grandcamp, not far from Pointe du Hoc; he was to move to Colombières early July. Eisenhower in turn came to the zone on the 7th of June to take stock of the situation, hugging the coast aboard a minelayer. Yet, for the time being, *Overlord's* headquarters remained in Southwick House, in England. The operation's Commander in Chief was only to establish his advanced command post in France early August, in Maisons, in the vicinity of Bayeux. However, in the meantime, he made increasingly frequent visits to Normandy to meet with General Bradley.

A week after the D-Day Landings, as combat was progressively moving away from the shoreline, a number of illustrious visitors came to the bridgehead. On the 12th of June, as Winston Churchill was on his way to meet Montgomery, Eisenhower accompanied the US Army's upper crust to Normandy, specially flown in from the United States for the occasion: Army Chief of Staff General Marshall, the commanders of the

A brief stopover for General Marshall and Admiral King on their way to Isigny.

US Air Force and the US Navy, General Arnold and Admiral King, together with Generals Spaatz (8th Air Force) and Royce (9th Air Force), Admirals Kirk (Western Task Force) and Hall ("O" Force). To fittingly welcome them on the morning of their arrival on *Omaha*, Bradley had "unpacked his first clean uniform". Transported in *command cars* amidst the convoys that meandered their way through the Normandy countryside, the group made halts at Isigny, Grandcamp and Pointe du Hoc, where they could contemplate the site's famous guns, unearthed in a hollow pathway. Bradley did nothing to hide his concern, "With General Marshall, King, Arnold, and Eisenhower bunched together in three open cars, an enemy sniper could have won immortality as a hero of the Reich."

On the 14th of June, a more disquieting visitor set foot on Norman soil: General de Gaulle. A few days prior to the landings, he had established the *GPFR - Gouvernement provisoire de la République française* (Provisional Government of the French Republic) and fully intended to impose his authority in this, "small portion of France recently freed by combat." He clearly expressed his aim to prevent the Americans from placing the country under AMGOT (Allied Military Government Occupied Territories) supervision, in other words an Allied military government. The somewhat prickly General brandished evidence of the "conspiracy", in the form of bank notes intended for use by Allied soldiers. Although these "Francs" represented, on one side, the French tricolour flag, their greenish appearance was highly reminiscent of the US Dollar and, more importantly, they had been issued without his consent.

If truth be told, the United States had no real intention of imposing the AMGOT. On the 9th of April 1944, Cordell-Hull, the Secretary of State, made it perfectly clear that, "The United States had neither the intention nor the desire to govern France or to administer its affairs, except insofar as it might be necessary for the purpose of conducting military operations against the enemy."

Marshall (seen turning his back), Eisenhower, Admiral Kirk and General Arnold before the Pointe du Hoc guns, found in a hollow path.

It is of the highest importance that civil authority in France be exercised by a Frenchman." Yet by no means did that mean that President Roosevelt was ready to give the "French house keys" back to a man who, in his view, had no genuine legitimacy and whom he considered, privately, to be an "apprentice dictator".

However, the enthusiastic welcome extended to de Gaulle in Bayeux on the 14th of June proved to be an excellent test. His unquestionable popularity among the Normans was manifest, as the SHAEF's information officers could but grant in their official reports. De Gaulle appeared as the "natural and indisputable leader of liberated France". Eisenhower, who was keen to concentrate on purely military affairs, without fretting over thorny political issues, discreetly pleaded the French general's cause to Roosevelt. Obliged to face reality, the President finally accepted to see de Gaulle in Washington on the 12th of July and to give *de facto* recognition to his legitimacy.

Whether they liked it or not, the Americans would need to put up with the presence of GPRF representatives in Normandy; first of all François Coulet, *Commissaire de la République* (Commissioner of the Republic), posted to Bayeux by de Gaulle on the 14th of June, followed

Bank notes printed by the Americans - "false money" according to de Gaulle.

by the new *Sous-Préfet* (Sub Prefect) of Cherbourg, Lucien Levandier, appointed on the 28th of June. This collaborative administration - which was not to escape the odd hitch - was therefore gradually set up between the new French authorities and the American Army.

Their priority: to get the port of Cherbourg back in working order

In the American plans, Cherbourg had not been granted a vast role. In fact, prior to the war, this major transatlantic and military port was only of secondary importance for merchant trade. With a total traffic of around a thousand tonnes per day, it ranked in 32nd position among all French ports. At the most, its capacity was capable of reaching 8,000 tonnes. The Americans were far more optimistic (17,000 tonnes) with regard to Breton ports such as Saint-Malo, Brest and Lorient, and even more so via their plans to redevelop Quiberon Bay (the *Chastity* plan). The delays accumulated by the 1st Army in the Cotentin were to offer Cherbourg

Deep-sea divers from the *Royal Navy* were rushed to Cherbourg where their demining skills were put to the test.

unexpected yet vital importance that was even to earn the port the historic name of the "port of Liberation".

However, first and foremost, the port needed to be restored. A vast undertaking given the sheer scale of the destruction and sabotage perpetrated by the Germans before their surrender. Many would have been disheartened by the prospect of the many months of work it required. However, time was short for the Americans absolutely needed a major port to directly transport to the Continent the necessary heavy equipment and supplies to ensure the success of operation Overlord. Mission impossible? Not according to the engineer corps teams quickly dispatched on site. For was their motto not, "The difficult, I'll do right now. The impossible will take a little while."

Work was conducted unremittingly, both night and day, by men from the 1056th Engineer Port Construction and Repair Group. Demining was their first priority.

A floating crane recovering the wreck of a tugboat, sunk by the Germans.

Risking their lives, the crews of British and American minesweepers, along with deep-sea divers detached from the Royal Navy, set to clearing the port's waters of hundreds of sinister and deadly weapons, some of which they had never come across before. With great difficulty, and with support from floating cranes, they also needed to refloat the dozens of wrecks - some of which were mined - that obstructed the port docks and channels.

Three weeks after the town was recaptured, they had already completed part of their work. On the 16th of July, four *Liberty Ships* sailed from the United States and anchored in Cherbourg's natural harbour. Unable to come any closer, their cargoes would need to be transshipped to dry land. The following day, barges and amphibious DUKW trucks ensured a shuttle service to and from the outer commercial harbour. On the 25th of July, the first fuel tanker moored at the Querqueville promenade terminal. On the 27th, unloading of railway equipment began on the Le Homet promenade... Although still limited, traffic had nevertheless resumed. Yet by late July, much work still remained to be done.

Over several weeks, demining and refloating operations continued; the swing bridge - shattered beyond repair - was dismantled for it blocked the entrance to the commercial port; it was replaced by a Bailey truss bridge; the arsenal docks were cleared; new landing stages were built at Mielles and, most importantly, the transatlantic dock quays were repaired in order to enable as many *Liberty Ships* as possible to berth, hence reducing stevedoring operations.

As work gradually progressed, Cherbourg's maritime traffic considerably increased. From 8,600 tonnes per day in August, it progressed to 11,800 tonnes by October, to reach a peak of 14,500 in November. It exceeded traffic on *Omaha Beach* as early as September. When the beaches were closed late 1944, almost all American supplies sent to Normandy were shipped to Cherbourg. However, the beaches still played a vital role throughout June and July.

Removal of the commercial port's swing bridge, which had been sabotaged and was no longer fit for use.

Repairing the quayside at the Mielles dock.

The first Liberty Ships arrive in Cherbourg

On the 16th of July, four *Liberty Ships* crossed the channel to the west for the first time, entered the natural harbour and moored in the safety zone, around 2 miles from the shoreline. Cranes were the first to be transshipped aboard LCT barges. Once on dry land, they were used to unload the cases of supplies that had been transported by a fleet of amphibious DUKW trucks. Given that their loading capacity did not exceed 2.5 tonnes, one can but imagine the sheer scale of the task they were to accomplish with the thousands of tonnes transported in each cargo.

Through demined and marked channels, they launched an incredible shuttle service between the cargo ships and Napoleon Beach, specially equipped for the purpose. It took several months before any large ships could enter the small natural harbour to dock at appropriate wharfs.

In the meantime, intense activity continued on and around Napoleon Beach and on the commercial port docks, where stevedoring was conducted by port battalions, essentially comprised of black soldiers, occasionally reinforced by civilian labourers and, later, by German POWs.

"The vastest supply warehouse in History" (Eisenhower)

Intense traffic continued on the beaches, at an average rate of 17,000 tonnes of supplies unloaded every day, i.e. a total of 490,000 tonnes for the month of July, compared to 290,000 in June. *Omaha* alone welcomed 56% of traffic, compared to 30% on Utah, 8% in the ports of Grandcamp, Isigny and Saint-Vaast and only 6% in Cherbourg where activity had barely resumed.

Although these figures were quite striking, they were nevertheless below expectations, often due to poor weather which, on several occasions, slowed down maritime traffic and unloading activities. Whereas food rations were in sufficient supply, the same did not apply to all types of goods. Vehicle spare parts, for example, were sporadically lacking. Insufficient construction materials were compensated for by the massive stocks left behind by the Germans.

Yet the most problematic shortage concerned ammunition, in particular shells of which the American artillery made far from parsimonious use. In July, combat during the war of the hedgerows proved costly in shells, bullets and grenades. Many automatic weapons, mortars

Advertisement singing the praises of the Army Service Forces and published in *Life* Magazine in July 1944.

and bazookas were lost or damaged during hostilities and needed to be replaced. Despite the absolute priority placed on ammunition transport, the balance between available stocks and consumption remained unsteady and serious shortage was feared on several occasions. Hence, around mid-July, due to poor weather conditions, only 3,000 tonnes were unloaded each day whilst the 1st Army demanded 7,500. Severe rationing was introduced by the military staff, restricting, for example, the number of shells to be fired each day by each army corps.

Fuel, "the red blood of war" according to Clemenceau's famous expression, was also crucial for the highly mechanised US Army, which consumed it in large quantities. For example, fuel

Departure point of fuel pipes at the west pier in Port-en-Bessin.

Pipelines through Étreham.

consumption for a GMC six-wheel-drive truck was 7 miles to the gallon, whereas for a *half-track* it was 4.7 and a *Sherman* tank only 1.2. Late July, the 1st Army was burning no less than 330,000 gallons every day! Over the days that followed the D-Day Landings, this precious liquid was transported in jerry cans and gas cans. In due course, two fuel supply systems were set up, both for land vehicles (MT 80 – *Motor Vehicle Gazoline octane 80*) and for planes (AVGAS – *Aviation gazoline*).

In particular, the "major" system provided - within the context of the "PLUTO" (Pipe-Line Under The Ocean) project - for the establishment of an underwater oil pipeline. Flexible 3-inch diameter pipes were to be unreeled on the English Channel bed, from the Isle of Wight to Cherbourg, i.e. a distance of over 60 miles. It was a genuine historic first, designed by the British, yet somewhat sceptically regarded by their Allies. Delayed by accidents and damage, this audacious and excessively complex project from a technical point of view, was postponed, to finally end in a fiasco. "PLUTO" only began operating in September, for a period of barely twelve days, to be abandoned on the 4th of October. Most of the necessary fuel destined for Cherbourg was, in fact, unloaded by fuel tankers moored at the Querqueville promenade, before being stored in reservoirs scattered across the surrounding countryside, then sent by pipeline to the open fuel depot in La Haye-du-Puits. The Americans were to wait until the 25th of July before seeing the first tanker, the *Empire Traveller* enter the port.

As such, the "minor" system was to play a role well beyond that planned for by the Allies. An initial system (the *Ship to Shore Pipeline*), set up in Sainte-Honorine-des-Pertes and codenamed "Tombolas", enabled fuel to be transferred from tankers anchored a little less than a mile from the shoreline to dry land, thanks to a flexible tube (*Sealine*) held in place via a system of floaters. Not far from there, the two piers in Port-en-Bessin were used - one on behalf of the Americans, the other on behalf of the British - by 1,300 tonne tankers. Fuel was transferred from their holds towards large tanks installed on the heights of Mont Cauvin, in Étreham. From here, it was dispatched by pipeline to depots such as those in Balleroy,

The *Empire Traveller* moored at the fuel terminal on the Querqueville promenade. The tanker's cisterns were connected to a pumping and land storage system.

Fuel depot in the Cotentin.

Tire warehouse in Écausseville.

Carentan and Saint-Lô, where tank trucks and jerry cans were duly filled. To compensate for delays sustained by the "major" system, daily supplies were doubled in

volume compared to forecasts and the total storage capacity at Sainte-Honorine and Étreham was increased from 2 to 4.8 million gallons. Despite such prowess, the overall gap had still not been filled. Nevertheless, up to the launch of operation *Cobra* and the American breakthrough, this situation was to have no major consequence. Consumption remained considerably lower than estimated, due to the narrowness of the bridgehead and the limited scope for Allied vehicle movement.

In February 1944, the Army Service Forces staff in charge of logistic matters had developed an ambitious plan for the six weeks following the landings. The staff had chosen a precise location, either in town or country, for each type of depot, and had defined their surface area and their configuration - indoor or outdoor - throughout a vast geographical zone which by mid-July was scheduled to stretch beyond Lower Normandy, Brittany, Maine and Pays de Loire. Forty days after the landings, the heart of this logistic system was scheduled to have covered a vast Rennes-Laval-Châteaubriant triangle. Ammunition stores were, in turn, to be developed at several different levels, across a 250-mile road network.

However, delayed progression on the front line had foiled this bold theoretical enterprise. The Allies would therefore need to establish their depots over an infinitely smaller area. Which they did in an empirical manner, or rather in a manner close to chaos and far from propitious to rational stock management. Incorrectly labelled shipments, sent to erroneous locations, were lost from sight. This was often the case with transmission and medical equipment. Lacking in appropriately scaled maps (1:25,000), trucks drove round in circles for hours amidst the Normandy bocage, in search of the right village or hamlet.

So where could they stock their countless cases of ammunition, food rations and equipment, not forgetting materials and vehicles? Cherbourg was the only major town that had fallen virtually intact into American hands; however, it was rapidly submerged by the influx of GIs and only a few rare buildings could still be used as warehouses, such as the Amiot factories for example. In Écausseville, near Montebourg, a former French Army airship hangar was also put to use. However, it was insufficient. The Normandy countryside was now overrun with depots: initially along main roads, before stretching deep into the countryside, by breaking through the hedges to enable trucks to move from one field

to another. It was an arresting sight that led Eisenhower to say, "The coastal zone, from the Cotentin to Caen, was transformed into an immense depot, the vastest ever set up in History on invaded territory." The tight space occupied by the bridgehead was close to saturation with - over and above depots - airfields, camps, parade grounds, equipment fleets, repair workshops, vehicle assembly lines, POW camps, hospitals, cemeteries...

Truck repair workshop.

Food ration warehouse.

Detroit... in Normandy?

In 1944, the small village of La Cambe, located on the RN13 trunk road to the south of Grandcamp and home to barely 700 inhabitants, became a genuine nerve centre for the US Army. Not only was it home to four hospitals, a vast cemetery and a fuel depot, but also two nearby airfields in Deux-Jumeaux and Cardonville.

Yet the creation of a truck assembly line amidst the pastures, placed under the responsibility of the 148th Motor Vehicle Assembly Company was surely among the most astonishing of undertakings. "Detroit, America's automobile capital, has been moved to Normandy," a war correspondent ironically reported. "France had never seen such an enterprise," one of the 150 specifically recruited French labourers told him.

In an aim to relieve the pressure on American plants, assembly lines had been decentralised to Europe, where they were supplied with spare parts. The experience had already been tested in England. It was to be continued in Normandy, in particular in Hardinvast and Querqueville, near Cherbourg, but also in the Bessin, where daily production included one hundred jeeps in Isigny and sixty 2.5-tonne GMC trucks in La Cambe.

Re-establishing communication

The hostilities throughout the summer of 1944 had ravaged Normandy: from the terrifying aerial bombardments conducted prior to and, to a greater extent, after the landings, to the devastating effects of artillery exchange, via the demolition operations perpetrated by the Germans and sabotage by the Resistance. Towns and villages had been reduced to ruins and communication networks had suffered: collapsed bridges, blocked tunnels, slashed railway lines, mined roads and pathways, cut telephone and power lines... After many weeks of destruction, the time had come for reconstruction. Within the bridgehead, a momentous task awaited the Engineers and the Transportation Corps.

Rail transport was, in due course, to become an absolute necessity for dispatching the tens of thousands of tonnes of supplies shipped via Cherbourg, the rear

The *Twickenham Ferry* rolling bridge.

base for reconquering Europe. Even before the town was recaptured, work had already begun on rebuilding bridges over the Taute and the Vire for example. After Cherbourg had fallen into Allied hands, restoration of the railway station was initiated. However, its capacity was soon to prove insufficient, leading to the necessity to establish two marshalling yards further south in Couville and Sottevast. Equipped with a total of 30 miles of track capable of welcoming close to four thousand wagons, they were operational by the autumn.

In the meantime, in July, the train shortage was the first problem to be solved. The war had left France with only three thousand of its 1939 stock of 17,500 locomotives. In Normandy, the Americans found a few trains still fit for use, but many were very old models. They consequently urgently needed trains to be shipped from warehouses in Wales or direct from the United States. Many were to arrive in Cherbourg. Several

An LST converted into a *ferry train* unloading wagons on the Mielles platform.

experimental methods were tried out for unloading rail equipment. The simplest was used on the Mielles platform and consisted in transporting wagons on rails by LSTs equipped with openable stems and in rolling them onto a junction, via a connecting ramp. Concurrently, two former British ferries the *Twickenham* and the *Hampton* were transformed by adding a loading system with a rolling bridge to their stern; this enabled locomotives and wagons to be hoisted and placed on tracks on the dyke in Le Homet.

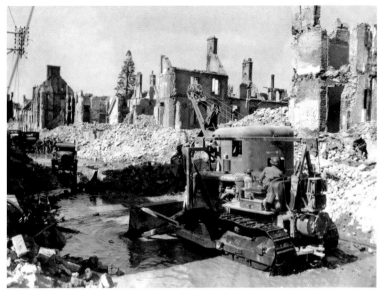

Clearing the streets of Saint-Lô.

28th July: the *Twickenham* unloading wagons on the Le Homet dock.

Heavier locomotives (75 tonnes) were shipped aboard two Seatrain rail carriers from the Great Lakes Fleet, *USS Texas* and *USS Lakehurst*. Equipped with powerful derricks, they were capable of hoisting and landing this type of equipment - or at least in principle - for when the *USS Texas'* derrick broke, it sent a locomotive thirty feet under, requiring a crane ship to be brought from England to recover it and to empty what remained in the ship's hold.

By late July, fifty locomotives and two hundred wagons had been imported to France from the United Kingdom. Many more were to follow. Traffic was progressively resumed on the Cherbourg-Paris line, at least as far as the Lison station and, a little later, Molay-Littry. The first rail link with Carentan was made on the

Unloading train locomotives and wagons in Cherbourg.

A stone crusher used for road maintenance near Carentan.

11th of July. On the 4th of August, an ambulance train transporting wounded troops from the 56th General Hospital left Lison to head for Cherbourg. Two junctions were connected on the main line: one towards the small ports of Barfleur and Saint-Vaast; the other towards Saint-Sauveur-le-Vicomte and Bricquebec. By late July, one hundred and twenty miles of track were available.

However, for the time being, rail transport was only to play a limited role, the vast share of traffic passing via the road network. Much work was also needed on the roads, to repair bridges, fill up the craters that had been created by bombs and to clear the towns of their ruins; work that was to be further complicated by intense traffic, trucks progressing bumper to bumper, despite road safety instructions. Normandy's roads were suffering. They required constant maintenance, frequent repair and even, occasionally, enlargement. The traffic statistics established by the Americans spoke for themselves: late July, thirty thousand tonnes of supplies were in transit every day between the beaches or warehouses and their final destination; on the day of the 18th of July alone, no less than 14,434 vehicles crossed the bridge between Isigny and Carentan, whilst an hourly average of 1,650 vehicles crossed the junction between the RD5 minor road and the RN13 trunk road...

The Signal Corps repairing telephone lines in Pont-l'Abbé.

Intelligence and psychological warfare

Long since had intelligence played a vital role in military operations, particularly in times of war. Indeed, it was essential to acquire the best possible knowledge of one's adversary. The US Army intelligence service, referred to as G-2, was present within each major military unit (army, army corps, division...).

Its principal mission consisted in gathering and quickly conveying, for use by the high command, any information gleaned on enemy troops, their organisation in the field, their intentions and their morale, all such information being transferred daily. To do so, a number of methods were deployed: interception of radio communication, aerial reconnaissance and photography, information provided by civilians and local Resistance fighters, recuperation of German documents and even interrogation of prisoners of war. Before recapturing Cherbourg, any men who fell into American hands were systematically subjected to questioning. Afterwards, the huge numbers of German prisoners rendered the task particularly arduous. "The information gathered from prisoners was a chief source of intelligence on enemy order of battle, morale, intentions and all other matters of importance", A 1st Army G-2 report stated. "An overwhelming number of the prisoners talked willingly. German officers, at first reluctant to talk, supplied valuable information after the invasion gathered force. In general, the morale of prisoners deteriorated, week by week and the PW cages of First US Army provided a sorry picture of Hitler's 'master race'."

Every day, several hundred pounds in weight of German documents (maps, reports or personal letters) were recovered and transmitted to a special G-2 service. Their analysis offered a wealth of information, "During the first

Questioning a German prisoner of war near Saint-Gilles.

These soldiers from the 3rd Armoured Division have made a sign out of a food ration box urging the Germans to surrender.
"Soldiers, surrender! You are surrounded."

Containers filled with leaflets being loaded onto an 8th Air Force *B-17*.

stage of the invasion the documents captured had been written with typical German thoroughness. Official papers were neatly typed and each document followed German Army regulations. Private letters captured welcomed the start of invasion as the opportunity the Germans had been waiting for to bring about final victory. A notable change took place after the fall of Cherbourg. The documents revealed that the Germans were less sure of themselves and also less security minded. Captured mail bags contained letters which had been delayed for many days for lack of personnel and transportation facilities.

Civilians were employed to roll up leaflets and to place them inside hollow shells.

There was no longer any talk of an early victory. At best there was hope for a miracle or the personal hope to conte out of the war alive. Letters from Germany clearly reflected the effects of our bombing, complained about long working hours and lack of food, and were gloomy in their outlook for the future."

Another of the G-2's missions involved counter-espionage. The Americans' main fear was the infiltration of enemy agents within their own lines, hence the multiplication of - more or less tolerated - security measures that affected the entire population, and the concurrent multiplication of controls at road junctions and town entrances. Collaborationist party members were hunted out, even if their numbers were thought to be low and that the most dangerous among them had already fled with the Germans. Special attention was paid to Todt Organisation workers, particularly abundant in the Cotentin. Many were interrogated, some of them treated like prisoners of war and sent to England, others forced to serve in the US Army.

A 1st Army interrogation centre for suspicious civilians was established in Saint-Laurent-sur-Mer as from the 12th of June, before being moved to the Isigny town hall on the 29th. Reinforced by OSS agents, it dealt with a total of 223 cases. Among them, nine German spies were identified and seventy-two other individuals, considered to be dangerous, were placed in the hands of the French authorities for further investigation in view of their referral to court.

Some of the information recovered by intelligence services was exploited by the Psychological Warfare Division, an inter-allied organisation placed under the direct orders of the SHAEF within the framework of operation Overlord. It reunited the combined experience of the American OWI (Office of War Information) and OSS (Office of Strategic Services) and the British PWE (Psychological Warfare Executive). Its aim had been clearly defined: to demoralise the German troops by all possible means.

Several techniques were used during the hostilities in Normandy. For example, radio trucks, equipped with powerful loud speakers regularly broadcast propaganda in the vicinity of the German lines, as Bradley explained, "Across on Gerow's front, a PW officer from the 2d Armored Division rare his sound track forward each evening to play Strauss waltzes for the homesick enemy across the Lines. At the end of each number he purred in German to ask if the soldiers remembered their homeland as it was before the war. 'You have fought well,' he told them, 'and you have conducted yourself honorably before your countrymen. But there is no longer any reason for fighting. Our bombers have destroyed your cities. You are faced with overwhelming strength. Surrender now and return safely to the loved ones you left behind. If you don't surrender and come over, we have no alternative but to give you more and more of this' With that, the divisional artillery dumped a 48-gun salvo into the German position."

Furthermore, the Allies massively distributed propaganda leaflets. Over the summer of 1944, the Americans scattered no less than 86 million of them over the German lines in Normandy. Generally

Empty 105mm smoke bomb cartridges could hold 500 leaflets, whilst 155mm cartridges could hold 1,500.

Safe-conduct signed by Eisenhower, for use by surrendering German troops.

Nachrichten für die Truppe, daily newspaper, printed in German by the Psychological Warfare Division.

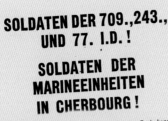

SOLDATEN DER 709.,243., UND 77. I.D.!

SOLDATEN DER MARINEEINHEITEN IN CHERBOURG!

Cherbourg ist eingeschlossen. Keiner von Euch kann mehr heraus—und niemand kann Euch entsetzen. See—, Land—und Luftweg sind gesperrt.

Eure Lage ist aussichtslos. Eure Führung hat Euch abgeschrieben. Ihr könnt die Lage nicht retten—aber wer will, kann sein Leben retten.

Wer sich alliierten Truppen ergibt, kann sich darauf verlassen, dass er anständig behandelt wird. Mehr als 15,000 von euren Kameraden von den anderen Einheiten in der Normandie haben die Erfahrung schon gemacht.

Kommt einzeln oder in kleinen Gruppen. Unsere Soldaten haben Befehl, auf niemanden zu schiessen, der sich ergeben will und etwas Weisses schwenkt oder den Helm oder das Gewehr.

Wenn Ihr nicht direkt zu uns 'rüberkommen könnt, verkrümelt Euch im Gelände und wartet bis wir kommen. Am besten wartet Ihr, bis unsere Infanterie da ist. Bringt euer Kochgeschirr mit.

ZG. 16

Generalleutnant von Schlieben, der Verteidiger von Cherbourg, verlässt seinen Gefechtsstand im Fort du Roule, um sich den Amerikanern zu ergeben. Die Lage war hoffnungslos. Auch Schliebens Tod hätte nichts daran ändern können. Deshalb setzte sich Generalleutnant von Schlieben, zusammen mit 18 000 anderen in der gleichen Lage, über den Führerbefehl hinweg, zu dem sie sich mit ihrer Unterschrift verpflichten mussten.

„dass sie ungeachtet der Lage ihren Platz mit Einsatz ihres Lebens bis zum letzten Mann und zur letzten Patrone zu verteidigen haben."

Generalleutnant von Schlieben und die 18 000 sind jetzt in England. Sie warten auf das Ende des Krieges und auf ein Deutschland, in dem solche erpresserischen Verpflichtungen unmöglich sind.

DIE NÜCHTERNE WAHRHEIT ÜBER KRIEGSGEFANGENSCHAFT

Deutscher Soldat: Wir versprechen Dir weder Utopien noch das Schlaraffenland, falls Du in Kriegsgefangenschaft gelangst. Aber — auf die folgenden Tatsachen kannst Du mit Bestimmtheit rechnen:

1. „FAIRE" BEHANDLUNG, wie es einem tapferen Gegner gebührt. Der Rang des Gefangenen wird anerkannt. Deine eigenen Kameraden sind Deine unmittelbaren Vorgesetzten.

2. GUTE VERPFLEGUNG. Viele Deiner Kameraden sind erstaunt, wie gut die Ernährung bei uns ist. Wir heissen mit Recht die bestgenährte Armee der Welt. (Manche Landser ziehen das deutsche Kommissbrot unserem Weissbrot vor, aber über unseren Kaffee und die Zubereitung unserer Speisen hat sich noch niemand beklagt . . .)

3. ERSTKLASSIGE LAZARETTPFLEGE für Verwundete und Kranke. Gemäss der Genfer Konvention erhalten Gefangene dieselbe Lazarettpflege wie unsere eigenen Truppen.

4. SCHREIBGELEGENHEIT. Du kannst im Monat drei Briefe und vier Karten nach Hause schreiben. Die Postverbindung ist schnell und zuverlässig. Du kannst Briefe und auch Pakete erhalten.

5. BESOLDUNG. Gemäss der Genfer Konvention behält der Kriegsgefangene das Anrecht auf seine Entlohnung bei. Für etwaige freiwillige Arbeitsleistungen erhältst Du aber selbstverständlich Bezahlung. Für das Geld, das Du erhältst, kannst Du verschiedentliche Marketenderwaren kaufen.

6. WEITERBILDUNG. Sollte der Krieg noch länger dauern, dann kommst Du wahrscheinlich noch dazu, Dich an den verschiedentlichen Bildungs- und Lehrkursen zu beteiligen, die von Kriegsgefangenen selbst veranstaltet werden.

Und selbstverständlich kommst Du nach Kriegsende nach Hause

ZG.39

SOLDATENPFLICHT

Fünf Jahre lang hat der deutsche Soldat an allen Fronten seine Pflicht erfüllt. Dabei hat er die schwersten Opfer gebracht. Die vielen Siege früherer Jahre haben ihm jedoch auf die Dauer nichts genützt.

Heute stehen die Russen auf deutschem Reichsgebiet in Ostpreussen. Sie haben Lemberg genommen, die Weichsel überquert und stehen vor Warschau. In Frankreich sind die Alliierten durchgebrochen und werfen immer neues Material in den Einsatz.

Angesichts der Übermacht auf allen Seiten kann Deutschland nicht mehr hoffen, den Krieg zu gewinnen. Es kann ihn nur noch verlängern.

Eure Soldatenpflicht ist getan

Eine andere Pflicht bleibt jedoch übrig:

Die Pflicht zur Selbsterhaltung

Eure Familie, Euer Volk und Euer Vaterland brauchen gesunde Helfer zum Wiederaufbau, nicht weitere unnütze Opfer für eine verlorene Sache.

Als Soldaten ist Euch gute Behandlung im Fall der Gefangenschaft nach den Bestimmungen der Genfer Konvention durch die Alliierten verbürgt.

Ihr seid jetzt abgeschnitten!

Um nutzloses Blutvergiessen zu ersparen, wird Euch dieses Flugblatt zugestellt.

Ihr seid jetzt abgeschnitten. Alliierte Einheiten stehen bereits weit hinter Euch. Ihr habt tapfer gekämpft, aber von jetzt an ist ein Weiterkämpfen nutzlos. Ihr müsst Euch ergeben oder knapp vor Kriegsende sterben.

Ihr erkennt die Lage. Es gilt jetzt, dementsprechend zu handeln. Jeder muss für sich selbst entscheiden. Es ist keine Zeit zu verlieren.

Die Alliierten wollen Euer Leben schonen und sichern Euch anständige Behandlung zu. Ihr müsst aber klar zu verstehen geben, dass Ihr aus dem Kampf scheidet.

HANDELT SOFORT!

Polnisch sprechende Wehrmachtangehörige!

Odezwa Armij Sprzymierzonych

POLACY!

1. Wcielono was gwałtem do armji niemieckiej. Najeźdźca napiętnował was hańbiącym mianem Volksdeutscha.

2. Odwieczny wróg Polski rzucił was na ten pas wybrzeża bez rezerw i transportu. Uczynił z was żywe miny, wysunięte przed niemiecką siłą pancerną.

3. Żołnierze, marynarze i lotnicy Narodów Zjednoczonych ruszyli do potężnego szturmu przeciw hitlerowskim Niemcom, do szturmu, który na zawsze złamie tyranię 'wspólnego wroga i położy kres niewoli Polaków.

4. Każdy strzał, wymierzony przez was w tych bojowników wolności byłby strzałem w serce Polski.

5. Każdy Polak, który zaprzestanie bezcelowej walki, zachowa swe życie dla siebie i dla Polski.

American leaflets targeting the German troops.

designed and produced in England, they were dropped in huge quantities over the enemy lines by 8th US Air Force bombers. Most of them aimed at convincing the German troops to surrender, reassuring them on the treatment that awaited them as prisoners. One special leaflet was even in the form of a safe-conduct, signed by Eisenhower himself and guaranteeing total security to any German wishing to make use of it. Another specifically targeted besieged or encircled troops. It was widely distributed within the fortress of Cherbourg prior to the American assault. After the town's recapture, a new leaflet with a picture of General von Schlieben's surrender was launched on the forts around the natural harbour, where a few pockets of resistance remained. Out in the field, another method was deployed, to a lesser extent, to reach specific targets and to quickly satisfy - in just a few hours - tactical battle requirements. It consisted in filling empty shells with leaflets drafted and printed on site by PWD teams. The shells were transported to artillery units in position on the front; they were fired above the hedges and exploded, scattering their contents across the enemy positions.

Within the framework of operation *Overlord*, one particularly spectacular project was developed. It consisted in printing no less than several hundred thousand copies of a four-page daily newspaper, drafted in German and targeting German soldiers on the Western Front. Dropped by planes at night, it needed to be ready every morning "in time for breakfast", hence largely beating the speed of the German press itself. The first issue of *Nachrichten für die Truppe* (*News for the Troops*) was published on the 25th of April and the last on the 7th of May 1945. In an effort to counterbalance propaganda broadcast by Dr Goebbels' services, the first page included an update of the latest news - which was generally accurate - from the various fronts on which soldiers from the Reich were engaged. Hence, the issue distributed on the night of the 6th to the 7th of June spoke of the D-Day Landings, with a five-column headline on the front page, "Atlantic Wall breached in several places." On the 13th of June, the troops in Normandy and elsewhere learned of the "noose tightening around Cherbourg"... The inside pages - decidedly more subversive - were devoted to what was going on in the meantime in Germany: reports of bombings over towns, with detailed descriptions of the streets destroyed; the "scandalous" behaviour of the Reich leaders and Nazi party dignitaries who indulged themselves in Berlin whilst the *Wehrmacht* soldiers were suffering and dying by thousands in both the East and the West... To draw its readers' attention, the paper even included the latest sports results, trivial events and a few sketches of scantily clad young ladies.

Measuring the impact of psychological warfare was a difficult task. Nevertheless, the intelligence services did endeavour to appreciate its effects by interrogating prisoners of war. According to a 1st Army G-2 study, from 70 to 80% of prisoners acknowledged having read the Allied leaflets and 40% even had them in their possession when they were captured; however, these statistics failed to convey their influence. In a report drafted at the end of the war, the PWD conceded that leaflets and loud-speaker announcements rarely had an immediate effect. Nevertheless, it did highlight that - over time - within the context of a deteriorating military position for the Germans, psychological warfare had an undeniable impact, predominantly among non-German soldiers enlisted in the *Wehrmacht*. Impact that became tangible as from late July, when the Americans launched operation *Cobra*.

A German prisoner reading one of the leaflets distributed by the Americans.

When he came across a group of GIs preparing the assault on Cherbourg late June, Ernie Pyle, a war correspondent, was struck by their appearance, "The soldiers around us had a two weeks' growth of beard. Their uniforms were worn slick and very dirty – the uncomfortable gas-impregnated clothes they had come ashore in. The boys were tired. They had been fighting and moving constantly forward on foot for nearly three weeks without rest - sleeping out on the ground, wet most of the time, always tense, eating cold rations, seeing their friends die. One of them came up to me and said, almost belligerently, 'Why don't you tell the folks back home what this is like? All they hear about is victories and a lot of glory stuff. They don't know that for every hundred yards we advance somebody gets killed. Why don't you tell them how tough this life is?' As we waited to start our advance, the low black skies of Normandy let loose on us and we gradually became soaked to the skin."

Indeed, the day-to-day lives of front line troops were particularly gruelling. They were of no comparison to those of the troops positioned to the rear, offering precious logistic support. Yet, the general mood on the front lines was frequently conveyed in the form of often callous remarks concerning those who were considered to have the "cushy job", "All those sons of bitches that are behind my personal hole." In an attempt to curb such prejudice, a "rear" soldier gave his own version of the situation to the newspaper The *Stars and Stripes*, "No one seems ever to think a soldier in QM ever gets to smell any gunpowder, dig any foxholes, get into any fighting, go without food, mail and the like. Our QM outfit hit the beach on D-Day right when the heat was on, and more outfits are hitting the beaches every day - to unload and load rations, ammunition, and all other equipment and supplies. Opening and running dumps under combat conditions is a tough job. We sleep in foxholes, wash and shave in helmets, and operate twenty-four hours a day - about fifty percent of that time in the rain and mud." Whether they were on the front or the rear lines, they all had the same day-to-day preoccupations: finding shelter, sleeping, eating, washing, resting, amusing themselves... Yet, however shared, accounts of these needs and expectations varied from one soldier to another.

Sergeant Williams from the 4th Infantry Division, exhausted by combat.

Life with a roof over your head, in a tent... or a hole in the ground

The men in the rear lines frequently became settled in their positions, particularly in July. Those posted in towns, such as Cherbourg, found accommodation relatively easily in houses or buildings, many of which were vacant following the evacuation of certain civilians before the landings. In the countryside, lucky troops found shelter in farms, barns or stables. However, most soldiers camped in tents, often two-by-two, each carrying half of the canvas in his kit bag. The most resourceful among them used odds and ends to build cabins which they often adorned with pictures of pin-ups cut out from magazines. On the front lines, the soldier's "lodge" consisted of a deep hole dug out in the damp earth, referred to as a *foxhole*, and offering - in principle - shelter from bullets or shrapnel. As they gradually advanced, and each time they stopped to establish a new position, the GIs swapped their rifles for spades and set to digging. This resulted, of course, in further fatigue for the already exhausted troops, unless they were lucky enough to use - with due caution - the hideaways the Germans had abandoned when forced into retreat.

Sainteny: Sergeant Chicos successfully installed an electric light in his shelter.

Private Battaglia with his *pin-ups*.

Between two attacks during the battle in the hedges, the GIs could spend extremely tense hours in their *foxholes*, always on the lookout, their fingers poised on their triggers and their grenades close at hand. Leaving or recklessly moving away from a shelter could prove fatal, for mortar and artillery fire was a constant threat, both day and night, not forgetting the enemy snipers perched up in the trees. During the First World War, soldiers could at least move around in their trenches. The GIs independent personal holes did not enable this and exacerbated feelings of isolation, even when shared by two, which at least helped them keep warm over the cold and damp Normandy nights. Every morning when they woke, they were stiff and covered with dew,

A moment's respite in a *foxhole* during the war of the hedgerows.

their skin clammy due to the condensation between their bodies and their clothes. In their narrow and uncomfortable *foxholes*, the GIs either slept very little or very badly. Their fatigue accumulated.

Men from the 9th Division enjoying a moment's respite during hostilities near Marigny.

Private Skagges' somewhat peculiar hideout.

Washing, shaving...
and changing clothes

"I felt older after so many days of incessant combat," the paratrooper Tom Porcella recalled, "We had no way to wash or shave. So, as the days went on we began to look and smell bad. Also, we had gas impregnated woollen OD's which we lived and slept in without even changing our under wear. I believe I had been in Normandy about three weeks. I had not bathed, changed my clothes. Back in England, the first thing I did was to take a long hot bath."

For men on the front, often huddled up in their *foxholes*, personal hygiene was frequently reduced to the bare minimum, their helmets serving as makeshift washbasins. Yet, they were wise enough to wait for a break in hostilities to avoid unnecessarily exposing themselves. They also had to wait for a long time before being able to change their uniforms, which were covered

Corporal Henry, from the 2nd Armoured Division, washing his feet in a canvas bucket after the battle to free Carentan.

with mud, sweat and sometimes blood. Such was the case for Private Jack Port who, just like his buddies from the 4th Division, had to wait for Cherbourg to be recaptured before enjoying a hot shower, a clean

Prétot - 20th July 1944. Re-equipping a 90th Division unit before its return to the front lines.

Changing uniforms in a 1st Army supply depot in July 1944.

uniform and - one pleasure leading to another - a hot meal. Troops from the 9th Division were more fortunate for, once they had reached the coast at Barneville mid June, they could bathe in the sea. Yet some of them were unaccustomed to and didn't really appreciate the salty sea water.

As they moved away from the front, various resources became available for improving personal hygiene. Rivers and ponds contributed considerably. Certain troops cobbled together makeshift collective showers in fields. Finally, the soldiers stationed in Cherbourg and the surrounding area were undoubtedly the best off for they could freely pay visits to public baths and showers.

Although worrying in June, the situation did improve in July with the arrival of mobile units equipped with showers installed on trailers. "After a hot bath each man was given a complete change of clothing, with the exception of shoes," a Supply Corps officer explained. "In my opinion this hot shower and provision for clean clothing, from the skin out, was one of the greatest possible morale-building factors. I saw men come out from under the showers looking like polished apples, with big smiles on their faces. Many had not had a bath or change of clothing for weeks."

However, these facilities were located to the rear of the front and combat troops could only access them periodically and in turns. For example, the 90th Division only released 2 to 3% of its troops at the same time, which meant each man could only take a shower once every three to four weeks! Although the 2nd Armoured Division made sure that its men were offered regular access to mobile showers, the 35th Infantry Division often had to content itself with Normandy's rivers. Other units set to improvising to offer their men the bare minimum in terms of cleanliness.

Captain Franklin enjoying a hot bath in a drinking trough, thanks to an oil-fired water heater.

Thirteenth field hospital in Saint-Laurent-sur-Mer: lunchtime for the nurses.

Before the D-Day Landings, the supply corps had, mistakenly, forecast that the harshness of the German occupation and the ravages caused by combat would leave Normandy on its knees, on the breach of famine. They consequently presumed that everything would need to be taken there to nourish the troops, including water. In addition, the high command had based its strategy on manoeuvre warfare in which there was no place for permanent facilities.

Dieticians therefore set to considering the GIs' food supplies in order to develop various packaged rations to satisfy a dual purpose: that of providing a maximum quantity of calories for a minimum volume; the concept was aimed at enabling units to benefit from the services of kitchens "on wheels", hence offering them great freedom of movement. During the first four weeks of combat, no less than sixty million rations were unloaded onto the Normandy beaches.

The K-ration, although far from the most popular, was to become the most famous. Originally designed for paratroopers, its contents were relatively sparse: three small cans (one per meal) containing meat, cheese and pâté, along with vitamin supplements, biscuits, sachets of stock... The GIs' verdict was final, "Anything was better than a K-ration." Its small size was its key advantage for it could easily be transported in a pocket or a haversack.

The more cumbersome, yet less consistent C-ration essentially comprised cans of meat and vegetables, available in three versions. One of them, made of minced meat, met with violent aversion. Whereas the K-ration was intended to be eaten cold, the C-ration could be reheated, directly in its metal container, on a small stove - whenever one was available. Failing which, the heat of a truck engine could also suffice, if there was one in the area. Although constantly on the go since they had landed on *Utah Beach*, the men from the 4th Division were only to enjoy their first hot meal after Cherbourg was captured. Neither ration was intended to be used for too long - six days at the very most for the K-ration

Sergeant Jenkins using his own home-made stove.

- to avoid monotony and revulsion. However, the reality facing the troops on the front line was often quite different. The D-ration, consisted of high-calorie and high vitamin content chocolate bars. It was supposed to be a survival ration, for use only in the case of absolute necessity. The B-ration in turn consisted of frozen meat, dry vegetables, fresh bread, milk, coffee, etc., and was exclusively reserved for garrison and camp troops.

Most rations included - over and above a main dish - sweets, cigarettes, chewing gum, dehydrated milk and instant coffee, a "strange mixture that even pigs would have refused" according to some. Dieticians were particularly attached to lemon powder, because of its ascorbic properties; however, it was unanimously hated by troops due to its acidity and bitter taste. It was, "barely good enough to scrub the pans," one sergeant exclaimed. The remaining sachets of "lemonade" that had not simply been thrown away were drunk with large quantities of sugar... or even alcohol!

The British 10-in-1 ration was indubitably the most appreciated by all. Delivered in 45lb cases, it was intended to feed ten men and included a more varied diet, with five different menus, bacon, cereals, tinned milk and even fruit in syrup. However, its weight and bulk meant that it was more appropriate for rear troops or for troops close to the front but with means of transport such as armoured or artillery units. However, it was far more difficult to supply it to front line infantrymen. When it did arrive - which was relatively rare - the men complained that only the less popular menus were left, accusing their buddies of keeping the best for themselves.

Although their nutritional quality was not to be criticised, the unappetising nature of the C- and K-rations, which were the most frequently consumed, was to have an impact on military operations, as overtly reported by the supply corps, "Men in combat need to be correctly fed, not only to preserve their energy, but also to overcome

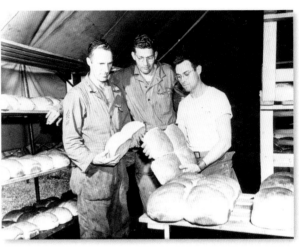

A mobile bakery in the Cotentin.

Engineers preparing their meal on a portable stove in one of Cherbourg's streets.

A quick "bite to eat" in an ammunition store.

fatigue and nervous tension. We have noticed that even famished soldiers, after severe hostilities, are reluctant to take in sufficient quantities of food that is cold and tasteless. And this lack of appetite can only weaken their physical resistance and intensify their fatigue. In contrast, we have observed that warm meals reinforce their fighting spirit."

On the front, the lack of fresh produce had a particular impact. The luckiest of those who ventured through the Normandy bocage came across abandoned farms, falling face-to-face with the farmyard animals and vegetable gardens, swallowing up eggs or voraciously devouring raw carrots, or even potatoes which - far from ripe - were likely to considerably upset their digestive system.

To the rear, days were generally punctuated, as in civilian life, by mealtimes. On the front, these familiar daily highlights were erased. The law was set down by battle and troops ate or slept only when the opportunity arose. Sometimes they were to wait for a long time.

Nevertheless, the odd godsend did arrive. Tom Porcella was a paratrooper in the 82nd Division, which had found itself isolated to the west of the River Merderet shortly after the landings and was soon to fall short of supplies, "Since D-Day, the only food I had eaten was a few chocolate bars, and I began to feel weak from hunger. We searched constantly for food, or for anyone who could give us something to eat. Some of the French people shunned us, but we were to find out later that they were under the threat of death if they were caught aiding us in any way. Looking out my *foxhole* one morning, I saw a trooper carrying a huge piece of meat. I asked him if the main part of the regiment had broken through and brought supplies. 'Hell, no. One of the troopers shot a cow and everyone is cutting up slabs of beef. You want some?' Of course I did, and he cut off a portion. I put it in my canteen cup with some water and boiled it. A residue formed on top of the water which looked and smelled too horrible to eat. I threw it away and still was hungry…"

The K-ration was often the only food available for troops in their *foxholes.*

Although the rear troops did not always escape standard rations and dehydrated food, somewhat half-heartedly prepared by cooks, they at least had the opportunity of somewhat improving their everyday fare with fresh produce. For Normandy, far from on its knees, abounded with victuals, all the more so since the trade routes to Paris - where a great share of local production was exported - had been cut. Meat, butter, milk, cheese, eggs and fruit were available in abundance. Units could also purchase goods to supply the "canteens" installed in tents in their base camps. Direct trade between soldiers and local farmers was, in principle, prohibited by the staff. However, farmers were happy to exchange their produce for fuel or various materials, which were often pilfered from warehouses and depots.

Rear troops also benefited from consumer goods that very rarely reached combat troops. First of all, fresh bread, from the restored industrial bakery in Cherbourg, employing thirty French workers, or the seven mobile bakeries deployed across the bridgehead and producing close to 12 tonnes of bread every day. Similarly, they could enjoy a top quality coffee, roasted and ground on site. Nevertheless, production failed to keep up with consumption, which proved well above expectations, due to difficulties in importing large quantities of *Coca-Cola* or tea and to the low popularity of "artificial lemonade". Among the other advantages, they also had easier and faster access to Red Cross *Clubmobiles*, trucks where pleasant young ladies distributed coffee and doughnuts (over 1.5 million in just two months). The same applied to PXs (*Post eXchanges*), stores managed by the Supply Corps and opened, for example, in Cherbourg and Berneville where troops could purchase cheap extra rations, chocolate, cigarettes, beer, *Coca-Cola*, razor blades, toothpaste and many other goods.

Projection of the film entitled *Casanova Brown* at the Eldorado cinema in Cherbourg, organised by the Special Services.

The US Army's Special Services were in charge of offering the GIs entertaining activities similar to those to which they were accustomed in the United States or the United Kingdom, starting with film projections. In Cherbourg, the *Eldorado* cinema, specially re-opened for the American troops on the 18th of July, was constantly full and other cinemas needed to be found to satisfy demand. Very few recent Hollywood pictures were available. Nevertheless, the projection of *Casanova Brown*, featuring Gary Cooper, was presented as a "world premiere". In the Cotentin and Bessin countryside, mobile units offered film projections in rather less comfortable conditions. Films were frequently in minimally furnished barns with a white sheet for a screen, and before an audience of soldiers who often had to sit on their helmets, no seats being available. Equipment was of poor quality and technical hitches frequent, each time earning the poor projectionist a chorus of cries and protestation, "Throw

that guy out!"; "Bring us a chap who knows how that damn machine works!"

The United Service Organization (USO), a private yet State-subsidised organisation, endeavoured to offer some solace to the American soldiers who were far from home. Upon the organisation's initiative, artists travelled over from the United States to offer the GIs stationed in Normandy a diversified entertainment programme, in particular wounded troops in hospitals. Among them, the highly popular actor Edward G. Robinson, famous for his gangster film roles. French productions also contributed, including *Les Grandes Tournées* by André Fleury from Paris, who had initially been invited to the Cotentin to entertain the German soldiers. Dance, theatre, concerts and song… were generally given a triumphant welcome. Entertaining the troops and, concurrently, boosting their morale, also consisted in offering them sports equipment and the radios they clamoured for to listen to their favourite music and to keep up to date with news from the United States or from across the globe. They were also provided with newspapers. The most popular was indisputably *The Stars and Stripes*, the US armed forces' official daily newspaper, written "for the soldiers". They also read *Yank*, a weekly and richly illustrated army magazine of which 75,000 copies were distributed across the bridgehead. Certain units, such as the 29th Division, published their own "papers", which were, in fact, simple duplicated sheets printed on both sides.

On this subject, as on that of many other day-to-day pleasures, combat troops were less fortunate. On the front, rest periods were - first and foremost - an opportunity for many to simply light up a cigarette as Ernie Pyle recalled, "Murph never smoked cigarettes until he landed in France on D-day, but after that he smoked one after another. He was about the tenth soldier who had told me that same thing.

A guy in war has to have some outlet for his nerves, and I guess smoking is as good as anything." Others took advantage of calmer intervals to read the letters or newspapers they more or less regularly received. Certain, less imaginative troops, cleaned their guns, ate or took a nap in an attempt to recover from so much lost sleep.

If truth be told, for GIs engaged in the front lines, the opportunity to forget the war - at least for an instant - was rare. It essentially involved their transfer, in turns, to *rest and restauration areas*, set up to the rear of the front, in Barneville for example. Quite a different life awaited them there. It was a long-awaited opportunity to take a shower, have a close shave, a change of clothing, but also for a few purchases at the PX, to see the odd film or USO show, to read one of the paperbacks published by the Armed Service Editions, or to quietly take the time to write letters, collect overdue parcels or attend religious services given by chaplains...

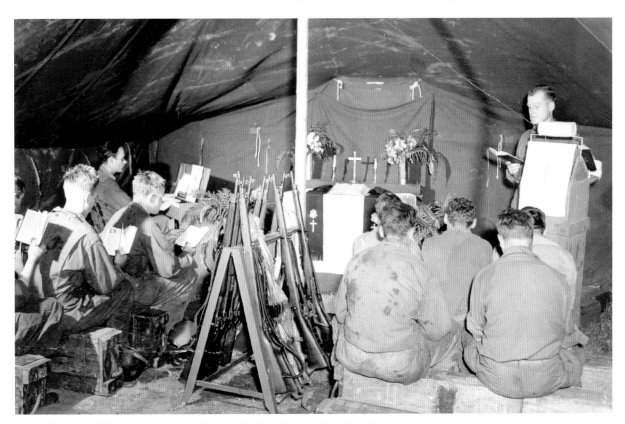

Father Bornheoft's "permanent chapel", set up in Vierville from the 9th of June.

A special link with "home": mail

In all armies across the globe, soldiers' lives are pleasantly punctuated by the arrival of mail. For the GIs, it provided a very special link with their families, thousands of miles from Normandy. On the other side of the Atlantic, wives, parents, brothers and sisters impatiently awaited news from France with mixed feelings of eagerness and genuine concern.

Here is Lieutenant John Allsup's moving account of these special moments, "The guys who didn't get mail went for the C-rations and the rest stopped what they were doing to catch up on home! With the arrivail of mail each of us became more vulnerable to sentiment. I had opened my mail and was lost somewhere between Chicago and Texas. God, but it was good to hear from my two girls!!! Sweet Mary, who was my life and sweet Mom, who gave me life. Mary's letter was full of news and love, oh my God she was precious, while Mom was full of sage advice and prayers for my safety. I had to chuckle when she warned me about 'keeping my feet dry and to be sure and have clear underwear on every day!' If only she could see her 'little boy' now."

Given the expected scale of exchanges between the United States and the armed forces positioned in Europe, the US Army proved to be particularly innovative by creating, as early as 1942, a mail system referred to as V-Mail (*Victory Mail*), aimed at reducing the volume of shipped mail and at speeding up its delivery. Soldiers

were provided with blank forms. After being censored, which could involve blue-pencilling dates, locations or officer names, letters were transferred to a mail processing centre and microfilmed - one reel containing up to 2,000 letters. Microfilms were flown to the United States, where each letter was reprinted on photographic paper, placed in an envelope and sent to its addressee. For mail heading in the opposite direction, a propaganda campaign was aimed at encouraging families to use the same system for keeping in touch with the "boys". As such, considerable time was saved. Letters sent by air mail were delivered around a week later, compared to a month if sent by sea.

Sergeant Stevenson from the 2nd Infantry Division writing to his family in Texas.

The Stars & Stripes

The Stars & Stripes had already been published for men from the American Expeditionary Force posted in France during the First World War. It reappeared in London during the Second World War in April 1942, to take the form of a daily newspaper in November. After the D-Day Landings, it was delivered to GIs within the bridgehead, though sporadically and often late for its air transport was not among priorities, which aroused a certain degree of criticism.

As early as the 16th of June, Charles F. Kiley , one of the paper's editors posted in Sainte-Mère-Église, published a continental issue - no more than a modest duplicated bulletin, designed as a simple supplement to the London issue.

When Cherbourg was captured, the *The Stars & Stripes'* Normandy team began actively looking for a printer. The very first continental issue - on just two pages due to paper shortages - was published on the 4th of July, thanks to the *La Presse cherbourgeoise* (formerly *Cherbourg-Éclair*) rotary presses. By mid August, the US Armed Forces' daily newspaper left Cherbourg to head for Rennes, within the premises of *Ouest-Éclair*.

The *Liberty Club* in Cherbourg. The Ratti department store in Rue Gambetta, converted into a club reserved for black soldiers.

Within the Normandy bridgehead, black soldiers represented around a third of total logistic troops enlisted in the Armed Service Forces (ASF). In Cherbourg, they even represented one in two troops, in particular within the vast majority of port battalions in charge of unloading freight from the *Liberty Ships*.

Given the tense race-related relationships between black and white troops and the difficulties already experienced in the United Kingdom, the high command was keen, more than ever, to maintain segregation. The aim was clearly to prevent, as much as possible, any contact between the two communities in order to avoid any tension - or even clashes - likely to compromise the port's smooth running and, concurrently, the United States' strategic interests.

Consequently, the majority of black troops were positioned in separate camps, often in tents pitched in fields a few miles from Cherbourg. Every morning, they had to go - often on foot - to their workplace, where a particularly gruelling day's work awaited them: twelve hour shifts, both day and night, seven days a week. However, the high command claimed that it was "the only possible way" to process the necessary tonnage.

Access to brothels in Cherbourg also posed a problem for the military authorities, due both to the risk of venereal disease and the fact that prostitution was illegal in the United States. It was finally decided that licensed brothels should be "tolerated". All that remained was to ensure strict medical and Military Police surveillance. Use of these establishments also required to be regulated. One of the "authorised" brothels was reserved specifically for white soldiers, whilst another was defined as "mixed", a somewhat hypocritical term which, in reality, meant that it would be exclusively used by blacks. The same problem arose on the subject of two clubs opened by the American Red Cross in Cherbourg in July, aimed at offering the GIs a little "healthy relaxation". After a disagreement in principle with the representative from the Red Cross, the army reached a conclusion. To "avoid any problems", the *Victory Club* was to be reserved for whites and - ironically - the *Liberty Club* for blacks. However, despite these "precautions", fighting did break out between blacks and whites, generally at night, and often in the town's most "heated" districts. All it took for a fight to break out was for white GIs to enter a café where black GIs were dancing with young French girls.

Black war correspondents paid visits to their coloured buddies to enquire about their activities, their health and their morale, in order to convey information to their compatriots back in the United States. In August, Benjamin O. Davis, the first - and at the time the only - black US Army general, paid a visit to the bridgehead. In keeping with the role he had been assigned by the high command, his mission consisted in inspecting black troops in European theatres of operation. As he meandered his way through the Cotentin and Bessin, he made frequent stopovers in camps, not only to question soldiers, but also to remind them of the importance of their role in the success of *Overlord*. Brigadier General Davis relentlessly pleaded in favour of better integration

for black troops in the US Army, in particular among combat troops. Yet, it was only in the very last months of the war that his pleas were finally heard.

Black soldiers from the Army Service Forces in charge of watching over German prisoners of war.

General Benjamin O. Davis (1877-1970), the first black US Army general.

Black soldiers in Normandy

Very few black troops were enlisted in the combat units engaged in Normandy. Two field artillery battalions and one air defence battalion were among the rare exceptions. Such were the consequences of racial discrimination in the US Army. In contrast, African Americans represented a major share, estimated to be a good third, of logistic troops.

Many black soldiers could also be seen behind the wheel of military trucks. Many others were in charge of stevedoring operations, especially in Cherbourg where they were particularly abundant among port battalions responsible for unloading cargoes. They were also employed for clearing and repairing roads, railway tracks and telephone lines, as nurses or stretcher-bearers in healthcare services, or as POW wardens, without forgetting the 320th Barrage Balloon Battalion, one of the rare "black" units to land on the 6th of June.

The role of black GIs in Normandy was often overshadowed by the more spectacular and glorious feats of white troops. They nevertheless provided an essential contribution towards the operational prowess of the American war machine.

AMERICANS AND NORMANS:
THE ENCOUNTER

1st of August 1944, near Avranches.

In the collective memory, Normandy's liberation is generally evoked in a similar manner. Certain representations are engraved in our memories and passed on from generation to generation: those of the GIs being welcomed with enthusiasm and emotion, covered with flowers and kisses and offered copious quantities of cider and calvados; those of the population discovering with surprise and wonder - not the British troops they were expecting - but those grand, friendly and nonchalant American soldiers - their equipment as abundant as it was surprising - forthcoming with children, generously handing out sweets, chocolate, chewing gum, cigarettes... Although these images, reproduced and shared at length by Signal Corps photographers, largely depicted reality, they failed to cast a convenient shadow over the overtly more complex relationships between the Normans and their liberators, which varied both with time and with location.

Canned food was distributed to civilians.

Rather awkward first contact

Although they had barely set foot on Norman soil, the GIS - overwrought by the violence of hostilities - frequently blindly opened fire, hails of bullets showering the bushes or closed doors, sometimes inadvertently killing civilians. On the 6th of June, paratroopers took up quarters in the Manoir de Brécourt, near Sainte-Marie-du-Mont, ousting out a German detachment. Michel de Valavieille, the family son, was shot down by an uneasy GI as he advanced to greet them. Seriously wounded, he was transported to England and, mercifully, survived this tragic incident. Without for as much always being quite so dramatic, early contact was nevertheless tense. A railwayman's daughter, who was 11 at the time, kept an indelible memory of a face-to-face encounter between her family and an American soldier on the early hours of the 6th of June, "My father had seen aeroplanes and parachutists

Cleaning operations after particularly fierce combat. For the GIs, caution was of the essence.

Sainte-Mère-Église.

in the skies around Sainte-Mère-Église. He rushed back home to wake the family and to fetch a bottle to celebrate. He turned to go down the cellar, but before he had taken two steps the kitchen door was suddenly kicked open from outside. Standing framed against the darkness was a strangely dressed man carrying a machine-gun, which was aimed menacingly at us. Here we were ready to kiss and laugh and celebrate; instead of which, this fierce-looking stranger, his jaw set, his gun trained on us, had burst in on us from nowhere. He kicked the door shut behind him, as violently as he had kicked it open. He didn't say a word. He just kept looking at us, as though waiting for someone to make a wrong move. My heart was pounding; I sensed, in that frozen moment, that if any of us did move then he would surely kill us on the spot... Finally the stranger broke the silence, 'Friend or foe?' he asked, in perfect French.

"Suspicious" civilians being transferred to England for interrogation.

What a silly question, I thought; as if anyone would ever answer 'Foe'! In the heavy silence, the intermittent roar of the planes contrasted strangely with the quiet, persistent ticking of our old clock. It was [six-year-old] Claude who finally answered him. 'Friends, Monsieur - we're all friends'. His high little voice echoed round the room as he walked straight up to the soldier, his hands stretching out towards the barrel of the machine-gun. 'Friends', the soldier repeated, lowering the gun at last. 'Really friends?' And he ran his grimy hand through Claude's hair. We all breathed again. Following my little brother's example, I went over to the soldier and kissed him on the cheek. He looked surprised, but pleased. The whole room now relaxed, and my parents came back to life and walked over to him. The soldier pulled a map from his pocket and laid it out on the table. 'Show me where the Germans are', he said."

On the same morning, Captain Chouvaloff, an officer from the 101st Airborne, asked Alexandre Renaud, the local chemist and mayor of Sainte-Mère-Église, to tell him where the German commander's house was, "I offered to take him there. He said, 'OK', and off we went. He didn't speak. A young local joined us. The Captain became suspicious and asked us to walk in front of him and, after he had pulled out his revolver, he asked the young man to break down the door. The commander had fled. A fortnight late, I reminded Captain Chouvaloff, by then my friend, of this anecdote. He apologised and said, 'We had heard so many stories about French collaborationists that we were kind of scared of you.'" Over the days that followed the landings, the GIs' maintained a suspicious attitude towards civilians. For the SHAEF's high command had, indeed, launched several appeals, by means of leaflets or via the BBC,

The GIs habit of, first of all, accepting Norman hospitality rapidly disappeared.

and deadly for civilians. General Bradley was perfectly aware of this negative psychological impact when, on the 9th of June, he entered Isigny - liberated yet horrendously devastated by naval artillery fire, "A few villagers searched sorrowfully through the ruins of their homes. From one, an aged man and his wife carried the twisted skeleton of a brass bed. And down the street, a woman carefully removed the curtain from a paneless window in the remaining wall of what had been the village café. For more than four years the people of Isigny had awaited this moment of liberation. Now they stared accusingly on us from the ruins that covered their dead."

Concurrently, the 1st Division progressed towards Balleroy, covered by heavy artillery fire and demolishing anything in its way. "A bewildering method to the Normans who watched them squander phenomenal quantities of projectiles, often on secondary targets," a Bessin inhabitant related. "To calm the tempest, brave Frenchmen went ahead of the Americans, guaranteeing the Germans had left, leading the march to save their villages. Some said, "They use their guns too much. A simple patrol would have sufficed to occupy the field."

for civilians to leave the coast. So were those who had chosen to stay not simply German sympathisers? How could anyone tell? A number of coastal inhabitants, considered as suspect by the Americans, were arrested and taken by force to England to be interrogated, before returning to Normandy a few days later. Many a soldier began by accepting a taste of the local produce or the friendly glass he was offered, which was only to add further incomprehension and frustration among their hosts. However, their behaviour was soon to change! Many Normans in turn were curious as to the outcome of combat. The Dieppe catastrophe in 1942 was still fresh in many memories. Faced with the premise of a victorious German counter-attack, caution was of the essence. It would take time before confidence reigned between both camps. Furthermore, the American combat methods proved to be both devastating

Amidst the ruins of Isigny.

"Initially distant, the Normans quickly became friendly"

In the autumn of 1943, the American military services had drafted a series of manuals intended for Civil Affairs officers and offering a detailed presentation of each region, its characteristics, its economy, its administrative officers... Zone Handbook n°9 dealt with Normandy and offered a depiction of its inhabitants, "The Norman, naturally taciturn and reserved, withholds his judgment "peut-être que oui, peut-être que non" is one of his favourite phrases. He observes. He observes inimically distrusting newcomers. He is a realist, and acts count with him. It is the bombing that they have minded most: that joined to the great spate of German propaganda might be expected to produce a fair amount of anti-Allied feeling. It seems neither widespread nor fundamental in character. However, one should be prepared for some degree of animosity: it will probably be concealed, but it will be there. Normandy is a rich country, and possessive people with a lot to lose cannot take kindly to bombing."

Montebourg. "The old churches have not been spared from Allied attacks."

Consequently, with the exception of Cherbourg, which was for a long time the only town to have been liberated virtually intact, the first contact between the Americans and liberated civilians was far from exuberant or demonstrative. "The Normans were initially quite aloof," an official 1st Army report resumed, adding immediately afterwards, "However, they have very quickly become friendly and cooperative." In an article entitled, "War comes to the people of Normandy" Life magazine adopted an indulgent outlook, "They were friendly but they had a certain provincial reserve. Many greeted the troops with mixed emotions. The Allies, after all, had brought the war with them. The rich dairy herd had been slaughtered in the fields by

bullets and shell fragments. Allied artillery had wrecked the lovely little towns. The ancient cathedral had been hit by Allied fire because Germans choose to use them as observation posts. Any allied wooing of the people

The language barrier.

was also complicated by the fact that the Germans in the area had been almost human."

When conversation finally did get going, and despite the language barrier, some Normans tried to help the GIs to grasp a point of view that they tended to have trouble understanding. Françoise de Hauteclocque, whose village - Sainte-Suzanne near La Haye-du-Puits - had just been liberated after bitter combat, was one of them, "Every one of those soldiers brought with him something good for France. They dreamt of an enthusiastic welcome, of flowers, of kisses. Some of them bitterly complained about the rather cold welcome extended by the Norman people. Yet those who fought here understood why. What did they meet with, in reality, in those devastated villages? A few poor stunned individuals, overwhelmed by fear, by noise, totally inert before their collapsed homes, their annihilated livestock and, often alas, their lost loved ones. Could those people truly hail them? Nevertheless, our little hamlet in Sainte-Suzanne rolled out the red carpet for them. Their response to our welcome was in the form of friendliness and generosity. Provisions and military rations of all sorts were distributed. They paid incessant visits, one after another. They wanted to see all those foreign civilians grouped together before them, to try to repair, by all sorts of kind gestures, the unintentional harm they had caused us. A few days later, a young artilleryman came to see us. He looked at my son's torn dungarees, then at his own khaki uniform. 'I think we're the same size,' - 'No please,' I retorted, 'Do keep your trousers,' - 'I've got another pair under those ones.' And the khaki trousers immediately became the property of my elder son. This gallant Yank was unfamiliar with the legend of Saint Martin. So I told him the story."

A surprising survey in the Cotentin

In June, the British newspaper the *Sunday Pictorial* published a vitriolic article against the Normans, written by a certain Rex North and entitled, "These people terrify me." He claimed that 60% of the population hated the Allies, that men spat when they walked by and even that mysterious women shot them in the back. This violent diatribe was to arouse much controversy in the British press and genuine concern among the Allied high command, including the American generals. They were consequently keen to glean more trustworthy information on the Normans' viewpoint.

"They dreamt of kisses."

A Psychological Warfare Division officer talking to civilians in Cherbourg.

According to survey, three people out of four expressed no criticism with regard to the Americans.

To clarify things once and for all, the Psychological Warfare division set to organising a survey among Cotentin inhabitants. Ten young enquirers were appointed to conduct the survey from the 11th to the 25th of July among a thousand inhabitants and following the Gallup representative sampling method; they questioned men and women of different professions and ages and from both rural and urban locations. Theirs answers were of no great surprise; but then how could they be? Normans are traditionally reserved, in particular when facing a totally new and hitherto unknown exercise. One of the enquirers spoke of "mistrustful" respondents who gave "trite or restrained" answers, and of many totally indifferent participants who "considered the survey of very little value."

The forty questions asked covered issues on information, supply provision and, of course, relationships between the Allies in general and the Americans in particular. Although 75% of respondents were delighted the landings had taken place, 17% were unhappy to see France back at war, with its wake of dead and wounded among civilians, not forgetting the risk Germans might return... and retaliate. Sixty-eight percent spoke of friendly exchanges with the Allies, against 1% who expressed a contradictory opinion and 9% - typical Normans - who claimed they had only seen them from a distance. Three quarters of respondents expressed no particular criticism aimed at the American soldiers, some of them even stressing the contrary; however 21% disagreed, accusing them of being unruly, excessively noisy, keen pilferers, of treating the German prisoners too well and - particularly on the subject of black soldiers - of drinking unreasonably and of exerting an excessively close grip on certain Norman ladies. A few cases of rape were even brought to light. The first dated from the 14th of June, in Vierville. The culprit, a black soldier named Clarence Whitfield, was hung two months later in the gardens of the Château de Canisy.

Civil Affairs entered into action

Civil Affairs teams, trained in the United States since 1943, set foot on Norman soil just a few days after the D-Day Landings. By late July, thirty-seven detachments were in place, essentially in cities and large market towns, reuniting around five hundred men, around half of whom were French-speaking officers. Their mission consisted in taking charge of the local population, in order to satisfy their urgent needs whilst waiting till the French authorities - with whom they hoped to establish excellent links - were ready to take over. The key aim was to prevent - to the rear of the front lines - any problems arising, of any nature whatsoever likely to compromise the smooth running of military operations, which Eisenhower had defined as the absolute priority.

One of the first tasks they were to accomplish - for obvious sanitary reasons - was to bury the many animals killed in the fields during combat. Civilians were called upon to complete the job. In an aim to restore "law

The Civil Affairs office in Trévières.

AVIS au Public

Jusqu'à nouvel ordre, tout déplacement à pied ou par n'importe quel autre moyen de locomotion à une distance supérieure à

SIX Kilomètres

du domicile est strictement prohibé.

Toutes les demandes d'autorisation de déplacement en dehors de cette zone de SIX kilomètres de rayon, doivent être adressées au Bureau des Affaires Civiles dont dépend le domicile du requérant.

and order" - to which Anglo-Saxons are traditionally attached - as fast as possible, courts were re-opened, police forces and French Gendarmeries set up, back-up troops offering appropriate support to all. Concurrently, Civil Affairs began to impose a series of military security measures to prevent espionage and sabotage operations: imposing curfews and black-outs, prohibiting moving more than six kilometres (4 miles) from home without permission, prohibiting the possession of weapons or carrier pigeons, prohibiting travelling with cameras or binoculars... These restrictions to personal liberties - painful reminders of the German occupation - were extremely unpopular and rarely abided by, much to the dismay of the Americans.

Civil Affairs, who were the only units to benefit from appropriate means of transport, consequently took on the problem of the thousands of refugees who were eager to return home as soon as possible, in particular those from Cherbourg. This proved to be a tricky operation given the congestion on the roads. Temporary transit camps were set up in the Château de Francqueville near Fontenay-sur-Mer, in the Château de Cavigny to the north of Pont-Hébert, in Blanchelande... Although relatively rudimentary, they nevertheless provided sufficient food, covers, pharmaceutical products and soap.

The local economy also needed to be rapidly revived. To do so, Engineer units were brought in to re-establish communication links, electric and telephone networks, not forgetting precious tap water. Banks and post offices were also re-opened, priority being placed on official mail. Along the coast, fishing was permitted as from late July, however only under certain conditions. Efforts to recruit civilian manpower, particularly in Cherbourg, were long to offer satisfactory results. Tension was quick to develop between the French workers, who were not particularly keen on their long working hours and mediocre pay, and their

Bread was scarce in Cotentin.

Civil Affairs in La Haye-du-Puits were in charge of bringing refugees back home.

American employers who considered them to be unruly, demanding, discontented and devoted pilferers. In contrast, the situation with regard to food supplies proved to be far less dramatic than expected. Official documents reported that the local population was on the verge of famine, "France has been pillaged by the Nazis to such an extent that people don't even have the vital necessities. Almost the entire French population is underfed and many have even died of starvation." The reality the Americans discovered - or at least in Normandy - was quite different; hence a few misunderstandings over certain demands, as reported by Major Maginnis, commander of the Civil Affairs detachment posted in Carentan, "The mayor came to me and said that the people were starving. I said, 'How can that be, M. Joret? You have tons of beef, butter and milk, and you have some fruits and vegetables.' 'Yes,' he replied, 'but we have no bread.' It seemed ludicrous to me that in this rich area of France people were going to starve just because of a shortage of flour."

The major was very probably oblivious to the fact that this breeding region did not produce wheat and that bread formed the very basis of the average Norman diet. Since there was, in reality, no major food shortage, there was consequently no need to massively import foodstuffs. Civil Affairs contented themselves with distributing bread and a few cans of food to the most needy.

Distributing canned food in Hiesville.

Controlling information

Whilst Civil Affairs were looking after material questions, the Psychological Warfare Division (PWD) set to tackling informing civilian populations, often deprived of up-to-date information since the landings. The priority was not only to bring to their attention the decisions made by military and civilian authorities, but also to inform them of wartime events, particularly in Normandy, in order to boost their confidence and to encourage the best possible alliance. *Liberator*, "the very first Allied daily printed on French soil" saw the day on the 16th of June. Drafted in French and printed in Isigny, this modest paper was sold for one French franc and profits were donated to the Red Cross.

Captain Dolan (to the right) and Daniel Yon, editor, discovering the first issue of *La Presse Cherbourgeoise*, printed on the 3rd of July.

In the Radio-Cherbourg studios.

The first newspaper to be published in Normandy by the US Army.

It was published up to the 5th of July, the date that marked the arrival of a "proper" newspaper. Captain Dolan, a PWD officer, took the initiative of publishing a new daily, *La Presse Cherbourgeoise*, printed by the *Cherbourg-Éclair* presses, following the prohibition of the latter for collaborationism. In the meantime, another team was busy setting up Radio-Cherbourg, the first radio station to be broadcast in liberated France, early July. Perched on the town heights, its range stretched over 45 miles. The daily two-hour programme included Civil Affairs press releases and retransmissions of BBC programmes. Unfortunately, throughout a large share of the Cotentin and Bessin, many families were unable to tune into these programmes. In March 1944, the Germans had requisitioned all wireless sets from throughout Normandy to prevent inhabitants from listening to the BBC and those who had succeeded in hanging on to their own did not necessarily have electricity. The Americans therefore decided to travel across the bridgehead with trucks equipped with loud speakers to publicly announce information. Every day, each vehicle drove through around thirty villages. Other methods were deployed for informing and boosting the population's confidence, within the context of what the PWD referred to as "consolidation propaganda". Photographs were displayed in shop windows, where crowds gathered to catch the latest update on wartime affairs. Posters printed in England were stuck on every wall, in every town and village. Their aim was to extol patriotism, "Freedom for the French", "Hail the Resistance... and forward march." Film projections were organised wherever possible, often using mobile resources. War films, such as *Desert Victory*, were screened, preceded by newsreels illustrating the Allied advance on all fronts.

A PWD soldier sticking new posters up in Colombières.

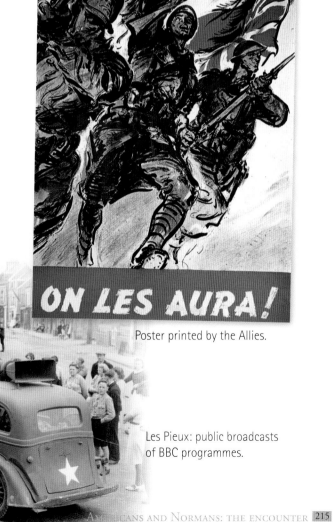

Poster printed by the Allies.

Les Pieux: public broadcasts of BBC programmes.

"Everything's old in Normandy"

During the summer of 1944, many young Americans discovered a land of which they knew nothing and which was to surprise them in many respects: the countryside, in particular, still cooped up in 19th century tradition, with its tiny fields bordered with hedgerows and its farmers with their very strange shoes - extremely noisy wooden clogs - and with no knowledge of how a tractor worked. Towns - or at least those that still stood - were equally astonishing with their small narrow streets, and their homes, as yet devoid of modern comforts. A genuine culture shock for the sons of the world's most influential economic power, most of whom had become accustomed to quite a different lifestyle.

Ernie Pyle was one of them, "Everything seems old in Normandy. The towns and cities are just as old and worn-looking. I didn't see a building in Normandy that appeared to have been built within the last three generations. Even Cherbourg was a surprise. All of its buildings are old and worn. A street scene in Cherbourg looks so much like the Hollywood sets of old European cities that the perspective is reversed and

Rubber-soled boots... and wooden clogs.

it seems that Cherbourg has just been copied from a movie set. It was a contrast to other war cities we passed through – Algiers and Palermo and even Naples – where much building and remodeling had been done in this century, and the new homes were shiny and modernistic, and the street fronts looked almost American."

Normandy seemed so remote and so different from the vast American landscapes and their wooden ranches, "Everything is of stone. Even the barns and cowsheds are stone and in exactly the same design and usually the same size as the houses. They are grouped closely together around a square, so that a farmer's home makes a compact little settlement of buildings that from a distance resembles a country estate." He even found the bocage landscapes far removed from those he had seen in England, "Everything there is less polished and more natural. The hedgerows are thick and ancient. The stone walls are sometimes so mounded over with earth you don't know there's a wall beneath. The trees in the apple orchards are mellow with moss so thick that it seems like a coat of green velvet. All our soldiers

Norman farms were very different
from western American ranches.

Papier-mâché copy of a Hollywood set, Cherbourg?

POCKET GUIDE TO

FRANCE

Encounter between two very different worlds in a Cotentin farm.

were impressed by the loveliness of the Normandy countryside."

The GIs also found themselves confronted with a population whose customs were unlike their own. For this very reason, the high command had provided each of them with a *Pocket Guide to France*, just like the one they had been given when they arrived in the United Kingdom. It included a few typical clichés, "The French are good talkers and magnificent cooks – If there still is anything left to put in the pot. French talk and French food have contributed more than anything else to the French reputation." It also abounded with good advice, "The French are not given to confidences, or to telling how much money they make. The French also shake hands on greeting each other. They are not back slappers. It's not their way." Equal efforts were made to enlighten young Americans on the fact that French women did not necessarily fit with their rather seductive reputation, "France has been represented too often in fiction as a frivolous nation where sly winks and coy pats on the rear are the accepted form of address. You'd better get rid of such notions right now if you are going to keep out of trouble. France is full of decent women and strict women. Most French girls have less freedom than girls back home. If you get a date don't be surprised if her parents want to meet you first, to size you up." They were encouraged to be wary of prostitutes due to the risk of venereal disease. The *Warweek* newspaper frequently broached the subject, "If you have a Don Juan attitude towards French women, don't be a fool. You've already been told – and you'll be told again – that French women are respectable. But there are whores in France, just as there are in most places. Whores look like whores. They're over-dressed, over-powered and over-perfumed. They smoke in public, and they don't hide their intentions. They're on the streets and in houses known as 'bordels'."

Conversation made easy thanks to the *French Phrase* Book.

On a different vein, with regard to progress in purely material commodities, France's relative lateness was highlighted without for as much coming as a surprise, "French provincial towns might have more charm and beauty than some of our small towns, but not necessarily as much entertainment. They are about like what your home town was when your father was a boy, before movies, the radio and the family car changed all that. Public entertainment in any French town centers in its cafés, called 'bistrots'. French beer is flatter than our beer. The French have never liked their drinks ice-cold just as they have never liked strong mixtures liked cocktails. They prefer aperitifs which are mostly cooked wines. To the French the café is much more and much less than a bar. It's the social center. The Frenchmen play belotte or dominoes. The workman, in his velveteen pantaloons and beret look more picturesque than his opposite number back home in the United States."

Language was an obvious and sizeable barrier to communication between the GIs and the Normans. Very few Americans spoke French and vice versa. Hence, over and above their *Pocket Guides*, American soldiers were also provided with *French Phrase Books*, small glossaries covering essential vocabulary and a few useful expressions. Translations were provided alongside English terms, together with a phonetic transcription to overcome the major difficulty of pronunciation,

Miss = Mademoiselle (Mad-mwa-zel)

Please = S'il vous plaît (Seel voo play)

I am thirsty = J'ai soif (Jay swaf)

I want to eat = Je voudrais manger (Juh voo-dray mahn-jay)

Many Americans were quick to make even simpler use of their phrase books, as Private Lloyd explained in a letter to his wife, "Of course, we have learned a few words of French. But we communicate especially by gestures. We have been given a small glossary. All we need to do is find the phrase we're looking for and point to it with our finger. The French then read the translation and they know what we want."

In Le Hommet-d'Arthenay, an old lady watching a 4th Division column from behind her rabbit cage.

The Norman-American "honeymoon"

At the end of the report summarising the results of the survey conducted in the Cotentin, an information officer reached the following conclusions, "In Normandy the Allies, up to late July, were living in a honeymoon period. To put it another way, they had a credit in their favor at the bank. The Allied landings were long expected and the uppermost emotional feeling was a sense of relief and optimism over the Allied successes and joy at the thought of coming freedom."

Fourth of July - Independence Day celebrations in Trévières.

Trying to get closer to a young Norman girl.

In fact, in the towns and villages that had been spared devastation following the hostilities, the Star Spangled Banner was flown on house windows and banners were attached to their facades, "Welcome to the Americans". Housewives had hastily made their children clothes that proudly boasted the American colours. Excited children shook small flags and offered flowers to the GIs. On the 4th of July, the French authorities and the population largely participated in commemorating Independence Day. In return, the American troops also took part in the Bastille Day celebrations on the 14th of July, in liberated French towns and villages. These scenes were an infinite source of inspiration for Signal Corps photographers, whose missions included portraying these demonstrations of Franco-American friendship and the warm welcome extended to the "boys", back in the United States.

However, contact between front line combat troops and civilians remained sporadic. For - in truth - on the battlefield, opportunities rarely arose. Many villages were in ruins and most of their inhabitants had been evacuated. "The only person I remember meeting and speaking with was a priest. I believe it was in Colleville. We gave him a present of cigarettes," admitted Michael Accordino whose case was far from exceptional. The *P-47 Thunderbolt* pilot Philip Wright, in turn, told of how he was totally absorbed by his mission, "We had received orders to crush Nazism. Firstly, we had no contact with civilians. Secondly, we slept, and when we didn't sleep, we bombed." Others, such as Jack Port from the 4th Infantry Division, appeared to have regrets on this situation for a very specific reason, "We had no time to flirt or have anything to do with the girls. The troops that carne later that were never in combat had a lot of time to play around. We had millions of condoms. Why I will never know, as we never used them for what they were made for, but used them for many other

The Bastille Day ball on the 14th of July in Cherbourg.

things. Such as over the barrels of our rifles to keep them clean, wrap our cigarettes in them, but never for sex as we were never in any one place long enough."

Because they were more firmly settled, men posted to the rear of the front lines had almost daily contact with the Normans, frequently in the form of bartering with local farmers: eggs for chocolate, milk for cigarettes, fresh vegetables for coffee, butter for fuel. As a result, the military staff soon discovered with astonishment a vast number of empty jerry cans scattered across the countryside, to such an extent that they were now lacking in the ranks. Children were therefore asked to collect and bring them to depots; in exchange they were offered "merit certificates" featuring Eisenhower's photograph and signature.

In order to respect Norman tradition, each transaction was an opportunity to "enjoy" a bowl of cider or a dram of calvados, which the GIs were quick to rename "the

devil's fluid". Ernie Pyle had a rather painful memory of it, "A little Frenchman filled our tiny glasses. We raised them, touched glasses all around, and *vived la France* all over the place, and good-will-towards-men rang out through the air and tears ran down our cheeks. In this case, however, the tears were largely induced by our violent efforts to refrain from clutching at our throats and crying out in anguish. In case you don't know, eau de vie is a savage liquid made by boiling barbed wire, soapsuds, watch springs and old tent pegs together. The better brands have a touch of nitroglycerine for flavor. I think every American who connected with a glass of eau de vie should have got a Purple Heart."

However, relationships between the Americans and the Normans were not restricted to simple mercantile exchange. Far more solid links were also forged. Germaine Fenand, a teenager from Trévières, recalled, "For us, the Americans were a bit like the Lord himself.

Children helped recover lost jerry cans.

Calva, "the devil's fluid".

When they drove by in their trucks, they threw out coffee, sweets, chocolate, cigarettes... My brother had an advance stock of least two hundred packets. That's when he started smoking. I didn't dare; my mother didn't want me to. Everyone in the whole country had adopted an American; every family had its own. They camped in the fields and, in the evening - after their day's work, they came to our house to eat and to chat with us. Fried eggs were their favourite. They also drank a lot of cider or calva and often left a little drunk. We spent hours with them. We learned a few English words and they learned some French. It was the same at all our neighbours'. One of them, who visited an old lady, called her his 'French mom'. After the war, we kept in touch for a while with the one who came to our house; his name was Angelo Murray. Despite all that had happened, despite all the destruction and death, we were happy to welcome them and I think they were aware of that."

Children and teenagers were, indeed, the most impatient and eager. They scurried round the American camps, their admiring eyes wide open. Some of them were adopted as the unit mascot. Charles Lemeland was twelve at the time, "It was as if they weren't really taking the war seriously, or at least not all the time. They had a great capacity for making the most of life whenever they could. As children, we had always stayed at a respectable distance from the German soldiers. With the Americans, a wonderful new life of laughter, play and freedom was open to us: as many sweets as we could eat, great fun climbing into tanks and other fascinating machines, being allowed to touch all those levers and pedals, posing for photographs, looking at pictures of their parents and their girlfriends, often in bathing suits - they looked like film stars."

Marcel Levéel and his friends in turn paid frequent visits to canteens, to discover - with much surprise - American cooking, "We very often had to queue for food and we

Vierville: children paid frequent visits to the US Army canteens.

For the time being, relationships appeared to be going well. Yet, forthcoming difficulties were already in the air, as described with lucidity by an information officer in his conclusion to the July 1944 survey, "Today, the Normans were still looking at the Allies through rose-tinted glasses. But our future policy and conduct will determine how inexhaustible the bank balance is. Their enthusiasm was likely to change in proportion to the length of our stay in Normandy." Indeed, over the months that followed, relationships gradually deteriorated, in particular in and around Cherbourg, where the GIs were abundantly present up to the end of the war, to such an extent that some even spoke of the "American occupation." But that's a different story!

were served like soldiers, in a mess tin, sometimes with rather unexpected mixtures. Turkey and chicken rubbed shoulders with peanut butter and marmalade. Delicious ham was served with sugary potatoes. Omelettes, made with powdered eggs, were to be eaten at the end of the meal, for they were also sweet. Steak was cut very thinly and served with particularly thick and sweet tomato sauce - our first taste of ketchup. All of this was very new to us and it was delicious, the bread in particular - it was whiter than white and looked like brioche, but was distributed parsimoniously. In contrast, coffee, which our hosts seemed to have a particular liking for, was available in unlimited quantities."

Sweets for the Isigny children.

How could the Americans escape from the "hedgerow hell"? Such was the question the US First Army's high command was tirelessly trying to answer. Bradley spent long hours in a vast and specially arranged tent near his command post, where he could liberally spread out huge maps across the wooden floor. But what plan should they implement to finally break through the German lines? A general offensive across the entire front, like the one they attempted early July, appeared once more doomed for failure. He therefore considered another solution: a massive attack over a narrower perimeter in order to open a breach his troops could surge and break through.

The American forces were to be reorganised for this crucial phase in military operations. Two armies were reunited within the XII Army Group, placed under Bradley's personal orders; he consequently delegated command of the 1st Army to his second in command, General Hodges. The Third Army was mobilised and entrusted to General Patton who had, so far, been idling in Néhou where he and his staff had established incognito quarters since the 6th of July.

General Bradley and his aide Major Hansen, in the company of US Air Force General Royce.

◀ Granville, early August 1944, before the Cours Jonville war memorial.

General Patton finally came out of the shadows late July 1944.

would have imagined. He originated from a wealthy, pious and well-educated family, readily supplementing his language and behaviour with a hint of brutality. He believed it was, "the best way to lead your men." His Sicilian escapades had earned him several months of purgatory in England. Yet Patton was, first and foremost, one of the most brilliant generals in the US Army and his contribution rapidly proved indispensible. His day was soon to come. In the meantime, he was champing at the bit, whilst the battle continued without him, jotting down in his personal diary a few petulant remarks on his colleagues, "Bradley and Hodges are such nothings." or even "Neither Ike nor Brad has the stuff."...

Bradley developed the *Cobra* plan

Georges S. Patton was a real "star". He willingly posed for photographers, proudly sporting his pearl-handled pistol on his belt or holding his bull terrier Willy on its leash. He was as partial to theatrical poises as he was to sensational statements to the press. Yet he had a complex personality. Behind the merciless commander his men had nicknamed "blood and guts", there was a far more sensitive and multifaceted man than one

Information in Bradley's possession, originating from intelligence services or from the French Resistance, proved that the Germans had not survived the war of the hedgerows intact, quite the contrary. They were

23rd July: infantrymen preparing to take up their positions for operation "Cobra".

short of men, material and ammunition and their defensive line had been perilously narrowed down. Once the front line broken through, they would be struggling considerably to thwart the American advance. The chosen location for the assault comprised a 5.5 mile-wide by 1.5 mile-deep strip to the west of Saint-Lô on the road leading to Périers, in the vicinity of the villages of Hébécrevon, La Chapelle-Enjuger and Montreuil-sur-Lozon. General Collins' VII Corps, which now comprised six divisions, two of which were armoured, was to lead the charge, reinforced on its flanks by three further army corps in charge of stopping the enemy in its tracks. The manoeuvre was to be completed by a turning movement towards Coutances, on the coast, in order to trap a share of the adverse troops. Concurrently, the major road routes leading southwards needed to be cleared to facilitate the progression of armoured and motorised vehicle columns. To break through the German front, Bradley undeniably

had powerful artillery at his disposal; however, it would be difficult to concentrate so many guns within such a restricted perimeter. He consequently opted for saturation bombing, essentially by 8th Air Force twin-engine planes. Each plane could drop an explosive charge equivalent to one hundred guns firing simultaneously. The plan was ready by mid July. Colonel Thorson, in charge of operations for the US First Army, baptised it *Cobra*.

On the 19th of July, Bradley went to the SHAEF air forces' headquarters in Stanmore, to finalise his bombardment plan. He planned for a formidable armada of 1,800 8th Air Force heavy bombers, together with 396 medium bombers and 360 9th Air Force fighter bombers. The attack was to rake the Saint-Lô to Périers road. However, the American troops would need to withdraw to avoid any accidents. For security reasons, aviation officers suggested 3,000 yards, whereas Bradley was looking at only 800, for fear of seeing the Germans

The 35th Division off to war.

Men from the 4th Infantry Division kept a confident eye on the air armada as it approached its target.

reconquer the vacant space. They finally agreed on 1,200 yards. By the end of the conference, everyone - mistakenly - believed that all of their problems had been solved. Operation *Cobra* was scheduled to be launched two days later.

However, persistent poor weather was to postpone the Allied plans. Bradley cursed the skies, "I'm going to have to court-martial the chaplain if we have many more days like this." Initially delayed till the 24th, the attack was, once more, postponed at the last minute. Nevertheless, certain bombers had already taken to the skies and, for some, the counter order came too late. Dropped under poor visibility, bombs fell on an ammunition depot, exploded on the Chippelle airfield and, in particular, hit the American infantry's front lines, killing or wounding 150 soldiers from the 30th Division. Bradley was all the more furious for, contrary to his orders, planes had dropped their projectiles perpendicular to the road - rather than parallel - at considerably greater risk of collateral damage. Yet despite his vehement protest, the airmen maintained a steadfast position. The other solution involved sending planes one behind the other, which would take far longer and would expose them to increased risks of attacks from the FLAK. Bradley and his staff finally accepted, keen to get the operation going again the next day.

Nurses from the 30th Division caring for the wounded after bombings on the 24th of July.

A deluge of bombs over the Germans... and the Americans

Mid-morning on the 25th of July, close behind the fighter bombers on their dive bombing run, the 8th Air Force's four-engine planes approached their target. Once again, Ernie Pyle was among the vanguard, "Our front lines were marked by long strips of colored cloth laid on the ground, and with colored smoke to guide our airmen during the mass bombing. A new sound gradually droned into our ears, a sound deep and all-encompassing with no notes in it – just a gigantic faraway surge of doomlike sound. It was the heavies. They came in flights of twelve, three flights to a group and in groups stretched out across the sky. They came in a constant procession and I thought it would never end. The first huge flight passed directly overhead and then the bombs came. They began like the crackle of popcorn and almost instantly swelled into a monstrous fury of noise that seemed surely to destroy all the world ahead of us. From then on for an hour and a half that had in it the agonies of centuries, the bombs came down. A wall of smoke and dust erected by them grew high in the sky. By now everything was an indescribable caldron of sounds. As we watched, there crept into our consciousness a realization that the windrows of exploding bombs were easing back toward us. Then we were horrified by the suspicion that those machines, high in the sky were aiming their bombs at the smoke line on the ground – and a gentle breeze was drifting the smoke line back over us! We stood tensed in muscle feeling trapped and completely helpless. And then all of an instant the universe became filled with a gigantic rattling. It was bombs by the hundred, hurtling down

through the air above us. We dived. Some got into a dugout. Others made *foxholes* and ditches. There is no description of the sound and fury of those bombs except to say it was chaos, and a waiting for darkness. The air struck us in hundreds of continuing flutters. At last the sound died down and we looked at each other in disbelief. Everything about us was shaken. The leading company of our battalion was to spearhead the attack. The company had been hit directly by our bombs. Their casualties were heavy. Men went to pieces and had to be sent back. I'm sure that back in England that night other men – bomber crews – almost wept, and maybe they did really, in the awful knowledge that they had killed our own American troops."

Indeed, news was catastrophic. Just like the previous day, certain bombs missed their targets. As a result, around a hundred more dead and five hundred wounded GIs from the 9th and the 30th Divisions. Among the victims, General Leslie McNair, Commander in Chief of the US Army who had come as an observer; he was identified only thanks to the stars he wore on his shoulder. Out in the field, General Collins'

War correspondent Ernie Pyle (1900-1945) was particularly popular among the GIs. He was killed by a Japanese sniper in Okinawa.

25th July: GIs freeing their buddies from the heaps of earth heaved up by bombs.

VII Corps had become disorganised and was struggling to advance. By nightfall, it had only gained a few miles. When Eisenhower - who had come to France specially to participate in operations - returned to England, tension among the military staff was tangible,

Yet Bradley's hopes were soon to be revived, "For although *Cobra* might have looked like a failure on the evening of July 25, it had struck a more deadly blow than any of us dared imagine. For though air had pummeled us, it had pulverized the enemy in the carpet to litter the torn fields and roads with the black hulls of burned-out tanks, the mutilated bodies of soldiers, and the carcasses of bloated, stiff-legged cattle." Around 4,700 tonnes of bombs had hit the German lines, giving the fatal blow to the *Panzer Lehr* stationed in the sector. Corporal Brooks and his buddies from the 30th Division found themselves before an incredible sight, "When we passed through the bombed area, it was the biggest mess I ever saw. It looked like a World War I battlefield. The destruction was terrific; there were no branches on the trees, no plants, no hedges, no buildings or roads. The dust was so heavy and thick you needed a mask to break through it."

The breakthrough towards Avranches

On the 26th of July, Collins' troops began to surge into the yawning gap in the German lines between Marigny and Saint-Gilles. The 27th marked dramatic change and commotion. As the 2nd Armoured Division charged southwards towards Notre-Dame-de-Cenilly, General Huebner's 1st Division progressed on the major route leading to Coutances, threatening Von Choltitz' LXXXIV Corps from the rear. As the Germans pulled back, General Middleton's VIII Corps took immediate advantage of the situation to recapture Lessay and Périers and to gain a ten-mile advance in just one day. The following day, the 28th of July, General Wood's 4th Armoured Division entered Coutances where the still intact cathedral loomed above a heap of ruins.

The Germans had escaped encirclement, but only for a while. In a vast sweeping movement towards the coast, the American armoured units thwarted their retreat. The remaining troops from the 2nd and 17th SS Divisions and the 6th Parachute Regiment found themselves

A *Panther* tank belonging to the *Panzer Lehr* division, rendered inoperative by Allied bombings.

trapped in the Roncey pocket. In an attempt to release the stranglehold, the Germans fought desperately in Saint-Denis-le-Gast and Cérences on the 29th of July. Although half of their men managed to escape, they did so leaving behind most of their material.

Determined enemy opposition was also encountered to the east, round Tessy-sur-Vire. However, the southern front was weakening. "Men were exhausted by combat and their cohesion was totally shattered," Von Choltitz resumed. "Since we had no further reserves, it was impossible to ward off our ill fortune." Swarms of fighter bombers droned above the roads and attacked the enemy columns amidst their frenzied retreat, leaving the roads littered with debris and destroyed vehicles. German documents recovered during the breakthrough, then analysed by intelligence services,

offered enlightening information, "Our rapid advance during the latter part of July produced reports and orders, frequently handwritten showing organizational and moral disintegration of the German forces. There were warnings and threats about the consequences of desertion and about giving information to the enemy after capture. Official reports about combat experiences in France never mentioned the word victory. The necessity of saving weapons, ammunition, and equipment was stressed."

The breach was turning into a genuine breakthrough. The American armoured units were thrusting forward towards Avranches, followed by infantrymen aboard trucks and *half-tracks*. The pockets of resistance established on major road junctions were effortlessly approached and overthrown. *Rhinoceros* tanks

American troops in Marigny, liberated on the 27th of July by the 1st Infantry Division.

Coutances, liberated on the 28th of July.

opened breaches in the hedges and continued their progression through the fields. When they encountered more cumbersome obstacles, tanks called upon the planes that flew permanently above them. In just one week, over 18,000 Germans were taken prisoner and evacuated to new transit camps. The Americans wreaked havoc along their way, in true cavalry charging tradition.

Throughout this fantastic cavalcade, the Normans rushed to congratulate their liberators, extending a welcome the troops had rarely experienced to date. Indeed, in the south of Manche, the population - relatively remote from the front - had not been evacuated and their towns and villages had suffered lesser destruction. Lieutenant Abrams kept very moving memories of the great

Abandoned German *Marder* self-propelled guns in front of the ruins of Roncey church.

A group of German prisoners near Avranches.

with wine and eider. If the wine happened to be sour or the eider watered, it made no difference. It was the same in every town and village. The little girls dressed in their Sunday best, tightly gripping a bouquet of daisies and reciting hesitantly, "welcome to les Américains", while their proud parents looked on and prompted them when they forgot. And Monsieur le Mayor with his cutaway and stripped pants and

enthusiasm the arrival of the 90th Division had aroused, "The people stood in the streets and cheered and waved and yelled until their throats were hoarse. They laughed until the tears rolled down their cheeks. American troops, riding in jeeps, on tanks, in trucks, were pelted with bouquets of flowers, presented ceremoniously his trimmed moustache waving frantically for quiet so he could make his speech. And then you moved on to the next town and the same thing happened everywhere you went, only sometimes the welcoming committee was a little put out because the Americans wouldn't stop long enough."

German prisoners evacuated in GMC trucks.

As Patton was waiting to take charge of his Third Army on the 1st of August, he was assigned the task of "supervising" the VIII Corps' operations. He was quick to impose a hectic pace upon Middleton's troops. As from the 28th of July, he had armoured units progress in front of infantry units. On the 29th, they crossed the River Sienne. General Grow's 6th Armoured Division recaptured Bréhal and was approaching Granville. The 4th Armoured Division, led by the intrepid General Wood, aka "Tiger Jack", thrust forward towards Avranches. On the evening of the 30th of July, the division entered the town, devastated by bombings on the 7th of June, driving back a German counter-attack throughout the night. In six days, Bradley's troops had advanced almost 40 miles. It was no longer the same battle. The war of positions had given way to a war of movement, an American-style *Blitzkrieg*.

A short rest on the road to Avranches.

4th Armoured Division reconnaissance units in Folligny (in the hamlet of Le Repas) on their way to Avranches.

Sainte-Marie-des-Bois

Percy

Saint-Sever

Canisy

Bréhal

Mont-Saint-Michel

Sartilly

Villedieu

Tessy

Juvigny

The Battle of Normandy became the Battle of France

On the afternoon of the 31st of July, the American vanguard took control of the, miraculously intact, bridge at Pontaubault. It was a genuine godsend since this old medieval bridge over the Sélune was the only gateway to Brittany. A German column left Saint-Malo, but arrived too late, with no choice but to make a U-turn, much to its expense. Patton's hour of glory had come. On the 1st of August, he thrust his Third Army ahead, paying no heed to usual tactical and logistic rules. Relentlessly, over three days, cars, trucks, engineer vehicles, tank carriers paraded across the Pontaubault bridge, bumper to bumper. A striking cascade of steel and dust that attacks from the *Luftwaffe* failed to deter. To accelerate the movement through this critical passageway, a few superior officers readily gave a helping hand to the Military Police. "I spent almost all my time acting as a road traffic cop," a division commander explained.

The fortress of Saint-Malo under siege.

Fougères.

Yet some were genuinely concerned: the Avranches "bottleneck" was very slim; the enemy could break through it with a simple flank attack. Patton paid no attention. During his first staff conference, he told his generals, "Don't worry about your flanks. We need to protect them, OK! But not to the point of doing nothing else. Some goddamn fool once said that flanks have got to be secure. Since then sonofabitches all over the globe have been guarding their flanks. We don't want any of that in the Third Army. My flanks are something for the enemy to worry about. I don't want to get any messages saying, 'I'm holding my position.' We're not holding a goddamned thing. We are advancing constantly and we are not interested in holding onto anything, except the enemy's balls. We are going to twist his balls and kick the living shit out of him all the time."

In 72 hours, 120,000 men and 10,000 vehicles had moved into the breach. Thanks to one modest bridge in Pontaubault, the Battle of Normandy had become the Battle of France. Beyond Avranches, Patton's army fanned out. Whilst Middleton's VIII Corps marched through Brittany, General Walker's XX Corps was heading for the Loire and Haislip's XV Corps was progressing towards Sarthe. The Americans liberated Rennes on the 4th of August; they were on the outskirts of Brest on the 7th, recaptured Le Mans on the 8th, Angers on the 10th, Nantes on the 12th...

As Patton's Third Army was revelling in glory, General Hodges' First Army, whose left flank was covered by the British Second Army, was busy with the far less gratifying task of ousting the Germans out of the bocage. Indeed, amidst this rugged landscape, progression was slow and laborious. The enemy was retreating, but was still intact. The Americans made optimal use of their powerful artillery, advancing along the Caumont-Villedieu route. However, they sustained heavy losses: some 5,000 men fell over the first week of August alone. On the 3rd, Collins' VII Corps took control of Mortain, then

Laval.

Near Nantes.

Saint-Pois and the Saint-Sever forest. General Corlett's XIX Corps took over Tessy on the 2nd of August and advanced towards Vire where a furious battle awaited them. After three days of bitter combat, the 29th Division finally entered the ruined town on the morning of the 8th of August.

La Ferté-Macé

Argentan

Rânes

CH SEREE

Alençon

Bagnoles-de-l'Orne

Beauvain

Domfront

On one of the heights that overlook Mortain.

On Hitler's orders, four German armoured divisions had joined forces the previous day to the east of Mortain to launch a counter-attack. Their aim was perfectly clear: to thrust forward towards the coast and the Mont-Saint-Michel in order to slash the Avranches "bottleneck" and to separate Patton from his rear troops and, consequently, his supplies. Operation *Lüttich* was launched in the early hours of the 7th of August. Amidst a blanket of thick fog, after reconquering Mortain, the German columns progressed a further 6 miles westwards. The US 30th Division in position in the sector was take by surprise

and driven from the field. Some detachments were reduced to seeking refuge on the heights that loomed over the town. However, the mist finally settled early afternoon on the 7th of August. Allied fighter bombers could enter the scene and attack the enemy tanks with their guns and devastating rockets. The American ground troops, reinforced by armoured units, reorganised their attack and stopped the German attack early in its tracks. The enemy nevertheless succeeded in holding its position for a few days, much to the dismay of the 120th Infantry Regiment's 2nd Battalion, isolated since the 7th of August on Hill 314, overlooking Mortain to the east.

Around seven hundred men, under Captain Erichson's orders, were gathered at the top of the hill, in a genuinely precarious position. For six days, they heroically resisted attacks by 17th SS grenadiers. Short of supplies, ammunition and first aid for the wounded, they nevertheless repudiated all calls for surrender. Several parachute drops were attempted to help them; however, a share of containers fell directly into enemy hands. The Americans then deployed a cunning plan consisting in vertically firing onto the hillside empty shells filled with medical supplies. On the 12th of August, Hodges' divisions had reconquered the territory they had lost and had liberated surviving inhabitants. Around three hundred men were still fit for combat; just as many had been killed or wounded. According to General Bradley, the "lost battalion's" resistance was to mark, "one of the epic battles of the war."

The same day, Hitler finally gave in to his generals' pleas and gave orders to retreat; however, it was too late, for the Allies were already deploying their deadly trap. Bradley observed the enemy positions on his maps and concocted an audacious plan that was to receive immediate approval from Eisenhower and Montgomery. He planned to encircle the German forces, already in a perilous position after the daring attack on Mortain. Hence, he aimed to surround them from the south thanks to a direct northerly movement by General Haislip's XV

Corps, from Le Mans to Argentan. Concurrently, the increased pressure exerted by the British and Canadian troops to the south and west of Caen, against a German stopper that had been weakened by the detachment of several armoured units to Mortain, enabled them to clear the plain and to advance past Falaise. In short, two jaws - one American to the south, the other Anglo-Canadian to the north - were gradually closing in on the majority of the German troops around Argentan. On the 10th of August, Bradley gave orders, "We'll shoot the works and rush east with everything we've got!"

However, the manoeuvre was hindered by a few coordination blunders between Allied camps. Two XV Corps armoured divisions, including General Leclerc's 2nd Armoured Division, made a spearhead advance and reached the outskirts of Argentan on the 13th of August. But the Canadians were behind schedule, still relatively far from Falaise. A good third of the 150,000 Germans under threat of encirclement managed to escape the, still largely open, pocket. Patton scorned and, in his very own style, declared he was ready to send Haislip to go and collect Montgomery's troops himself, "Let me go on to Falaise and we'll drive the British back into the sea for another Dunkirk." Bradley harshly stopped him in his tracks.

Montgomery then proposed to close the pocket, which was tightening day by day, to the east of Argentan, between the villages of Trun and Chambois. This time, the Americans were late to make the junction, some of their divisions having hastily left to head for the Seine. By the 21st of August, the trap had been irretrievably sealed, even if around 100,000 Germans had managed to flee. They had nevertheless left some 40,000 prisoners and from 5,000 to 6,000 dead troops behind them. Eisenhower visited the "corridor of death" a few days later, "The battlefield at Falaise was unquestionably one of the greatest 'killing grounds' of any of the war areas. Roads, highways, and fields were so choked with destroyed equipment and with dead men and animals that passage through the area was extremely difficult.

Forty-eight hours after the closing of the gap I was conducted through it on foot, to encounter scenes that could be described only by Dante. It was literally possible to walk for hundreds of yards at a time, stepping on nothing but dead and decaying flesh."

The Americans and Canadians joined forces in Elbeuf.

Orléans.

With the Allies on their heels, the Germans withdrew and crossed the Seine late August, from various positions around Rouen, leaving a vast share of their heavy equipment behind. Their retreat towards the frontiers of the Reich was to accelerate for a further threat had emerged since the 15th of August. General Patch's Seventh Army, within which General de Lattre de Tassigny's French troops had been integrated, had landed in Provence and were making fast progress northwards along the banks of the Rhône.

Henceforth, the breakthrough turned into a pursuit and the Allies made impressive progress. Whilst Montgomery's troops hugged the Channel coast on their way to Belgium, the Americans fanned out from the Loire to the Seine, liberating Dreux, Chartres, Orléans... By the 23rd of August, Hodges' First Army had established a bridgehead at Mantes-Gassicourt on the right bank of the Seine. Patton's Third Army did the same the following day between Fontainebleau and Melun. Between the two: Paris - a new source of political embarrassment with General de Gaulle.

The Americans crossed the Seine in the vicinity of Mantes.

29th August: the 28th Division parading through Paris.

Paris avoided or Paris liberated?

"Tactically the city had become meaningless," Bradley explained. "For all of its past glories, Paris represented nothing more than an inkspot on our maps to be by-passed as we headed toward the Rhine. Logistically it could cause untold trouble, for behind its handsome façades there lived 4,000,000 hungry Frenchmen. The diversion of so much tonnage to Paris would only strain further our already taut lines of supply. Food for the people of Paris meant less gasoline for the front." Yet he had failed to pay due consideration to de Gaulle's national pride, for the French general firmly intended for the capital city, where the French Resistance had already instigated an uprising against the occupant, to be quickly liberated, and by French troops! Increasingly insistent, he finally obtained Eisenhower's approval to entrust the mission to General Leclerc's 2nd Armoured Division. Attached to General Gerow's V Corps, the division set off from Argentan on the morning of the 23rd of August. Several columns were progressing towards Paris, although they were slowed down not only by German resistance nests but also by over-enthusiastic local populations. It was another opportunity for one of Bradley's ironic remarks, "Neither could I wait for

them to dance their way to Paris. To hell with prestige!" Hence, he ordered Gerow to, "Tell the 4th to slam on in and take the liberation," whilst dispatching General Barton's 4th Division to the front. "Fearing an affront to France," Bradley continued, "Leclerc's troopers mounted their tanks and burned up their treads on the brick roads." On the 25th of August, most of the 2nd Armoured Division had entered Paris, covered by the 4th Division whose vanguard had reached the steps of Notre-Dame just before midday, before securing the eastern half of the capital.

On the 26th, de Gaulle invited Leclerc's division to participate in a grand parade on the Champs-Élysées, much to Gerow's distaste, the US general ordering Leclerc to continue his advance without delay - to which he replied that he also owed obedience to his "political" chief. His insubordination was to be of no consequence. Yet the Americans had no intention of letting the French take all the credit for the liberation of Paris. On the 29th of August, they consequently organised a triumphant parade through the streets of Paris by one of their own units, General Cota's 28th Division. Now that the scores were even, the eastward advance could continue.

Before the gates of the Château de Versailles.

After having crossed the Seine, the Allies headed immediately for the Rhine. Exhausted and disorganised after their defeat in Normandy, the Germans were incapable of establishing new and efficient defensive lines. Montgomery's 21st Army Group entered Brussels on the 3rd of September and took control of Antwerp the following day.

The division's right flank was covered by General Hodges' First Army, which had in turn liberated Soissons, Laon, Compiègne, Cambrai, Valenciennes, Maubeuge... Early September, they encircled the few remaining German units in the Mons pocket, taking 25,000 to 30,000 prisoners before continuing on to Liège and the Albert Canal. Further south, they besieged Ardennes and liberated Luxembourg.

The Third Army's advance, to the east of Allied operations, was no less spectacular. Troops marched through Marne, meeting with no opposition and reconquering Châlons, then Reims before reaching Verdun, on the banks of the Meuse, on the 31st of August. The next day, the Americans reached Saint-Mihiel, a historic site where their forefathers had bitterly fought in September 1918. Although temporarily hindered by fuel shortages, Patton's divisions were soon to resume their advance towards Moselle, reaching the outskirts of Metz and Nancy.

By mid September, one hundred days after the D-Day Landings, the front stretched from the Saône to Antwerp, over a position that SHAEF forecasts had only envisaged 330 days after the landings, in other words, only by early May 1945! After they had crossed the Seine, the Americans accomplished a momentum leap, progressing 150 to 200 miles in just two weeks. On the 12th of September, the vanguard of General Patch's Seventh Army, on their northward march from Provence, joined forces with Patton's Third Army to the north of Dijon. A vast share of French territory had now been liberated. However, Allied progression was soon to decelerate. As days went by, the "tyranny of logistics" weighed heavier and heavier on the Allies.

29th August: parade on the Champs-Élysées.

Reims.

2nd September: the 3rd Armoured Division entering Louvroil, near Maubeuge.

The "tyranny of logistics"

After their victory in Normandy, the Allies took the crucial decision of taking full tactical advantage of the German collapse. Their priority was to advance as quickly as possible towards the frontiers of the Reich. Logistics would simply have to keep up! However, day by day, the distance between the supply depots in Normandy and the combat troops increased. Supply chains were becoming dangerously long and were struggling to keep up with the hectic pace of the two American armies. The return to a war of movement had upset the order of things, as Bradley himself explained, "During our late August and September pursuit of the enemy across France, gasoline formed the bulk of our tonnage. For as we rolled on against spotty rather than organized resistance, ammunition expenditures declined. Whereas in Normandy an armored division might ordinarily consume four tons of ammunition for each ton of gasoline it burned, now the proportion was reversed." In July, daily fuel consumption barely exceeded a million tonnes - by late August it had been multiplied by three! On the 25th of July, the pipeline network from the Querqueville reservoirs only stretched as far as La Haye-du-Puits. It took a fortnight to extend it to Saint-Lô, before continuing southwards towards Alençon.

It was an immense task, occupying 7,000 men from Engineer units and 1,500 German prisoners. Three 6-inch diameter tubes - two for fuel to supply ground units (MT 80) and one for aviation (Avgas) - ran parallel, up hill and down dale, generally alongside existing roads and pathways. Technical difficulties were frequent and problems of all sorts accumulated: accidents, burst pipes, etc., not forgetting sabotage by dishonest civilians looking to steal fuel. By late August, the pipes had reached Alençon. Only one (the MT 80) was continued as far as Chartres, Dourdan then Coubert, to the north of the Seine, a destination it reached late September. As the network extended, the flow declined to a maximum of 330,000 gallons per day, and the American armies were still a further 150 to 220 miles away.

Air routes also contributed. Their speed was an unquestionable asset; however, the limited capacity of planes offered but modest results: barely more than a few hundred tonnes per day, and only weather permitting. Yet, in the case of urgency, the Air Force could offer crucial support. Consequently, a genuine airlift was established early September between Querqueville and Reims - over five days and five nights - in order to overcome acute fuel shortages.

The installation of pipelines attracted many curious spectators.

weeks. Yet such unscheduled long distance transport remained to be organised. However the Americans had a tremendous capacity for adaptation and, on the 25th of August, they initiated a system that, just like the "holy road" during the Battle of Verdun, was to go down in History: the Red Ball Highway. Two one-way tracks - one northward, the other southward - were to provide a link between Saint-Lô and a vast depot zone located around Chartres. The first route passed by Vire, Domfront, Alençon and Mortagne, to return to Normandy via Nogent-le-Rotrou, Mamers, Mayenne and Mortain. As from the 10th of September, a new route was opened slightly

Given its transport capacity, the rail network appeared to be the most appropriate solution for supplying adequate quantities to satisfy demand. Yet it was in need of repair and associated delays meant that it was impossible for it to keep up with the XII Army Group divisions. Over and above railway tracks and stations, the major setback was the need to repair the many rail bridges destroyed by the Germans or by the Allied aviation. Out in the field, the Engineers deployed over 18,000 men who spared their sleep whilst multiplying their efforts. Hence, Folligny was connected with Le Mans, via Fougères and Mayenne (over a distance of 125 miles), in just five days! Yet, on the 17th of August, the Third Army was still a long distance ahead.

Until such times as the rail network was once more operational, another solution needed to be found for supplying Hodges' and Patton's armies. Roads were consequently to play a crucial role for the following six

further north, leading to Soissons (First Army) and Sommesous (Third Army) over a return distance of over 600 miles. The Red Ball very quickly demonstrated its efficiency. From the 29th of August, it ensured the daily transport of some 12,342 tonnes, a record that was never to be broken. Of the 100,000 tonnes of supplies (excluding fuel) Patton had demanded by early September, the road alone provided 82%, compared to 18% by rail. The system nevertheless proved to be a costly one, not only due to wear and tear of equipment but also to exorbitant fuel consumption.

Mid September, despite the efforts deployed and the system's technical prowess, its use was rationed due to shortages, of fuel in particular. Patton was at a standstill on the outskirts of Metz and, considering himself more ill-treated than others, he proclaimed his indignation, "Bellowing like an angry bull," he marched into Bradley's headquarters, letting loose streams of abuse, "To hell with Hodges and Monty, we'll win your goddam war if you'll keep the Third Army going." And he was no less impertinent when he met Eisenhower a few days later, "My men can eat their belts, but my tanks gotta have gas!"

In fact, the Allies were victims of their own swift progression. The Germans were quick to take advantage of the situation, reorganising defence around their frontiers. Some - over-optimistic - had bet on the end of the war by Christmas 1944. Disenchanted, they were yet to face long months of bitter combat, in the Ardennes and the Ruhr, before forcing the Reich to capitulate on the 7th of May 1945.

Pipelines were built across the valley.

Repairing a rail bridge near Saint-Lô.

SOURCES

UNITED STATES ARMY IN WORLD WAR II, OFFICE OF THE CHIEF OF MILITARY HISTORY

Pogue (Forrest C.), *The Supreme Command*, 1954.
Smith (Elberton R.), *The Army and Economic Mobilization*, 1959.
Millet (John D.), *The Organization and Role of the Army Service Forces*, 1954.
Harrison (Gordon A.), *Cross Channel Attack*, 1951.
Blumenson (Martin), *Breakout and Pursuit*, 1961.
Ruppenthal (Roland G.), *Logistical Support of the Armies, May 1941 - September 1944*, 1953.
Beck (Alfred M.), Bortz (Abe), Lynch (Charles W.) Mayo (Lida), *The Corps of Engineers: The War against Germany*, 1985.
Cosmas (Graham A.), Cowdrey (Albert E.), *The Medical Department: Medical Service in the European Theater of Operations*, 1992.
Mayo (Lida), *The Ordnance Department: On Beachhead and Battlefront*, 1968.
Ross (William F.), Romanus (Charles F.), *The Quartermaster Corps in the War against Germany*, 1965.
Raynor (Thompson George R.), Harris (Dixie R.), *The Signal Corps: The Outcome (Mid-1943 through 1945)*, 1966.
Bykofsky (Joseph), Larson (Harold), *The Transportation Corps: Operations Overseas*, 1957.
Treadwell (Mattie E.), *The Women's Army Corps*, 1954.
Lee (Ulysses), *The Employment of Negro Troops*, 1966.
Coles (Harry L.), Weinberg (Albert K.), *Civil Affairs: Soldiers became Governors*, 1964.

AMERICAN FORCES IN ACTION SERIES, WAR DEPARTMENT - HISTORICAL DIVISION

Omaha Beachhead (6 June - 13 June 1944), 1945.
Ruppenthal (Roland G.), *Utah Beach to Cherbourg (6 June - 27 June 1944)*, 1948
Taylor (Charles H.), *St-Lô (7 July - 19 July 1944)*, 1946.

REPORTS OF OPERATIONS, UNITED STATES ARMY

First US Army, *Report of operations 20 October 1943 – 1 August 1944.*
First US Army, *Report of operations 1 August 1944 – 22 February 1945.*
Third US Army, *After action report 1 August 1944 – 9 May 1945.*

MEMOIRS AND WITNESS ACCOUNTS

Eisenhower (Dwight D.), *Crusade in Europe*, Doubleday & Co,1948.
Bradley (Omar N.), *A Soldier's Story*, Henry Holt and Co, 1951.
Sylvan (William C.), Smith (Francis G. JR), *Normandy to Victory – The War Diary of General Courtney H. Hodges & the First US Army*, The University Press of Kentucky, 2008.
Allsup (John S.), *Hedgerow Hell / L'Enfer du Bocage*, Editions Heimdal, 1985 Bilingual edition]
Ingersoll (Ralph), *Top Secret*, Harcourt, Brace and Co, 1946.
Maginnis (John J.), *Military Government Journal – Normandy to Berlin*, University of Massachusetts Press, 1971.
Pyle (Ernie), *Brave men*, Henry Holt and Co, 1944.
Pyle (Ernie), *G.I. Joe*, Overseas Editions, 1944
MacVane (John), *In the Air in World War II*, Morrow, 1979.
Drez (Ronald J.), *Voices of D-Day: The Story of the Allied Invasion told by those who were there*, Louisiana University Press, 1994.
Kaufmann (J.E.), Kaufmann (H.W.), *The Americain GI in Europe in World War II - The March to D-Day*, Stackpole Books, 2009.
Kaufmann (J.E.), Kaufmann (H.W.), *The Americain GI in Europe in World War II - D-Day, Storming ashore*, Stackpole Books, 2009.
Kaufmann (J.E.), Kaufmann (H.W.), *The American GI in Europe in World War II - The Battle in France*, Stackpole Books, 2010.
Miller (Russell), *Nothing less than Victory – An oral history of D-Day*, Michael Joseph Ltd, 1993.
Neillands (Robin), De Normann (Roderick), *D-Day, 1944 - Voices from Normandy*, Weidenfeld & Nicolson, 1993.

THE US ARMY AND THE GIS

Ambrose (Stephen E.), *Citizen Soldiers - The US Army from the Normandy Beaches to the Surrender of Germany*, Simon & Schuster, 1997.
Henry (Mark R.), *The US Army in World War II*, Osprey Publishing, 2001.
Hoyt (Edwin P.), *The GI's War - American Soldiers in Europe during World War II*, Cooper Square Press, 2000.
Kennett (Lee B.), *G.I.: The American Soldier in World War II*, Scribner, 1987.
Reynolds (David), *Rich relations - The American Occupation of Britain, 1942-1945*, Phoenix Press, 2000.

D-DAY AND THE BATTLE OF NORMANDY

Ambrose (Stephen), *D-Day, June 6, 1944 - The Climatic Battle of World War II*, Simon & Schuster, 1994.
Beevor (Antony), *D-Day: The Battle for Normandy*, Viking, 2009.
Carafano (James J.), *After D-Day - Operation Cobra and the Normandy Breakout*, Lynne Rienner Publishers, 2000.
Man (John), *Atlas of D-Day and the Normandy Campaign*, Penguin Books, 1994.
McManus (John C.), *The Americans at Normandy*, Tom Doherty Associates, 2004.
Quellien (Jean), *Normandy 44*, OREP, 2011.
Tute (Warren), Costello (John), Hugues (Terry), *D-Day*, Sidgwick & Jackson Ltd, 1974.
Wieviorka (Olivier), *Normandy – The Landings to the Liberation of Paris*, The Belknap Press, 2010

ICONOGRAPHICAL SOURCES

Archives départementales de la Manche (Manche Departmental Archives)
Normandie 1939-1945 Archives: (http://www.archivesnormandie39-45.org)
Jean Quellien - personal archives
The Library of Congress
Normandie photographic gallery:
(http://www.flickr.com/photos/photosnormandie/with/3801426688/)
Getty Images
Imperial War Museum
Mémorial de Caen